Léopold Sédar Senghor
and the Politics of Negritude

Léopold Sédar Senghor

and the Politics of Negritude

IRVING LEONARD MARKOVITZ

Atheneum NEW YORK

1969

For Ruth

Acknowledgments

THE cooperation and effort of many people and institutions made this essay possible and it is my added pleasure to here acknowledge their support. A generous fellowship from the Ford Foundation's Foreign Area Program provided the opportunity to spend most of 1964 and 1965 gathering material in Paris, Senegal, and West Africa; a grant from the Committee on Comparative Urban Studies of the City University of New York allowed for a return visit to West Africa during the Summer of 1968. James L. Gould of the Foreign Area Program was particularly encouraging when this project was far from completed.

In Paris, the resources of the Fondation Nationale des Sciences Politiques, the Centre des Hautes Etudes Administrative sur l'Afrique et l'Asie Moderne, the Bibliothèque Nationale, and the Compagnie d'Etudes Industrielles et d'Aménagement du Territoire were particularly important.

Within Senegal, the Office of the Presidency of the Republic, the University of Dakar, and the director and staff of the National Archives extended courtesies essential for the visiting scholar that were far beyond the demands of their ordinary duties. The officers of IFAN (Institut Fondamental d'Afrique Noire) generously made available a *chambre de passage* for myself and my family, as well as their excellent research facilities.

My obligation to Professors Carl G. Rosberg and David Apter, my teachers at Berkeley, is particularly great. William Bascom, Henry Morton and Edward Schumacher also read the entire manuscript, as did Olga Sapir. In Senegal, Olga and David

Acknowledgments

Sapir, Bruno and Colette Le Cour offered the benefit of their friendship, as well as many helpful suggestions. Jonathan and Nancy Barker helped us get settled in Paris and Senegal and shared with us their knowledge of Senegal.

Bob Zenowich, my editor at Atheneum, prodded me in the direction of more active sentences and helped impart whatever readability this study might have.

Many Senegalese at all levels of government and administration provided indispensable aid and hospitality. Without their cooperation, nothing would have been possible. It is therefore particularly difficult not be to able to include them by name in this book.

Above all, my wife, as critic and friend, typist and editor, has contributed more than anyone else to whatever is good about this study. Her company, and that of Amy and Jonathan, was important to me.

All matters of fact, judgment, and interpretation are, of course, my sole responsibility.

Contents

CHAPTER I / page 3

*Léopold Senghor and the Functions of Ideology
for Developing Nations*

CHAPTER II / page 40

*The Changing Social Functions of Negritude
as an Ideology: 1931–1966*

CHAPTER III / page 80

*France and Senegal: The Appeal of Colonialism
for Dependent Countries*

CHAPTER IV / page 102

Autonomy, Nationalism and Independence

CHAPTER V / page 119

The Definition of Senegalese Socialism

CHAPTER VI / page 155

Development and Socialism

CHAPTER VII / page 194

Democracy and Economic Development

CHAPTER VIII / page 212

Technicity and the New Humanism

BIBLIOGRAPHY / page 241

INDEX / page 291

Léopold Sédar Senghor
and the Politics of Negritude

I

Léopold Senghor and the Functions
of Ideology for Developing Nations

JEAN-PAUL SARTRE has hailed Léopold Senghor as foremost among those black intellectuals who produced "the
true revolutionary poetry of our time." [1] Other observers have
called Senghor one of Africa's foremost architects of a reinvigor-
ated, dynamic socialism; they have held him responsible for a
dramatic cultural and moral break with the values of Western
civilization and the creation of a new, uniquely African civilization and system of values. [2]

Politically, on the other hand, Senghor has gained in reputation because of his caution and moderation. He has advocated
cooperation with colonial authorities and autonomy within a
broad French Community rather than isolated, nominal independence. His practical politics emphasize the absence of any
mass nationalism, toleration for a carefully paced rate of economic expansion rather than experiments with authoritarian
measures of radical social reorganization, and reliance on technical management and scientific expertise.

Senghor has been praised for his ideas and damned for his
politics—and, conversely, praised for his politics and damned for
his ideas. This study explores the relationships between Senghor's ideas and his politics, as well as the relevance of his theories and values to the political and social situation of Senegal.

Allegedly Senghor's ideas seem either to contradict his poli-

3

tics or to be irrelevant to them. Any such contradiction is only apparent. In fact, Senghor has developed an ideology which justifies his politics.[3] Further, this marriage of ideas and politics in Senegal sometimes results in unintended consequences for Senghor's great humanitarian and socialistic objectives—making them difficult, if not impossible, to achieve. This, however, is not surprising given the history of Senghor's successes in accommodating his ideas and policies so well to the governing coalitions of both colonial France and independent Senegal.

African leaders like Senghor, who have argued the uniqueness of their historical conditions and cultural traditions, have declared the necessity for philosophies, governments and social systems that truly reflect the peculiarities of their situation. Yet the existence or meaningfulness of ideology in Senegal stimulates frequent debate. Negritude (a "black is beauty" doctrine originated by black intellectuals in pre-World War II Paris to assert the unique contributions, values and characteristics of black men and black civilization) is often criticized as a mystification, or Senghor's private philosophy; socialism is dismissed as a doctrine for wealthier societies; economic development is sought through scientific, not philosophical, innovations. In the countryside, problems of development are usually discussed in terms of inches of rainfall, soil acidity, the cost of hauling peanuts, lack of trained personnel, the balancing of budgets, etc., rather than in ideological categories.

Yet, ideology comes into play whenever a potential problem in the coordination of men, government and resources exists. Ideology accompanies the determination of any of the classic political questions of who gets what, when, where and why. Ideology becomes essential whenever more than the simple question of *how* to do something arises. Ideology assumes a class structure and conflict, decisions favoring one interest over another, the organization of society with groups in differential positions of influence, and technology manipulated to exploit productive resources. Hence, the problem is never simply one of economic growth or development, but one of "development for whom"?

4

In Senegal today, as in all the recently independent African states, the basic problems of ideology deal with unity, stability and economic development.[4]

The Need and Uses of Ideology

How are the leaders of the new nations to put their countries on the road to development and create unity after the indifference and inability of generations? They must arouse interest in the midst of apathy, project a vision where none had existed before, stimulate in the population a sense of self-awareness and encourage people to work to help themselves. Improvement, intervention, alteration—the invention of a meaning so that the world can be seen with fresh eyes and turned inside out by men working to improve it and themselves—these are among the objectives of the new African elites. *Prise de conscience*, "killing the old Negro," "Negritude," "African Socialism," "Pan Africanism," "moral tension"—all these concepts deal with these objectives.

Senghor has argued for the necessity to stimulate in all the people of Senegal a new awareness, sense of commitment and "moral awakening" in order to achieve unity and economic development. Accomplishment of these great objectives demands new values and outlooks as well as machinery and technological resources. An abundance of capital or skilled personnel does not, contrary to common belief, guarantee success. He has stated the problem this way:

> . . . more than cadres and financial means, *we lack a moral tension.* Our cruelest lack is genuine faith, a true commitment to the service of our country. It is this that I consider the most difficult task among all those that I have undertaken: to instill in my people, in all of my people, that taste for work well done, that minimum of honesty and civic consciousness, that sense of

5

the public good, without which nothing lasting can be accomplished.[5]

Thus ideology emerges as one major instrument in the moral battle against "the vast indifference," in the effort to create a "moral tension."

Today, in new nations, issues ranging from slums to sanitation are of national concern, an industrial infrastructure must be created virtually overnight, and the need for improved health and educational facilities is dire. Thus, skilled technicians, planners and bureaucrats (and politicians who know how to use their skills) command crucial positions. Two processes in emergent nations form the context for dealing with these problems of unity and development: (1) the creation of new administrative structures and the emergence of bureaucratic elites to fill positions within them; and (2) what the French call the *encadrement* of the population—that is, the reorganization of the population into a framework which makes the resources of the community available for efficient development. Theoretically, the first of these processes takes place to aid in the unfolding of the second.

These processes involve restructuring the countryside (rationalizing production methods and satisfying unfulfilled aspirations which stem from increased awareness of new material possibilities) and the "decolonization of mentalities"—sloughing off feelings of inferiority and dependency, and adopting the cluster of values first prominent in sixteenth- and seventeenth-century Europe having to do with a belief in progress and nature's amenability to rational manipulation.

Policy-makers can find ideology relevant to solving these problems in each of five crucial steps. First, to accumulate knowledge: decisions by policy-makers fundamentally aid in creating knowledge through material support for research, and in determining what knowledge ought to be disseminated. Second, to educate the personnel capable of demonstrating this knowledge—a problem involving middle-level cadres. Third, to stimu-

6

late the peasant to give the technicians an audience. Fourth, to encourage the peasant to experiment. And fifth, to induce the peasant to utilize innovations systematically.

This process should result in changes both in the mentality and the conditions of the peasant—not simply in a rise in production or a statistical change in the gross national product. Increases in the gross national product can be off-set by lower commodity prices on the world market or by a rising birth rate. Despite his increased efforts, the peasant may also get a lower return because of an unequal distribution of revenue, i.e., any increase in production going to functionaries and politicians rather than to the actual producers. The peasants in Senegal realize this. They have an intense feeling that differential beneficiaries existed in the post-independence period, with the common farmers gaining the least. Therefore, simply to increase productivity does not suffice. The peasant must enjoy the fruits of his labor. Measures such as improvement in the system of distribution and restricting or eliminating landlords and moneylenders achieve both substantive and symbolic significance in this respect. They help to establish the legitimacy of the government in the eyes of the peasant.

If the establishment of developmental policy is not done for the peasant, and with his participation, government will have to rely increasingly on force and not simply authority. If the peasant is shown something good and how to acquire it, there is no need for coercion to increase production. If the technicians and political savants always had perfect knowledge, there might also be no problem. But as development and new changes take place, the variety and complexity of problems increase. The failures of governmental omniscience become strikingly apparent. The necessity increases for reciprocity of information and influence.

To maintain a fever pitch of excitement on a day-to-day basis for day-to-day objectives has proved impossible in practice. The *Investissement Humain* projects in Mali and Guinea, for example, experienced severe disappointments and discouragement with the government when results were not immediate. In these respects, most developing societies encounter the problems

7

of *encadrement* and restructuring. In practice, however, the question arises: does ideology in Senegal actually meet these problems or, in its accommodation with established interests, simply safeguard the existing power structure?

To an extent rare in Africa, under the guidance of Senghor the governing politicians of Senegal have exercised a remarkable capacity in building durable coalitions out of traditionally non-cooperative and mutually suspicious social strata. Senghor is the great compromiser, the great builder of coalitions. He has accommodated his policy to what seems to be possible. He has gained room for maneuver by balancing one group against the other. He has always tried to see the larger picture while taking into account the specific interests of diverse groups. What, however, is really involved in this kind of politics? Is nothing more involved than moderation and compromise, or is there the sacrifice of radical change, the abandonment of any prospects for rapid change? In other words, is ideology in Senegal really an instrument for greater national unity and economic development, or is it primarily a mask for the existing "establishment"?

These questions gain in clarity when understood against the background of evolving French colonial and Senegalese political history as well as within the context of Senegal's traditional and religious social structures.

The Historical Background; the Changing Social Context

Colonial policies vary, and French policy has varied more than most because of a history of revolutions and counterrevolutions in France itself. Depending on the political spectrum and social forces in power, *France officielle* liberated, dominated, tyrannized, cultivated, uplifted, exploited or enslaved the peoples of its overseas areas. The basic attitudes of paternalism, elitism and manipulation, however, remained constants. Even as France held out the goal of complete equality, liberation was to be achieved through assimilation—*not* self-government or independence. For this, Africa is indebted to the most advanced European thinkers of the eighteenth century.

Philosophes of the Enlightenment effectively defined the rules of the French Imperial system. When properly nurtured, Reason embodied in Man would explode the chains of convention and the bonds of selfish interests to create a Brotherhood of the Universal. From Condorcet's cell-bed sprang the hope of progress, freedom, self-realization and liberation from the tyranny of repressive regimes.

From the eighteenth century on, therefore, the reformers and radicals of France attempted to change the nature of French government and society, rather than to break away from it. Virtually to this day in France the Left seeks to cause through control of the state structures the same universal vibrations the Enlightenment caused in the eighteenth century. Thus, no political tendency in France (including the Communist Party) demanded independence for the colonies until well after World War II. The past contained a clear message for those who wanted revolution and for those who wanted to be free: go to Paris; participate in the institutions of the mother country, even while seeking their overthrow.

Senegal was one of the earliest beneficiaries of this system. The French Revolution not only terminated the slave trade and slavery (only to have Napoleon restore them in 1802, and the revolutions of 1848 finally abolish them), but granted full French citizenship to all the people of Senegal and offered active representation in metropolitan institutions. This first grant of citizenship was short-lived. Nevertheless, earlier than in any other African country, France established in Senegal partly representative government and institutions providing significant opportunities for political participation. By so doing, it guided and channeled (and entrapped) political activity and political activists.[6]

By 1789 a sizable number of Senegalese—almost wholly *métis* (persons of mixed European and black African descent)—

had grown relatively wealthy acting as middlemen between the great houses of Bordeaux and up-country Africans. They looked to France for standards of behavior, and habituated themselves to styles of dress and cultural values determined by the ruling elites of Paris. Intermittently from 1848 (continuously from 1879), Senegal alone of all African countries (until 1946) sent a deputy to Paris. Until 1914 the powerful *métis* community controlled this office, as well as most other positions on the general and municipal councils.

In 1879 the colonial administration also established the first Territorial General Council in Senegal, with limited powers in local administrative and financial matters. Between 1872 and 1887 four communes (Saint-Louis, Gorée, Dakar and Rufisque) were converted into fully incorporated municipalities with their own additional councils. Before the turn of the century, therefore, elections by universal suffrage (available to anyone able to prove five-year residence) effectively politicized most of the African inhabitants of the four communes. Long before the formation of an indigenous political class in the British colonies, despite the purported English goals of self-government, a small Senegalese elite emerged—politically self-aware, but swirled into the vortex of French affairs.[7]

In 1914 citizens of the four communes elected the first full African deputy, Blaise Diagne, who defeated six *métis* and European opponents. Citizen, Catholic, Serer* and minor official in the customs service, Diagne went on to become the first African to participate in the French government in a high ministerial position.[8] Elected at the outbreak of the First World War, his eminence coincided with the need of the French government for an African army. In 1927 Diagne was appointed Commissioner of the Republic and placed in charge of conscription in West Africa. Over 180,000 men were recruited in one way or another

---

* President Senghor is a member of the Serer tribe, numbering about 500,000 people and accounting for approximately 14 percent of Senegal's population.

and sent to fight in Europe, with a tremendous rate of casualties.[9]

While prepared to defend the privileged position of the citizens, he soon acquired a reputation as an apologist for the colonial regime, to the extent of justifying forced labor and the total lack of democratic rights outside the four communes. At the end, his reputation for being a defender of colonialism, a tool of the administration and a spokesman for European big business stimulated an African opposition against him. Lamine Gueye, the first African lawyer in French West Africa, headed this opposition.

Throughout his career, until independence, Lamine Gueye attacked the autocratic and discriminatory aspects of colonial rule—never colonial rule itself. He helped develop a socialist action and study group which in the 1930's transformed itself into a Senegalese branch within the French socialist party—one of the earliest political parties in French West Africa. His political career was motivated by one major desire: acceptance of an African elite as the equals of French citizens with the same rights and duties to the point of social, economic and political assimilation.

Rejecting the solution of eventual independence adopted even before the war by Holland for Indonesia and Great Britain for the Gold Coast, he argued that "there is only asked of France a strict equality of treatment in the application of its own laws." [10] Léopold Senghor was never so complete an enthusiast in his support for France. In Lamine Gueye there is nothing counterposed to the all-pervading legitimacy and saliency of French institutions and civilization. There is no theory of Negritude, no inkling of an African personality, no indication that Africans as members of a non-Western civilization had any values, concepts or concerns worth mentioning. His close ties with the French prevented him from seeing clearly enough that Senegal was entering a period of transition. He found himself in perfect harmony with the administration and the urban bourgeoisie at the time when the countryside was assuming greater political importance. Senegal obviously needed a philosophy, a rhetoric, a person, to be a transition between country and city, between administration and the peasant, between black Muslim religious leaders and European Catholic political leaders, between France and Senegal.

Coming at different times in colonial history, representing different constituencies, Gueye and Senghor made different demands and had differing approaches to the colonial government. At the same time, these differences should not be overstated, for both men (like Blaise Diagne before them) were willing to work within the French system. Neither ideologically nor in terms of their constituencies did they feel any pressure to leave the French community or demand independence.

Senghor, in fact, had begun his political career as the hand-appointed protégé of Lamine Gueye. At first they were running-mates for the positions of Senegal's two deputies. Later, when they split apart, Senghor founded his own party and then defeated Gueye for the same position—deputy to the National Assembly. Senghor attributed their separation to the fact that Lamine Gueye had become increasingly alienated from the people and too close to the French administration.

The rise of Senghor's career coincided with the rise of conditions for a new type of politics in Senegal. These conditions resulted from an expansion of the politically relevant elements of the population to include the rural areas, as well as from both quantitative and qualitative changes in the nature of Senegal's elite. From the end of the war, France gradually extended the franchise first to veterans, civil servants, chiefs, holders of school certificates, gradually including more and more special categories until the universal franchise became law in 1957. By the end of 1951 the balance of votes had changed from the four communes to the countryside.

Senghor, born in Jaol, outside of the four communes and hence of "subject" origin himself, made a much more convincing appearance in the "bush" than did city-bred, bourgeoisified

Lamine Gueye. Senghor was also able to present himself with clean hands, free of the entangling alliances with *citadin* interests that had been the basis of Gueye's support for more than three decades.

Agricultural conditions were particularly difficult in Senegal from World War II until the Korean War, and Senghor addressed himself to the needs of rural interests. Although concerned with legal aspects of citizenship and equality, he did not have Gueye's almost total preoccupation with these matters (which were of concern almost exclusively to civil servants and city-dwellers).

After the Second World War, changes in suffrage appeared to introduce mass politics into Senegal. For the first time in her history a majority of the population was brought into the political arena. Nevertheless, the countryside remained highly structured. The net effect of the "liberalizing" measures, therefore, was to strengthen the power of the traditional and religious leaders. Assertions that these powers would be undermined by the forces of "modernization" proved conspicuously premature. Indeed, Senghor turned precisely to these rural elites in his search for a new base of support.

Traditional society in Senegal is unexpectedly unlike that found in most other parts of the continent today—yet of special interest because it indicates one very important pattern of possible evolution for many other countries. Long before the first French settlement in 1638 and seizure from the Dutch of the small island of Gorée in 1677, three African *bours*, or kings, of Cayor, Baol and Sine—states powerful and fearful by any Western standard of the time—traded and negotiated as equals with the merchants and princes of Europe.[11] Earlier, in 1444, Prince Henry's slavers explored the mouth of the Senegal River. By 1460 the Portuguese had well staked out a growing commerce in slaves, gold and other commodities. By the beginning of the seventeenth century, competition for the business of these African states between Portugal, England, France and Holland created a thriving international commerce. Thus, the impact of the West on Senegal's traditional society has acted over a period of more than three hundred years.

Again, unlike most African countries, rural Senegal has experienced three waves of conquest—which have left behind them elements of three separate ruling groups. The ancient conflicts between these groups are sometimes manifested in contemporary political struggles. Legitimacy of many present-day politicians finds its origin in this past.

Warrior invaders in the first wave of conquest created strongly hierarchical states in most of Senegal. Religious holy wars followed in later centuries; then came the imposition of a *Pax Française*. Chiefs appointed by the French succeeded the reigning families of the traditional African states. A new wave of men of economic and political power—the technicians, politicians, university graduates, businessmen and intellectuals—has today joined the *marabouts*, those religious leaders of the traditional Islamic brotherhoods who are simultaneously teacher, prophet and savior.

In a country with a population estimated at 3.4 million, Senegal contains Wolof, Serer, Peulh, Toucouleur, Mandingue, Bambara, Diola, Sankole, Mandjaque, Balante, Bassari, Coniqui and Lebou peoples.[12] Despite the long period of trade and contact with capitalist-industrial civilizations, traditional identities remain important. Toucouleur deputies predominated in the leadership of the National Assembly. The Serer, located near the coast, resisted Islam and converted to Catholicism. In a country where 80 percent of the population were Moslem and the vast majority illiterate, large numbers of the Serer—including Blaise Diagne and Senghor—became educated and entered the civil service or prospered as merchants. The Diola of the Casamance —a district separated from Dakar by climate, vegetation, distance, poor communications and transportation facilities—constituted the major element in the main organized opposition.

Another minor grouping, the Lebou, while numbering less than one percent of the population, had been tightly organized since the end of the eighteenth century. The Lebou "community" negotiated with the French and established treaties granting territorial concessions which today have made them owners of the most valuable property in Dakar.

In terms of understanding the role of ideology in modern Senegal, however, the most important grouping is the Wolof. The Wolof, with more than a million people, illustrate in their history and social structure some of the difficulties that face Senegal's modern rulers. Having had contact with Europeans for centuries, the Wolof have long enjoyed a far larger percentage of political and administrative positions than their numbers alone would warrant, as well as a predominance in economic control stemming from the production of peanuts. These reasons warrant a brief but more extended examination of Wolof history.

Traditional Wolof society stressed authoritative allocation of land rights and a hierarchy of caste and family. The caste system has broken down in contemporary Senegal, although the concept of caste still operates. Only an insignificant number of highly placed professionals are of low-caste origin.[13]

Today, the consequences of caste origins are more indirect, but nonetheless quite real. Slaves cannot be bought and sold, yet the social status and life-chances of individuals of slave origin continue to remain disadvantaged. Similarly, it is hardly surprising that the men who were at the top of traditional society seem, by and large, to have come out not too badly in their modern relationships as well. Caste is still of the greatest significance in modern Senegal.[14]

The nature of class relationships and chieftainship changed as chiefs became instruments of French rule. After 1887 only the French administration could remove living chiefs. Thus, no segment of the African population had the power to exercise restraint on their chiefs. Since the French wanted clear-cut lines of authority and were dependent on the chiefs to get things done, the colonial administration concentrated all power in their hands. This effectively resulted in cutting off the French from all other communication with the people. There was no way to go beyond the chief and check up on him.

15

While the French had the power to pick whomever they wished for chiefs, usually they tended to respect the traditional rules of succession. The administrative reorganization of 1898 signified the final establishment of a neat hierarchy of authority, with chiefs appointed by the administration and receiving salaries from it.

Not until the middle of the nineteenth century did the Wolof state system break down. Then, at roughly the same time, the French established their political rule rendering ineffectual the traditional chiefs (from 1850 to 1900), as Islam fulfilled a massive work of conversion. Much of the ancient power of the Wolof kings appears to have passed to the *marabouts*. The Wolof as a whole, however, did not succumb to Islamic proselytizing until the nineteenth century.[15]

Islam succeeded in large measure because it provided the religious, political and social framework most capable of shaping the new historical realities. The rise of African commerce was one of these new realities. With the continued spread of commercialization under continuous contact with the West, the feudal warrior aristocracy declined. It is in this context that one must understand the success of the *marabouts*; with the availability of new opportunities, conversion to Islam was a way of legitimizing a breaking away from the more traditional social system. Hence, the *marabouts* have to a great extent replaced the traditional leaders in the countryside.

In Senegal, adherents of Islam are divided into a number of brotherhoods or *confréries* that are based not only on sectarian differences but also in part on ethnic lines. Tidjane, Mouride and Quadriya are the three most important groupings.[16] They differ in history, doctrine and custom, discipline, political alliances and personalities. Yet, all of the brotherhoods have two factors crucial to Senegalese politics in common: first, a *marabout-talibé* relationship (i.e., a leader-follower relationship) in which the *marabout* guarantees salvation in the next world for his disciples as long as they are faithful in attentions and obedience to him personally; and, secondly, all of the brotherhoods share not only a general *weltanschauung,* but an intense mysticism which consecrates the *marabout-talibé* relationship and makes highly salient the religious criteria of this philosophy. While some young people are beginning to feel that the *marabouts* speak only *ex cathedra* on secular matters, no politician in Senegal seriously seeking a mass following can attack these religious precepts.

Of the Islamic brotherhoods in Senegal, the Mourides have shown the most spectacular growth and are the most powerful in terms of internal effectiveness and the obedience given the *marabouts* by the *talibés.* Today, estimates on the number of Mourides in Senegal vary from 400,000 to over a million. A French commentator, Abel Bourlon, puts the source of Mouride power very succinctly when he states that they have brought to their *talibés*

> . . . a simple and practical solution to that question, agonizing for all men, "what will become of us after our death?" Every Mouride who has worked for his Marabout and has given him his tithe will go to Heaven, because his Marabout prays for him and will save him without any need for the person to do anything for his own salvation, and even if he has sinned.[17]

Talibés are those who, in theory, although not necessarily in fact, have renounced father and mother and chosen to go to paradise. Adherents of the *marabouts* are supposed to be like a "cadaver in the hands of the washers of the dead." This means—and this fact should be emphasized—that a large proportion of the population of Senegal is highly committed and tightly organized on the basis of personal, charismatic relationships built on irrational emotional appeals.

The maraboutic dogma of "sanctification" through work provides another source of Mouride influence; it is not only agricultural work which sanctifies, but also commercial, industrial or political work. Today some *marabouts* have tens of thousands of *talibés* in the cities—civil servants, skilled and unskilled workers, whose earnings are far greater than the peasants', but who are

17

still equally faithful in carrying out their obligations.

There is no doubt that the *grands marabouts* and the great brotherhoods play a crucial role in contemporary Senegalese politics. One French commentator has said that the religious brotherhoods "are the ones who presently represent the principal force capable of opposing the modernistic elite with whom they and the political movement they express must seek an accommodation." [18] Commentators have held the leaders of the religious brotherhoods primarily responsible, among other things, for the "Yes" vote in 1958 on the French-sponsored referendum rejecting immediate independence, and for the ouster of Mamadou Dia.[19] In 1964–65 President Senghor received as official visitors more *marabouts* than members of any other non-governmental or party Senegalese group.

In addition to their great spiritual and political power, the religious brotherhoods have tremendous economic power. The Mourides alone probably control considerably more than half of the peanut crop, which accounts for over 80 percent of Senegal's gross national product. *Marabouts* have also succeeded in many cases in taking over control of the new rural institutions, such as Cooperatives, and (in at least some cases) running them with more than average efficiency.

Even some of the most radical politicians (African as well as European) were attracted to the *marabouts* for the purposes of constructing socialism. They looked to the brotherhoods to provide a framework of organization for the *encadrement* of the population as well as for a motivating force, an ethic of industry and work. They minimized the risks of cooperating with conservative interests, assuming that the introduction of Western rationality, the creation of new economic stimuli and relationships, and the increased strength of the secular state would cause the power of the *marabouts* to wither away.

For their part, however, the *marabouts* were perfectly aware of all of the dangers of erosion of their strength from within. For example, until they understood the implications of secular education and how to cope with it, they refrained from sending their children to the public schools. Once they grasped the necessity for modern education, the schools were swamped. Regardless of what deals were offered them, the *marabouts* refused to cooperate in a basically hostile environment. Despite protestations of friendship, they distrusted those elements of the modernistic elite who based their programs on individual rationality and equality. They were also suspicious of politicians opposed to French business and colonial interests, for these latter were major friends and allies of the *marabouts*.

The *marabouts* did not object to rapid economic change in the sense of quickly increased productivity, or to new institutions such as the Cooperatives, for what counted was how these institutions affected the relationships between *marabouts, talibés* and the central government. Insofar as the *marabouts* could become presidents of the Cooperatives, learn how to conduct the technical organizations, engage in trade themselves and keep control of these institutions in the countryside, they could actually strengthen their power.

In the towns, Senghor was at first less successful in drawing new allies. In 1945 less than 5 percent of school-age children in the Federation of French West Africa (A.O.F.) attended classes. Few Africans received a university education and many of those who did came from Senegal. The first African "elite" consisted of those who, in reality, possessed little formal education beyond an ability to read and write: clerks, secretaries, interpreters, lower civil servants—humble occupations by contemporary standards, but important because they acted as bridges between the African population and the colonial administration.

A small class, this first elite derived status from the colonial establishment and held itself aloof from the mass of the people. However, as the quality of education improved and the absolute number of highly trained Africans increased, fewer and fewer Africans accepted the goal of assimilation to French values and styles of life. The Senegalese elite, nevertheless, continued to aspire to the legal and administrative rights of Frenchmen, as well as to the artifacts of a higher material standard of living.

19

most. Dakar, as its capital, had reaped special administrative and economic advantages that left her with a surplus of civil servants and industries designed for a much broader market than her own hinterland. The 1958 Constitution did formally provide that those states in the Community who wished to regroup could do so, and in January 1959 Senegal, Soudan, Dahomey and Upper Volta formed the Mali Federation. Dahomey and Upper Volta defected even before the Union came into formal existence, and the ties between Mali and Senegal lasted only until August 1960, when Senegal dropped out and the Soudan retained the name Mali.

Although the de Gaulle Constitution of 1958 held out the possibility of independence to be decided by a popular referendum, the President of the French Republic made clear that independence meant isolation and the complete elimination of all *ties* with France, including technical assistance, economic aid and preferential tariffs. Guinea was the only Francophone state to "opt" for independence, and France, true to her promise, eradicated her presence to the extent of pulling telephones off the walls and medicines out of the hospitals.

Senghor actually had committed himself for a brief moment to the goal of independence in 1958, but then quickly retracted. This was at an interterritorial meeting in Cotonou in July 1958 of virtually all the political parties of West Africa. Calling themselves the *Parti du Regroupement Africain* (P.R.A.), the Congress, led by radical young newcomers, passed a resolution calling for independence. These "young men of the left" had been brought into Senghor's party despite their ideological dissonances in large part because of the difficulties of success.

When Senghor broke with Lamine Gueye, he formed the *Bloc Démocratique Sénégalais* (B.D.S.) in 1948, with Mamadou Dia as Secretary General. Dia was a "subject" schoolteacher stationed in the Sine-Saloum region. Son of a policeman and allegedly of low-caste origin, Dia was proficient in Wolof and had sat at the feet of Amadou Bamba, founder of the Mouride brotherhood.

In 1951 the B.D.S. won 69 percent of the votes cast; in 1956, 76 percent. However, the party still had a number of major difficulties. Most of the votes came from the countryside. Dakar and Saint-Louis remained strongly Gueyeist. Once in power, the B.D.S. desperately needed trained Africans to staff the civil services, as well as literate organizers for the "bush." Yet the lawyers, doctors and other established members of the liberal professions and the civil service backed the socialists. And men like Assane Seck (geographer and first African member of the staff of the University of Dakar), Abdoulaye Ly (historian and vice-director of Institut Français d'Afrique Noire—I.F.A.N.) and Amadou Moctar M'Bow (professor of history) rebelled against what they considered the bureaucratic, conservative, nonideological nature of the governing party.

For a brief period the intellectuals, along with students, members of youth organizations and trade-unionists, were enticed to enter Senghor's party in 1956 when it changed its name to the *Bloc Populaire Sénégalais* (B.P.S.). Early in 1958 Lamine Gueye finally cemented a new unity by merging his P.S.A.S.* into what is today Senegal's governing party—the U.P.S., *Union Progressiste Sénégalaise.*

This radical faction within the U.P.S. demanded a vote for independence in the referendum. When Dia and Senghor succeeded in turning the party to a policy of continued alliance with France, the "radicals" again went into opposition, in September 1958. Drawing upon reconsolidated strength in youth and student groups, labor, technocrats, professional personnel and upper civil servants, they called themselves *P.R.A.-Sénégal* after the Cotonou Conference.

After 1959, after the lessons of Indochina, Morocco and Tunisia, self-government for India and independence for Ghana, the Algerian war still dragged on, and France was faced with her own domestic turmoil. The French government then amended

* Lamine Gueye founded the Senegalese branch of the Section Française de l'Internationale Ouvrière (S.F.I.O.) in 1936. In February 1957 its name was changed to Parti Sénégalais d'Action Socialiste (P.S.A.S.) to re-emphasize its autonomy and Senegalese identity.

the metropolitan constitution to enable a state to become completely sovereign yet remain within a community renovated along the lines of the British Commonwealth. Only then, in 1960, did Senegal and the other Francophone states—with the blessing of France—become independent.

After independence, the tasks of producing internal cohesion, coupled with the necessities of economic development, increased tensions within the U.P.S. In 1962 Dia and Senghor had a falling out, in large part over strategies of economic development, with Dia driving for a rapid social reorganization and intensification of government efforts. Senghor, with the aid of the army, succeeded in winning a brief power struggle and removing Dia to prison exile in a remote corner of the countryside.

By 1965, however, the U.P.S. faced virtual disintegration into warring clans, and tremendous difficulties in reorganizing the population. In a new bid for unity, Senghor invited the opposition P.R.A. back into the U.P.S., creating a new façade of harmony. In 1968 only the illegal self-styled Marxist-Leninist *Parti Africain de l'Indépendance* (P.A.I.), founded in 1957 by radical students back from France, still semiexisted outside the realm of the governing party's consensus. Many Dia-ists persisted throughout the administration and country; and part of the *Bloc des Masses Sénégalaises*, led by Cheikh Anta Diop, remained aloof (although the majority joined the U.P.S. in 1963).

Clearly, however, Senegal had arrived at a new stage in its political evolution. The P.R.A. had recognized the impossibility of gaining power through the polls, and the uselessness of continued political activity outside the dominant party. The *parti dominant* had given way to the *parti unique*, and Senegal had followed the path of most other African nations.

However, even though France finally granted Senegal independence and Senegalese politicians refashioned her party system, the legacy of these struggles, the colonial past and the traditional and religious structures have all contributed to producing a growing chasm within Senegal's society that profoundly affects the nature of her present politics and the future prospects for economic development.

In terms of world history, mass participation in politics is a relatively limited and recent phenomenon, dating in the West in any significant fashion only from the French Revolution, and in any systematic fashion only from the mid-nineteenth century. In modern times, however, mass politics may be a basic prerequisite for the *encadrement* of the population and the implementation of various processes of change.

Yet, in Senegal two nations exist as distinctly and separately as ever they did in Disraeli's England. A privileged class, for the most part consisting of higher civil servants, but also including businessmen, politicians, teachers, scientific personnel, lawyers, doctors and other members of the liberal professions, is set apart from the unskilled and low-skilled workers, clerks, peddlers, traders, artisans, migrants, vagabonds, nurses, cooks, "boys," beggars, lepers and unemployed, who constitute the mass of the city populations. Elite and mass are separated not only by occupation and income, but by dress, food, style of crime, health, housing, play, education, language and every other important ingredient which goes into the composition of a style of life.

A few illustrations may not be amiss. Two hospitals exist in Dakar—Dantec and Principal—because there are two standards of health care. At one time, Dantec was reserved for *Europeans*—who were mainly "functionaries." Today, Dantec is used by *Africans* who are mainly "functionaries." Principal is the hospital that has a low percentage of malaria and acute malnutrition patients in a land where these diseases are endemic. There is room for only more serious problems.

Some of the villas overlooking the sea and basalt-studded beaches would be considered charming by any standard. Members of the top elite survive not badly in the elegant skyscraper apartment buildings and town houses with their well-watered lawns and bougainvillea. Lesser "functionaries" must be content to live more modestly, yet also have privileges in government-sponsored projects where the houses are becoming increasingly sumptuous.

25

However, most Africans live in the Medina, originally a completely segregated low-income African quarter. Emil Lengyel describes how the Medina was created by Europeans fearful of catching the diseases and other contaminations of Africans. Today there are a few modern buildings in the Medina. Huts built of broken concrete blocks, weathered scraps of lumber held together by chicken wire with tin roofs, predominate along crowded streets filled with swarms of goats.

Only one or two murders annually occur, on the average, in all of Senegal. Physical violence of any type has been rare; crime involving property, on the other hand, is rampant. Again, styles differ; among white-collar workers the crimes are embezzlement, the fix, pay-offs and influence peddling. "Have-nots," in their turn, have perfected housebreaking to the level of a sport. Fancy residential sections are often protected by dogs, high fences, round-the-clock guards (a symbol of prestige is to have a government-appointed watchman) and theft insurance. Break-ins in the Medina are even more common, but are seldom reported because of the feeling that there is nothing the police can do.

Direct taxes have always been easy to avoid if you know the right people. Tax-collectors—indeed high tax officials—have been known to bring their stamps and make out the forms for favored clients in the clients' homes or places of business. In dealing with the less favored, tax collectors have, without warning, driven to the door of a house, in the middle of the day when no men were home, and loaded everything not tied down—first sorting out the valuables in which they were personally interested.

Language, next to education, is a fundamental distinguishing characteristic. An infinitesimal percentage of Senegalese speak French in their homes, and less than 10 percent of the population speak French at all. Obviously, the influentials will be chosen from among these.

University graduates will enter the cream of the elite, followed closely by those with their baccalaureates. Literacy and education are the prerequisites of entrée into the administration and other opportunities. The occupations of fathers of students at the University of Dakar indicate the extent to which they are members of the privileged class. Equally surprising is the large percentage of civil servants in Senegal today whose fathers were also members of this privileged or upper stratum.

Thus, it would appear that not only are there two fundamentally different strata, but also the privileged class is further separated from the mass by being self-perpetuating, rather than relying for its continuity on outside recruitment.

Fundamentally different styles of life, ways of living, leisure-time activities, patterns of eating, dressing, speaking and working threaten to increase the gulf between the "haves" and the "have-nots" of Senegal. If such a gulf exists in Senegal's cities, the peasantry is even more in an immobile, stricken world apart.

The problems of unity are thus clearly linked to the problems of economic development, and the growth of social schisms to the political and institutional evolution of French-Senegalese relations. All of this is reflected in the changing thought and interests of Senghor.

Recently, to prevent the gulf between elite and mass from growing larger, Senghor has been making more of a concentrated effort to reach the people. In this respect, as in several others, there have been a number of important changes of emphasis in his thinking over the years.

Senghor: Ideology in Evolution

From the French Community to the Federation of French West Africa, to the Mali Federation, to Senegal, Senghor has shifted his attention from the concerns of a wider community to those of his own nation-state. Changing circumstances have forced Senghor's growing concentration upon the problems of Senegal alone. At the same time, he has increasingly turned from abstract philosophy to technical and pragmatic methodology for development. Increasingly, an assertion of the necessity to be

27

non-ideological becomes the prevailing ideology.

Originally, Negritude served the psychological needs of intellectuals in the Paris of the thirties. Today Senghor attempts to re-create Negritude into a new type of education for rural Africans. He now hopes to address himself to the mass of the peasants and not just to be an intellectual elite, to tell them to re-create and strengthen the old-fashioned type of community, and to throw off colonially induced bourgeois attitudes and training. Increasingly, Senghor speaks of "casting-off" and not of "synthesis," of action and not of culture and philosophy. From the doctrine of poets and philosophers, Negritude now attempts to justify the creation of engineers and technicians. A romanticization about the past appears as an instrument for the creation of the future. The success of this new shift of approach, given the historical complexities that have been constructed into Senegal's social fabric, is questionable.

The French created philosophers and intellectuals whom, Senghor now claims, the country did not need, instead of the skilled workmen it required for development. This recent perception might sound like hand-biting, but Senghor has never been the simple French acolyte that his most violent detractors would picture him. Over the years, he has assumed a number of differing stances in regard to the relations between Senegal and France, including a threat to declare for independence in the immediate postwar period.

Always a staunch foe of imperialism, Senghor was intensely concerned with racial discrimination felt above all by the civil-servant class. Only after independence did he become primarily and directly concerned with the welfare of the mass of the population, as economic development became his major preoccupation. Senghor began to place more emphasis on class; he re-interpreted the conflict between Europe and Africa in terms not of color, but of domination of poor by rich nations. Today a nuance of additional emphasis on race separates the French as whites from the Senegalese as blacks. In general, one can detect a slight cooling toward the French as Senegal becomes more involved with economic development and France cuts subsidies; as Senghor becomes more involved with the people of the rural areas and his connections with the French intelligentsia become less important. A trend toward broader identification by Senegal with non-French areas—as evidenced by trade figures showing the expansion of European, American and Commonwealth connections[20]—ideologically accompanies concepts (such as Portuguese-African civilization and Maghreb-African civilization) emphasizing the contribution of other cultures to African development.

A new emphasis on practical technology constitutes still another recent development in the evolution of Senghor's thought. Increasingly, he hails technology as the key to Senegal's future. Science, he argues, applied systematically, will make the physical universe yield its riches in increasing quantities. This belief in science and technology has influenced his attitudes and policies toward mass-elite relationships, socialism, capitalism, the political party, the administration, social reform and the strategy of economic development.

But faith in the efficacy of technology has important political consequences: if productivity can be increased by calling in a firm of French agricultural engineers to teach the farmers how to plant their peanuts two inches closer together and three inches deeper, why mobilize the population? What does it matter if the rural masses cannot understand learned illusions and the concept of Negritude, as long as they pour on the fertilizer? Then, logically it would follow that the strongest forces within society, those that should have the government's ear and provide its major support, should be those best able to administer the programs laid down by the rural engineers—the technicians.

Significantly, then, Senghor has increasingly relied more on the bureaucracy than the political party to carry out his program. He has found the political party too filled with factions, self-aggrandizing politicians who possess little mass support and who are bent on filling their own pockets. Within the administration, two new trends have been: (1) a further political neutralization of the agencies most directly concerned with the countryside, to the extent of bypassing the *animateurs ruraux* (once called the crux of Senegal's construction of socialism in the countryside) in favor of foreigners who in no way even pretend to participate in other than the technical aspects of rural life; and (2) an increased role for the army. The military are seen, first, as great patriots, defenders of the fatherland, and secondly as technicians —they are not to judge any particular party or policy, but to uphold the power of legally constituted authority, no matter what their personal opinion. Systematically, skillfully and with the proper means at their disposal, the military should carry out their assigned tasks with loyalty and devotion. Moreover, engaged in the concrete tasks of economic development, they will function not simply as mass laborers providing a type of cheap forced labor, but rather as construction engineers earning superior pay and privileges. Furthermore, military officers may play a certain political role. Particularly, they will police certain troublesome areas in the frontier region. A number of army officers have already been made prefects. They could also be made governors of regions or hold other important positions. Indeed, Senghor may tire of the bickering and roadblocks erected by politicians not entirely in sympathy with his objectives. He may come to despair of the possibility of significantly curtailing the privileges of the civil service, and might turn to the army for more direct aid in governing the country.

In this connection, another trend in Senghor's writing has been an increasing emphasis toward authoritarianism. Never fundamentally a democrat, he reveals more tolerance of a single-party system instead of the dominant-party theory that he previously expounded. At the same time, rationalization of the bureaucracy was also part of the process by which Senghor aimed at more effective, centralized control.

In the countryside, the success of socialism depended ultimately on the spread of Cooperatives. This would result not simply in better marketing procedures, but in the democratization of social structure and the spirit of a non-exploitative, humanitarian society. But from the beginning of his political career Senghor sought out the support of *marabouts* and other traditional leaders in the countryside who otherwise might act as social and economic obstacles to innovation. Instead of a suicidal frontal attack on these political allies, Senghor sought to undermine their authority and convert them to his interests and perspectives. He has believed that the power basis of the traditional leaders would wither away with the spread of education and additional opportunities. The emancipated peasants would turn to a secular, scientific authority with its promise of humane abundance. This strategy has remained constant in Senghor's thinking. Indeed, his faith in it has increased. Senghor's perspective, however, as revealed by his new image of capitalism, has changed. Gone are the days of the student and the French National Assembly, when he viewed capitalism primarily as a morally abhorrent, exploitative system, regardless of its accomplishments. Now he places more emphasis on investment and distribution because of their value in contributing to economic development. This important change of emphasis relates to his desire for increased technicity.

For a socialist engaged in national reconstruction and confronted by classical capitalism, the obvious solution is classical socialism. However, if the problem is viewed from the perspective of a technician—that is, as one of simply increasing production—the solution is quite different, for there is the absence of any moral perspective. Technicity involves the displacement of emotion by rationality.

This establishes a fundamental conflict between the requirements of technology and Senghor's personal and philosophical predilections: the poet as *beau idéal* is confronted by the technician, emotion by reason, the rhythm of the tom-tom by the rhythm of the machine, complexity by uniformity, coalition by centralization, and the full development of the individual by the individual as a unit in the productive apparatus.

Paradoxically, we resolve these apparent tensions if we view Senghor—who sees in emotionality the essence of Negritude and

who has been a leading political figure for decades—as foremost
among Africa's new breed of technicians. Senghor's technicity is
both most evident and most necessary in the field of nation-
building and economic development. His skills and understanding have aided in the creation of bureaucracies, the *encadrement*
of the peasant, rational organization and scientific planning. Senghor as political broker has been the great technician of politics.
He has created and balanced great coalitions of the most diverse
groups; he has emerged as the calculator of interests, the synthe-
sizer of opposites and the formulator of the lowest common denominator.

Senghor: His Style and Appeal

The political coalitions and policies of Senghor sometimes
have the unintended effect of undermining these socialist goals,
while his personality and political "style" may also make it difficult for him to mobilize his people for action toward these ultimate
ends.

Senghor has earned the highest honors of the greatest universities, cultural societies and governments of four continents as
well as the most important political positions and highest esteem
for his poetry and cultural achievements. Despite his honors, he
refers to himself in addressing his people as "this humble Serer"
and asks self-effacingly for their support. In the classical image,
he has been a man of honesty and integrity, faithful to his com-
rades, generous with his enemies. In contrast to changes in his
moods, his friends, his politics and his ideas, he maintains a remarkable consistency in his temper, constancy in his tones, and
faithfulness to his original aspirations.

Yet, in his own terms, Senghor is a tragic figure. His highest
responsibilities lie not with the promulgation of abstract theses
for the edification of the world, but with the realization of his
ideals within the immediate universe of Senegal. As he himself
has written:

> But if I must choose at the hour of
> testing . . .
> I have chosen my toiling black people,
> my peasant people . . .
> To be your trumpet! [21]

Despite Senghor's earnest desire to become the "trumpet of his people," to arouse them to achieve the goals of socialistic economic development, his personal and political style seem little suited to the tasks of mass stimulation. Mercer Cook, former United States Ambassador to Senegal and a close friend since their student days, describes Senghor's style as follows: "From Heraclitus to Hegel, from Marx to Mauriac, from Engels to Einstein, from Lincoln to Lenin, from François Perroux to Gaston Berger, from Teilhard to Gaëtan Picon, he cites passages that one would hardly expect to hear analyzed at an African political rally. Refusing to 'Africanize at a discount,' he shuns neither the difficult nor the unpopular. Always the teacher, he has the patience to explain, the intellectual honesty not to oversimplify, and faith that the lesson will be understood." [22] Senghor insists, for the most part, in addressing his countrymen in the same style and level of French which in the National Assembly caused him to be made Official Grammarian of the Constitution. [23]

Perhaps it is these qualities of Senghor that make him seem at once so attractive to Western audiences and critics and so questionable an entity in an underdeveloped country. For there is in Senghor a spacing of emotion, a marching of feelings single-file. In his politics as in his poetry, Senghor draws back from passion, from overstimulating his audience, for he seeks to move without arousing. Always in the background we sense a calculating presence, a man of Reason recording his sentiments.

As his situation and condition have changed, Senghor has written for different audiences to fulfill different needs. In the thirties he addressed primarily a highly educated, highly sophisticated audience that was mainly French. He desired not to arouse these people to *do* anything, but to inform them. Senghor's talent lay in his ability to communicate the moral experiences of African intellectuals living in the surrealistic pre-Nazi Paris of the thirties, and their longing for a more idyllic, noble past. His failure today lies in his inability to communicate a new morality appropriate to constructing a nation and raising the poor into material possession—a morality which, undoubtedly, he personally feels very deeply.

All of his erudition, all of the complexity of his philosophical exegesis and the abundance of the quotations from learned sources work only to create a barrier. Senghor's doctrine remains inaccessible to the mass of the population. Significantly, all of the populist revolutions of the past have had simple slogans like "Land, Bread and Peace." To insist upon talking in the most sophisticated terms to unlearned men about "Negritude," "African Socialism," "Economic Development" and the "Civilization of the Universal," on the grounds of not talking down to them, is not to talk to them at all.

Senghor's authority suffers because of this. He is widely regarded as a "good" man, yet this in itself is not sufficient to make people want to obey him when he expresses his wishes. Knowing this inhibits the type of orders he gives as well as his readiness to give orders at all.

As Catholic, Serer, intellectual and Francophile, Senghor's moral experiences do not touch upon those of the vast majority of his countrymen. He has found no way to fill this lacuna. He has found no dramatic way to symbolize or communicate with the society as a whole.

For reasons of personal taste as well as because of the necessity of his coalitions, Senghor cannot advance *himself* as an all-embracing symbol. Hardly a charismatic leader, he is not apt to demand unquestioning faith or to stimulate a personality cult. The complexity of his ideology combine with Senegal's complex of social arrangements and political conditions to further the separation between Senghor and the mass of the population.

Conclusion

Thus, never has Senghor attuned his personal or political style to stimulating mass political participation. The same is true of his philosophy. His ideas have undergone a change from the kind of abstraction which appealed most to a humanistically educated intelligentsia to a new pragmatic reliance on science and technology. However, for the most part this new technicity involves an appeal to a technological and administrative elite, and not to the mass of Senegal's population.

Indeed, those very groups in fundamental disagreement with Senghor on ultimate philosophical objectives find the existing ideology most functional, as long as the mass of the population does not participate in politics. Because he needs support from some organized quarter, Senghor seeks cooperation from interests such as the religious leaders and merchants. He considers them vital to the regime for the moment, and seeks their cooperation not as a final end, but for immediate assistance only. Paradoxically, however, the increasing strength of these interests (which are fundamentally exploitative of rural areas) renders the peasants ever more quiescent, as well as impoverished. Senghor's ideology can attract and suit the program of privileged groups and maintain their loyalty. Thus, it can function to buttress and maintain the regime, but again paradoxically, all this is done as the objectives of the government are subtly altered and deferred.

The proper understanding of Senegalese politics and the role of ideology begins with an analysis of Senghor's first major philosophical endeavor—the ideology of Negritude.

NOTES TO CHAPTER I

1. *Black Orpheus* translated by S. W. Allen (Présence Africaine, Paris, N.D.), originally published as a preface, "Orphée Noir," to L. S. Senghor, *Anthologie de la Nouvelle Poésie Nègre et Malgache de Langue Française* (Presses Universitaires de France, Paris, 1948). Over the years Sartre's definition of rev-

olutionary has changed. Cf. his introduction to Frantz Fanon, *The Wretched of the Earth* (Grove Press, New York, 1963).

2. Among the most extravagant statements see, for example, the assessment of André Malraux at the 1966 Dakar World Festival of Negro Art, "Discours à l'Ouverture du Colloque," reprinted in *L'Unité Africaine*, Dakar, April 7, 1966, p. 6. See also Albert Maurice, "Sénégal Terre d'Humanisme," *Bulletin de l'Académie Royale des Sciences d'Outre-Mer*, 4 (1964), Brussels.

3. For the purposes of this study, I have used the broad definition of Joseph La Palombara, who says of ideology that:

> it involves a philosophy of history, a view of man's present place in it, some estimate of probable lines of future development, and a set of prescriptions regarding how to hasten, retard and/or modify that developmental direction. While the concept, ideology, is certainly one of the most elusive in our vocabulary, we can say about it that, beyond the above, it tends to specify a set of values that are more or less coherent, and that it seeks to link given patterns of action to the achievement or maintenance of a future, or existing, state of affairs. What makes such formulations of particular interest to political scientists is that ideologies frequently insist that in order to achieve or maintain desired ends, deemed to be morally superior and therefore desirable for the entire collectivity, public authority is expected to intervene. ["Decline of Ideology: A Dissent and an Interpretation," *American Political Science Review*, Vol. LX, No. 1 (March 1966), p. 7].

This article also contains extensive bibliographical references to recent writings about ideology. Palombara's definition goes beyond that of Mannheim, when Mannheim defines ideology as "more or less conscious disguises of the real nature of the situation" (*Ideology and Utopia*, Harcourt, Brace & Company, New York, 1954). While this aspect of ideology is not neglected, this study is further interested in ideology as an instrument in its own right as a tool of unity and economic development.

La Palombara's definition, developed in the course of a debate with the "end of ideology" theorists (see S. M. Lipset's rejoinder, "Some Further Comments on 'The End of Ideology,'" *American Political Science Review*, March 1966), is particularly apt for Senegal because of its scope and emphasis on development.

Cf. the definition and discussion of ideology in terms of the "crisis of modernization" in the introduction by Paul E. Sigmund, Jr., to his (ed.) *The Ideologies of the Developing Nations* (Frederick A. Praeger, New York, 1963), pp. 3–40. Sigmund argues that:

> The leaders of the group of nations, variously described as "new," "uncommitted," "emerging" or "developing," share many political, economic, and social ideas as to the type of society they are building. Although they may differ regarding the appropriate methods for reaching their goals, these leaders (with the exception of those in the most backward and tradition-bound areas) are united by a group of beliefs that give expression to common feelings about the past, present, and future.
>
> These beliefs correspond to our definition of ideology in that they elicit an emotional commitment by the leadership and their followers and are directed toward action—the development of a new society in a certain direction, in conformity with certain goals. [P. 4]

Sigmund is interested in those elements that all of the leaders of the emergent areas have in common; he emphasizes "development" as a key goal. This study is interested in the uniqueness of Senghor's ideology, in what distinguishes it from all other ideologies. While development is a key goal of this ideology, rather than assume this from the start, I am more interested in the functions Senghor's ideology fulfills in a particular sociological-historical context.

David Apter argues that he is "inclined to the view that ideology helps to perform two main functions: one, directly social, binding the community together, and the other, individual, organizing the role personalities of the maturing individual. These functions combine to legitimize authority." (Apter, ed., *Ideology and Discontent* [The Free Press of Glencoe, New York, 1964], p. 18, *passim*). See also David E. Apter, *The Politics of Modernization* (University of Chicago Press, Chicago, 1965), especially Chap. 8, "The Formation of Political Values," and Chap. 9, "Ideology in Modernizing Societies," pp. 266–357.

4. Ideology can be an aid in the fulfillment of certain requisites for economic development. Among these are: inducements to curtail immediate consumption, incitements for reinvestment, increased efforts to create a philosophy of planning, invention of a technical apparatus (including a bureaucracy) inherently in accord with announced objectives, motivation for middle-level bureaucrats and other social groups, a *prise de conscience* among the people. See, further, Eugene Staley, *The Future of Underdeveloped Countries: Political Implications of Economic Development* (rev. ed., published for the Council on Foreign Relations by Frederick A. Praeger, New York, 1961), pp. 215–220, for an economist's discussion of the "will to develop," as an important factor in economic growth. Also pp. 203–208 and *passim*.

For other discussions by economists relating to ideological problems of economic development, see W. Arthur Lewis, *The Theory of Economic Growth* (Richard D. Irwin, Homewood, Ill., 1955), especially Chap. II, "The Will to Economize," pp. 23–57; also by Lewis, "Science, Men and Money," pp. 24–33, in Ruth Gruber, ed., *Science and the New Nations* (Basic Books, New York, 1961). See also Paul Baran, *The Political Economy of Growth* (Monthly Review Press, New York, 1957); and W. W. Rostow, *The Stages of Economic Growth* (Cambridge University Press, New York, 1961).

These economists of widely differing political viewpoints are agreed on the importance of ideological and non-economic factors in development.

5. *Ouverture de la Deuxième Conférence des Chefs de Mission Diplomatique Sénégalaise*, Dakar, mimeo, N.P., March 18, 1963.

6. On the history of French colonial policy in Senegal, see for example, Félix Brigaud, *Histoire du Sénégal des Origines aux Traités de Protectorat* (Editions Clairafrique, Dakar, 1964); Michael Crowder, *Senegal: A Study in French Assimilation Policy* (Oxford University Press, New York, 1962); Georges Hardy, *La Mise en Valeur du Sénégal de 1817 à 1854* (Emile Larose, Paris, 1921); J. D. Hargreaves, "Assimilation in Eighteenth Century Senegal," *Journal of African History*, Vol. 6, No. 2 (November 4, 1965), pp. 177–184.

7. On the development and practice of organized Senegalese politics see Thomas Hodgkin, "Background to AOF," 9 articles in *West Africa*, January 2, 1954–March 6, 1954; G. Wesley Johnson, "The Ascendency of Blaise Diagne and the Beginning of African Politics in Senegal," *Africa*, Vol. XXXVI, No. 3 (July 1966), pp. 235–252; W. J. M. Mackenzie and Kenneth E. Robinson, eds., *Five Elections in Africa* (Oxford University Press, London, 1960); Ruth Schachter Morgenthau, *Political Parties in French-Speaking West Africa* (Oxford University Press, London, 1964); Jean-Louis Seurin, "Etudes Sociales et

Partis Politiques," *Annales Africaines* (Université de Dakar, Paris, 1958); Bakary Traoré, Mamadou Lo and Jean-Louis Albert, *Forces Politiques en Afrique Noire* (Presses Universitaires de France, Paris, 1966).

8. See Robert W. July, *The Origins of Modern African Thought* (Frederick A. Praeger, New York, 1967), especially Chap. 19, "The Assimilation of Blaise Diagne," pp. 392–414; also G. Wesley Johnson, *op. cit.* Charles Cros provides the most sympathetic treatment of Diagne in *La Parole est à M. Blaise Diagne* (privately printed, Paris, 1961), which also contains extensive selections from his speeches; a critical account is that of Thomas Hodgkin in "Background to AOF," *op. cit.* January 16, 1954, pp. 31–32.

9. Robert Delavignette and Charles-André Julien, eds., *Les Constructeurs de La France d'Outre-Mer* (Editions Correa, Paris, 1946), pp. 420–447.

10. Cf. Lamine Gueye's own account of his career *Itinéraire Africaine* (Présence Africaine, Paris, 1966). On his strong feelings of identity with France and proposals for reform see also his *Etapes et Perspectives de l'Union Française* (Editions de l'Union Française, Paris, 1955).

11. Cf. Martin A. Klein, "The Relevance of African History; A Case Study from Senegal," unpublished paper prepared for the African Studies Association Meeting, Philadelphia, October 1965 (mimeo).

12. Sources: *Sénégal Faits et Chiffres, Nouvelle Edition,* 1965, "Le Pays et les Hommes," pp. 1–9 (République du Sénégal, Commissariat à l'Information, à la Radiodiffusion et au Tourisme, Dakar, 1965), which refers to the still unpublished 1961 census.

Rapport Général sur les Perspectives de Développement du Sénégal, Première Partie, 3rd ed., January 1963 (first publ., July 1960, CINAM et SERES à Dakar), pp. 1–1(38) and Chap. 1, "Cadre Physique et Humain," pp. 12–50.

Cf. *Recensement Démographique de Dakar,* 1955, Résultats Définitifs (Vol. 1, Haut Commissariat de la République en Afrique Occidental Française, Paris, 2nd., 1958; Vol. 2, République du Sénégal, Ministère du Plan, de la Statistique, Paris, 1962), pp. 23–51.

13. On the caste system in Wolof society see for example David P. Gamble, *The Wolof of Senegambia* (International African Institute, London, 1957) and Ousmane Silla, "Persistence des Castes dans la Société Wolof Contemporaine," *Bulletin de l'IFAN,* 28 (B) 3/4 (July-October 1966), pp. 731–770.

14. See for example Luc Thoré, "Mariage et Divorce dans la Banlieue de Dakar," *Cahiers d'Etudes Africaines,* Vol. IV, No. 16, pp. 479–552. The official view of the government admitting that castes are significant *in the countryside* is found in *Sénégal, Faits et Chiffres, Nouvelle Edition,* 1965 (République du Sénégal, Dakar, 1965), p. 8.

15. Vincent Monteil, *L'Islam Noir* (Editions du Seuil, Paris, 1964), particularly Chap. 3, "Les Fétiches ont Tremblés," pp. 49–104, and Chap. 5, "Marabouts en Noir et Blanc," pp. 121–149. Also Martin A. Klein, *Islam and Imperialism in Senegal: Sine-Saloum 1847–1914* (Stanford University Press, Stanford, 1968).

16. For a discussion of differences between and within the various brotherhoods and a history of their origins, see Monteil, *L'Islam Noir, op. cit.,* and M. Chailly *et al.,* *Notes et Etudes sur l'Islam en Afrique Noire,* CHEAM, (J. Peyronnet et Cie, Paris, 1962).

Cf. F. Quesnot's two articles in this latter collection. "Les Cadres Maraboutiques de l'Islam Sénégalais," pp. 127–195, includes a discussion of various factions within the brotherhoods, as well as extensive biographical sketches of a large number of important *marabouts.*

To give an example of this type of internal conflict: Today the Tidjaniya —which includes more than half of Senegal's Moslems—are divided into a number of branches. While the nominal leader is Khalifa Abdoul Aziz Sy, an important competitor is Seydou Nourou Tall. Much more distinctive, although still formally Tidjaniya, are the followers of Ibrahim Niasse.

Some idea of the size of the various brotherhoods can be had from the following:

Tidjane	1,029,577
Mouride	423,273
Quadriya	302,457
Layene	15,430
Hamalliste	7,511

Total Population of Senegal, 2,260,136 (CHEAM, *op. cit.*, p. 194). These figures are only very rough estimates. Today the total population of Senegal is estimated at over three million. Monteil says that there are 400,000 Mouride males, etc.

A recent illustration of conflict *between* brotherhoods concerned the election of an Iman for the new Great Mosque of Dakar. El Hadj Abdoul Aziz Sy, Khalife Générale of the Tidjanes, supposedly elevated by an assembly of all the heads of all the mosques in the Cap Vert region, was contested by the followers of El Hadj Amadou Lamine Dieme. See "Tension au Sein de la Communicante Musulmane de Dakar," *Le Monde*, May 14, 1964.

17. Abel Bourlon, "Actualité des Mourides et du Mourides," *L'Afrique et l'Asie*," First Quarter, 1959, pp. 10–30.
18. Seurin, *op. cit.*, pp. 141–142.
19. Cf. Seurin, *ibid.*, André Blanchet, "C'est le Vieux Sénégal Qui Répondait Oui le 28 Septembre," *Le Monde*, September 15, 1958. Ruth Schachter Morgenthau, *Political Parties in French West Africa*; Paul Thibaud, "Dia, Senghor et le Socialisme Africain," *Esprit*, September 1963, pp. 332–348.
20. See Jean-Bernard Mas, Serigne Lamine Diop, Oumar Thiaw, *Rapport Provisoire sur les Comptes de la Nation des Années 1959 à 1962* (République du Sénégal, Ministre du Plan et Développement, Service de la Statistique, Dakar, 1963).
21. From "For Koras and Balafond," dedicated to René Maran, one of Senghor's earliest published poems written in October-December 1939 and included in the collection *Chants d'Ombre*; translated and reprinted in *Léopold Sédar Senghor: Prose and Poetry*, John Reed and Clive Wake, eds. (Oxford University Press, London, 1965), p. 110.
22. Mercer Cook, Introduction to *On African Socialism* by Léopold Sédar Senghor, translated by Mercer Cook (Frederick A. Praeger, New York, 1964), p. x.
23. See, for example, the series of radio speeches to the nation, *Messages au Peuple Sénégalais*, "Premier Message au Peuple Sénégalais," September 6, 1960, mimeo, N.P.; "Second Message au Peuple Sénégalais," December 31, 1960, mimeo, N.P.; "Troisième Message du Président à l'Occasion des Fêtes de l'Indépendance du Sénégal," April 4, 1961, mimeo, N.P.; etc. Also interesting is *Guinée Matin* of September 26, 1958, which contains an analysis of Senghor's style of campaigning in the countryside.

II

The Changing Social Functions of Negritude as an Ideology: 1931–1966

THE PHILOSOPHY of Negritude is the first systematic set of ideas whereby Léopold Senghor oriented himself to a foreign, European-dominated world. Negritude must be understood as a part of the changing social contexts and intellectual climates in which it took shape. As a student and young intellectual in prewar Europe, for example, Senghor was sensitive to accusations of membership in a race without culture or pride; as President of Senegal, he seeks to unite a nation in harmonious and rapid development. Senghor has adapted Negritude to these purposes. What began as a way of facing the world has become a way of changing it. Commentators who see Negritude primarily as a revolutionary philosophy of self-discovery and rejection of Western civilization have failed to evaluate these changes in the nature of Negritude as an ideology.[1]

Actually, only very briefly at the beginning of his intellectual career, when a strong racism characterized his thought, did Senghor's conception of Negritude have the potential of a revolutionary doctrine. As he became increasingly an important figure within the French literary and political establishments, Negritude, even with all its emphasis on the singularity of the black's contribution to civilization, became an instrument for

40

furthering collaboration between colonial and African elites. Throughout its historical development Senghor's Negritude has been, above all, a bridge to the colonial establishment. It must be seen in relationship to other aspects of his philosophy which favor close French-African ties—his attitude toward the entire French Community, autonomy, independence, cooperation, etc.

The evolution of Senghor's conception of Negritude occurs in three distinct periods—the era preceding World War II, the period of achieving independence and the epoch following independence. Throughout, this analysis focuses on the elitist nature of Senghor's concepts and their relationship to the kind of close French-African cooperation he sought.

Negritude: An Overview

Senghor argues that the work of the black has distinction not in substance or subject matter, but rather in a special approach, method and style. One must look for the Negro's uniqueness in the Negro himself. Negritude arises first from singular racial characteristics of the black.

> Negritude is the whole of the values of civilization—cultural, economic, social, political—which characterize the black peoples, more exactly, the Negro-African world. It is essentially *instinctive reason*, which pervades all these values. It is reason of the impressions, reason that is "seized." It is expressed by the emotions through an abandonment of self and a complete identification with the object; through the myth of the archetype of the collective soul, and the *myth primordial* accorded to the cosmos. In other terms, the sense of communion, the gift of imagination, the gift of rhythm—these are the traits of Negritude, that we find like an indelible seal on all the works and activities of the black man.[2]

Negritude was an important movement before the period of nationalism. It continued to affect Senghor's philosophy, but with a change in emphasis, after independence. At first a movement born of psychic suffering, Negritude now attempts to stimulate programs and propaganda for social action. At different times in the history of its evolution as an ideology, Negritude stood for a number of things: a critique of imperialism; a revolutionary African development distinguished from the proletarian revolt; the birth of a new black civilization; a philosophy of life; an ideology for African unity; a methodology for development; a justification for rule by indigenous elites; a defense of the dignity of cultured blacks.

In Senghor's hands, however, Negritude became above all an appeal to the French.[3] Its success had little to do with any forceful revolutionary appeal. Rather, Negritude served as a type of "passive resistance." It "worked" because it contained a moral appeal to the French intelligentsia couched in terms of their own culture and tradition. Negritude attracted not only intellectuals of the Left, such as Jean-Paul Sartre, but also the more general French intellectual and political establishment.[4]

This appeal succeeded because Negritude, from its origins, was conceived within the scope of the French colonial myth. French colonial policy had never maintained that the colonial peoples were racially inferior or inherently different in any manner. Like the Greeks, the French had always proclaimed to the peoples of the world that when they had achieved the level of French civilization, they would be equal. Negritude attempted to show that this level was attained. It was a demonstration in abstraction, erudition and sensitivity. Negritude may have been rebellion, but not revolution.

Black Intellectuals in Paris During the Thirties: Genesis of an Elite

Above all, Negritude was a Paris invention. Gathered together from many countries, different continents and diverse cultures, the young intellectuals who met in Paris had four things in common: the color of their skins, a language (French), their colonial background and their residence in Paris.

African writers, poets, and men of letters were in many respects the black Jews of Paris. They were not merely transient visitors—many who did not settle permanently stayed ten, fifteen years or longer. They functioned as marginal men in French society. Knowing France through personal experience in the period of their greatest self-conscious, self-discovering adolescence, they had to seek information about their countries of origin through books and ethnographic accounts. Most of them did not feel a patriotic or even sentimental attachment to any particular segment of overseas France. Intellectuals spoke about "Africa" rather than Senegal, the Ivory Coast or Gabon. How could it be otherwise? Descent, tribe, caste were more important and real than artificial European-imposed national boundaries. French administration also focused, in Africa, on federations (Afrique Occidentale Française, Afrique Equatoriale Française) rather than individual countries. But education separated them from their indigenous countrymen and brought them together in Paris.

Education would have been enough to set them apart from their compatriots. The critically self-conscious intellectuals formed a still smaller minority within the educated elite. Out of these "free-floating" intellectuals came the purveyors of Negritude. Instead of turning their analytic skills to use as social critics, however, they rediscovered their past.

At a time when any agitational activities would have appeared futile, the opening of fantastic cultural opportunities counted importantly among the reasons for their political quies-

43

cence. The ethnological and artistic discoveries of the time precipitated the re-evaluation of African civilization. The work of Frobenius and Delafosse proved a past worth writing about. African history became an intellectually valid pursuit. European artists made black sculpture respectable and worthy of comment. A new field blossomed for intellectuals.

Senghor has written extensively about the need for a basic feeling of self-respect which had to precede any meaningful political actions. To African intellectuals, then, came the chance to be both God and Moses—to create a people, and then to show it the way to the promised land. They also had political opportunities which, historically, are denied to marginal intellectuals. For the blacks, marginal in French society, usually came from highly privileged situations in their homelands. Education, of course, strengthened their positions. Intellectual skills, like every other Western commodity, were in short supply.

The Appeal to the French: Negritude as a Link Between French and African Elites

Finally, French traditions of intellectuality and culture provided a universe of discourse that invited invention of categories of civilization such as Negritude and *Africanité*. Intellectual movements and conditions of the times were ripe for such novelties. At the same time, even colonial administrators tended to be cultured men who used Cartesian categories and a Rousseauean vocabulary.[5] With this in mind, Negritude might have appeared as a weapon for use in the French National Assembly against those who still thought Africans were racially inferior. It could have been a shield against the superiority of French culture— both a defense and an attack on the colonialists' own grounds. Even so, it would still have been a doctrine directed to the French.[6]

Negritude could appeal to both governmental intellectuals and administrators and to the critical intelligentsia alienated

leaders to understand and sympathize with each other's objectives, despite conflicts. Each could understand and sympathize with how the other felt, as well as with his goals. This facilitated communication and trust. Political intercourse obviously became easier.

The Evolution of Negritude

To see this process unfold, one must follow the evolution of Negritude through its various phases. Although Senghor has maintained in his philosophy of Negritude a remarkably consistent core of values and concepts, marked changes of emphasis do occur over time. These changes have accompanied changes in Senghor's objective situation, as Senegal has moved from political independence to a period of concern with rapid development.

The evolution of Negritude progresses through three general historical periods. The first period begins with the gathering of young black intellectuals in Paris in the thirties and continues until the Second World War. During this time Senghor belonged to a group of students, young intellectuals and politicians who were still seeking their *personal identities*.[11] The second period runs from the war until Senegal's independence in 1960. Senghor became a recognized African leader sitting as a representative from Senegal in metropolitan institutions. At this time African leaders dealt with the central problems of establishing *national identities* and defining the relationships between the overseas territories and France. The third period follows independence. Negritude grew into an ideology for unity, economic development and cultural growth.

I. NEGRITUDE BEFORE THE WAR: THE
"PRE-ESTABLISHMENT PERIOD"

In prewar Paris, when the theories of Negritude first took shape, Negritude had some of the characteristics of revolutionary potential which many commentators still ascribe to it. Then

Negritude came closest to being an ideology of racial superiority —a militant racism accompanied by a stance of withdrawal and an attitude of total noncooperation which could possibly have barred communication and accommodation with the French. Very quickly, however, these elements were modulated. By the outbreak of the war Negritude became an ideology more suitable for dialogue with the colonial power.

In October 1961 Senghor, in a remarkable speech at Oxford University, discussed the origins and evolution of Negritude in psychological, historical and sociological terms.

To understand the birth of Negritude, he stated, one had to go back to the Latin Quarter during the period between the wars. Negritude originated in the student quarter of Paris with the young black intellectuals and their quest for a sense of personal identity.

Senghor began his discourse by raising the question "Wasn't Negritude a new racism?" His direct answer is ambiguous.

> I will confess to you, in effect it [Negritude] had been at the beginning of its elaboration, "an anti-racist racism" as Sartre defined it in *Black Orpheus*.[12]

Immediately Senghor continued with an analysis of the situation of the black students.

> Assume a black skin for five minutes. I know that this is difficult for you, but there is no other way to have a living experience of our *situation*. Take yourself back some thirty years to the years between the two wars. We were the black students of the Latin Quarter with the pride, passion, and also the naive ignorance of youth.[13]

Frustrated by prejudice, they saw themselves viewed as black-skinned men devoid of talent or values coming as beggars to the white man's table. Originally unconscious of color, as students they defined themselves as idealistic youth. Europeans, however, viewed them in racial terms as black.

> They had taught us at the Lycée that we didn't have any civilization, having not been invited to the Banquet of the Universal; that we were a *tabula rasa*, or better, a soft wax to your fingers of demi-urges. You would offer to us the only way of safety, which was to allow us to assimilate.[14]

The burden, the unfairness of being judged by so superficial a characteristic as one's skin color, can be appreciated only if one tries to "assume a black skin." Senghor doesn't ask that you "take his place" (that is, his existential position in society) but rather his skin—which imposes a burden, regardless of status or work situation. Years later Senghor is fascinated by the experience of the white American John Griffin, who adopted the role of a black by dyeing his skin and ventured into the American South. Senghor projects a sense of his black skin acting as a prison, locking in his true personality and filtering outside contact through a screen of pigment. Only rarely does Senghor's writing arouse the prickly feeling that such physical things are more important than Reason, Culture, Civilization. Usually, moreover, Senghor is boastful in his poetry about the positive aspects of black beauty; physical self-defensiveness is virtually nonexistent.[15] Yet the reminiscences precipitated by Griffin's adventures force Senghor to recall the shame his color caused him because of the colonial world. Such powerful feelings of shame almost guaranteed a reaction:

> Paradoxically, it was the French who forced us first to seek and then to reveal ourselves to ourselves. . . . Very early we had attested in ourselves the failure of assimilation: we had been able to assimilate the French language and mathematics, but we weren't able to slough off either our black skin or our black soul. Thus

we were led in search of a passionate quest for a Holy
Grail: our *collective soul*.[16]

Senghor and his companions reacted against their situation
of shame and their intended assimilation by French culture.
They did not necessarily react against absorption into French society; indeed, they did not discuss or reveal whether this existed.
A search for a "collective soul" makes a lot of sense when
one remembers that Senghor, Césaire and Damas were of highly
different backgrounds. Coming from different parts of the world
and being of different social conditions, they had little in common except their color, their despair and possibly—historically—
a common origin and culture. Since their "spirit"—their psychological condition—bothered them, what better thing to look for
than their "collective soul"?
France itself helped them in the search for their "collective
soul." Not, to be sure, the "official France" of the politicians,
who, through interest and conviction, defended assimilation: "it
was suggested to us by this handful of crack intellects—writers,
artists, ethnologists, prehistorians—who make the cultural revolutions in France."
Senghor continued:

What did we learn from these writers . . . ? [We
learned] that the introduction of colonization, and especially, the slave trade had burned Black Africa like a
brush fire, producing a vast carnage of images and values; that Negroid civilization had flourished . . . that
discursive reason by itself could not comprehend the
world in order to transform it; that it was necessary to
add intuitive reason, which penetrated facts and things
beyond the surfaces.[17]

"I confess it," Senghor continues in talking about the effect of
these scientific discoveries about Africa.

We came out, drunk from this revelation, spilling over
into racism. And militants of Negritude, Senegalese

sharpshooters, we threw ourselves like an unleashed sword into an assault on European values that we summed up by the trilogy: discursive reason, technology, the market economy, i.e. Capitalism.[18]

Thus, Negritude found its origins in passion, not polite intellectual disagreement or academic contribution.

> . . . at the beginning of the Revelation, we had the intransigence of neophytes, accentuated by all the resentments born of the colonial regime. We refused any cooperation; we delighted in a radical opposition to Western civilization.[19]

Théodore Monod, as professor at the National Museum of Natural History in Paris during the thirties, had been instrumental in influencing Senghor to return to Senegal to study African linguistics. Senghor in 1965, in conferring on him one of Senegal's highest honors, said of Monod that he had succeeded in giving to Negritude a "Humanistic overture." "I owe you personally," Senghor said, "in large part for having guarded me against Racism." [20]

Intellectual ferment at the time between the two wars, the reaction against the scientism of the nineteenth century, the questioning of European rationalism, had the effect of turning the black African students away from everything Western toward the sources of Negritude. In another retrospective speech, Senghor said:

> This return to the sources . . . the defiance in regard to European values, turned quickly enough into scorn; why hide it, into racism. We would think, and we would say, that we were, we Negroes, the salt of the earth, that we were the bearers of an extraordinary message that nobody else could proffer except us. Unconsciously through osmosis and reaction at the same time, we would speak like Hitler and the Colonialists, we

would extol the blood. . . . After the negation of
white values, the affirmation of Negro values.[21]

However, the militant racism of Negritude in its formative
years quickly died. Senghor goes on, in the Oxford speech, to
note the change during the late thirties away from emphasis on
racial superiority.

> The excesses of Nazism and the catastrophe that it pro-
> voked worked to sober us. These hates, these violences,
> and above all, these tears and this blood, which were so
> contrary to our genius, to our need to love, nauseated
> us.[22]

While the theories of innate racial differences were never
dropped from Negritude, Senghor began to moderate them with
increased emphasis on cultural differences. By the outbreak of
the war, he had reached the position that, although innate racial
differences exist, they do not necessarily involve the questions of
racial superiority or inferiority, and that, further, the main task at
hand was the cultural regeneration of the black man.

In the thirties, assimilation reverberated as the great issue
challenging young African intellectuals. Previously both black
and white accepted assimilation without question as the only legitimate goal for the members of the black elite. Senghor shone
forth as a radical at the time, above all in that he rejected assimilation as a solution to the problem of either the black intellectual
or the colonial relationship. From the beginning, nevertheless,
he saw the problem of assimilation primarily in terms of culture.

Any political radicalism on his part would have collided
with the fact that the French administration itself increasingly
emphasized a policy of association rather than assimilation. Obviously, the mounting numbers of educated colonials would not
be admitted as equals into the institutions of the *métropole*.[23]
Senghor, however, focused on the cultural dimension of the
problems.

In the first major public speech that attracted attention outside of his personal coterie, Senghor addressed a meeting in the Chamber of Commerce in Dakar in September 1937. He began his speech by asserting that it wasn't his intention to convince his essentially European audience of his opinions, but only to provide the proper perspective on the problem of culture in French West Africa—"the greatest problem of the hour."

Culture Senghor defined as:

> . . . a racial reaction of man on his milieu tending towards an intellectual and moral balance between man and this milieu. As the milieu is no more immutable than race, culture becomes a perpetual effort towards a perfect balance, a divine balance. Education is . . . the instrument of culture. It consists for the child of the acquisition of experience accumulated from previous generations under the form of concepts, of ideas, methods and techniques.[24]

Senghor argues here that culture is more than a veneer achieved in a few years of French schooling. Africans differ from Europeans because of the experience of generations spread over centuries. Those blacks who later became intellectuals in France were raised in a distinctly African environment. Africans cannot, therefore, be treated simply as black Frenchmen.

Black intellectuals, for their part, have a special duty. For a long time African values have slumbered. They have lain dormant. The African peoples have lain quiescent to the point where they have lost their zest for life and personality as men. If culture is a "racial reaction," then the black intellectuals "have as their mission the restoration of black values in their truth and excellence, the awakening of their people to the taste of bread and the play of the spirit by which we are men." [25]

Senghor, like other African nationalist leaders, intended the creation of a new African man. In the thirties he was beginning to construct with a vision and an image. He announced the necessity for a psychological and cultural regeneration and restructuring. He engaged in the same type of process that all nationalist leaders have undergone. He also spoke with the self-confidence of a member of an instrumental elite: he was going to help create the new Black Man of the future.

Senghor expected an adverse reaction from the European audience. To distinguish between cultural and racial differences is obviously to introduce the possibility of a new schism. Later, Senghor argued that the racial differences had always existed. By recognizing them in a friendly way, he did not push the races further apart, but brought them closer through a better mutual understanding. Senghor emphasized a *Europeans'* perception, "the sweetness of being different and together." [26]

Europeans had reason to fear that demands for political independence would follow those for racial and cultural independence. But in 1937 Senghor was willing to say, "Let us make of the West African politically a French citizen."

By 1937 Senghor had emerged from the early period of political and racial militancy of his first student years in Paris. He spoke of race, but did not argue for racial supremacy; he asserted the necessity of cultural autonomy, but foresaw only French-African political cooperation. Except for his first brief student period of intense racialism, Senghor seems quite correct to note in the works of Negritude: "It is remarkable that here anger was never hate nor grimace; that the racial sentiment was anti-racist." "You will find in the works studied here," Senghor told a conference on African literature in 1963, "a remarkable permanence of themes: beyond the revolt of the colonized, the appeal of man to man, to the great elementary needs of justice, brotherhood, love. . . ." [27]

There are three possible approaches to race: (1) The theory of racial superiority—that some peoples, because of biological or other factors, are inherently superior, mentally, culturally or physically. (2) The theory of common experience—all peoples of a race or civilization have undergone the same historical process, hence have shared perspectives, customs and attitudes. Significant differences between peoples are only the result of changes in the historical and social environment. (3) The theory

of innate differences between people of diverse cultures and races
—differences between peoples exist, but don't necessarily involve
a question of superiority. Whatever the original scientific cause,
these differences must be recognized.

This latter theory became Senghor's position. He accepts,
but goes beyond Sartre's thesis that the blacks are a race in their
common suffering and have developed unique feelings and
values. According to Sartre:

> Negritude appears as the weak stage of a dialectical
> progression: the theoretical and practical affirmation of
> white supremacy is the thesis; the position of Negri-
> tude as antithetical value is the moment of negativity.
> But this negation moment is not sufficient in itself, and
> the blacks who employ it well know it; they know that
> it seems to promise the way for the synthesis or the
> realization of the human society without racism. Thus
> Negritude is dedicated to its own destruction, it is pas-
> sage and not objective, means and not the ultimate
> goal.[28]

This passage explains why Sartre is not afraid of Negritude.
What is to be feared by a nonracist racism, one which proclaims
its own self-destruction? Negritude is a doctrine directed against
the other fellow, the white racist colonialist, not the white liberal
or existentialists. Ultimately, their objective is to be "white like
me." Fanon said that when he had read the above passage, he
felt that "one had stolen from me my last chance. . . . One had
appealed to a friend of the colored peoples and this friend had
found nothing better than to show the relativity of their action.
. . . J.-P. Sartre in this study has destroyed the enthusiasm of
the black." [29]

Sartre, nevertheless, demonstrated how the Negritude of
Senghor was acceptable to the French intelligentsia and assimi-
lable by any good middle-class intellectual. Once Senghor had
rejected any notion of racial supremacy, an accommodation with
the French became possible. It is not coincidental, or simply a

question of rabble-rousing, that some of the most radical politicians and vehement nationalists are also racists. Racism provides the most direct and most sensitive way of intensifying conflict and making accommodation difficult. Race as an issue involves the mass of the population because it touches everybody. "Polite" racial disagreements are difficult. Race as an issue is not the style of the bourgeoisie, and race as an issue was finally rejected by the leaders of the culture of blackness. The short-lived feeling of racial superiority of the authors of Negritude coincided with the change of their social condition from students to more recognized members of legitimate political and intellectual circles.

II. NEGRITUDE AFTER THE WAR—PERIOD OF INDEPENDENCE

After the Second World War began a new period that culminated in political independence for most of the countries in the underdeveloped world. Paul Niger and Guy Tirolien, members of the original group around *Présence Africaine*, bitterly criticized the content of Negritude upon their return from a "pilgrimage to the ancestral sources." They were disenchanted before the Africa of the "Beni-oui-oui" (the "yes men"), "the Africa of the sleeping men waiting as a favor the opening of the cask, the Africa of the *boubous* floating as the flag of capitulation, of dysentery, of pest, of yellow fever and chiggers."

Bitterly recalling their Parisian discussions, Paul Niger said:

> We had lived an unreal Negritude, made out of the theories of enthnologists, sociologists, and other scholars who studied man under glass. They have injected the *Negroite* with formaldehyde, and pretended it was a type of happy man.[30]

Senghor, in one speech during this period, went so far as to call for independence. On the whole, however, he continued to develop those theories and those aspects of Negritude that further facilitated dialogue and accommodation with the colonial power. In this respect, the ideologies of the Francophone Africans during this period did not differ functionally (at least in part) from those of the English-speaking Africans.

Post-independence experience reveals, with increasing clarity, that all African countries and their leaders had more in common in terms of mutual problems, past experiences and outlook on the secular Western world than any differences stemming from diversities in colonial policy, regional variations or personal philosophy of industrialization. Previously assumed fundamental differences between French and British colonial policy appear incorrect. Thus, in practice, the French colonial system of direct rule and the British arrangement of indirect rule both resulted in the decline of power of traditional authorities. Both the French and British held out the promise of some type of equality; neither thought it desirable to identify with large masses of Africans. Both powers willingly granted political independence and gave grants of aid and money for social and economic development projects.

Variations in metropolitan policies turned out to be only subtleties. The situation of dependence dominated all niceties of tactical policy. Africans were dependent for political liberty, economic development, advancement in every realm. These common problems persisted in the post-independence period. Not unexpectedly, they created a certain basic similarity in the ideologies and philosophies of African leaders. Yet a final myth persists, an insistence on fundamental differences between the thought of French-African and English-speaking African leaders. The former were considered abstract and philosophical, the latter pragmatic and concrete. An extension of this myth is the reference to "French Africans," but not "English Africans"—only Nigerians, Ghanaians, etc. Africans from Francophone Africa, according to this view, have been assimilated to France and thus use French categories of thought. The categories used by English-speaking Africans usually are unspecified, leaving only generalizations about their pragmatism and nationalism.

The proponents of this view do not realize that the pragmatism and concreteness of the English-speaking African political leaders are as much a part of the ideological equipment of Britain as Cartesian abstraction is of France. Instead of talking about culture and civilization, the English-speaking leaders talk about social justice, equal opportunities, freedom from want, etc. But with the Francophone Africans they have a common history which has produced some measure of community of interest, taste and habit between the colonial power and African leaders.[31]

English-speaking African leaders, during the postwar period, increasingly developed an ideology involving nationalism, mass movements and participation in the political process, separate internal development and independence.

Francophone African leaders in power during this time, for the most part, downgraded these problems. They continued, for example, to seek self-knowledge rather than stimulate mass enthusiasms. In this respect Sartre, coming to praise the originators of Negritude's revolutionary poetry, produced a fine analysis of why Negritude was not revolutionary. He immediately indicates how British and French-African ideologies of the period differed. Sartre writes:

> Without doubt, the oppressed class must first take conscience of itself. But this taking conscience is exactly the opposite of a re-descent into one's self; . . . United by an oppression which weighs upon all, by a common struggle, the worker scarcely knows the interior contradictions which fertilize a work of art, but which, on the other hand, tend to vitiate action. Parain has shown that the language of revolting parties is pragmatic; it serves to transmit orders, words of command, of information; if it loses its vigor, the party defeats itself. . . .[32]

The French Africans, however, did not ignore political problems and economic advancement. To the extent that the Senegalese, for example, accepted an identity of interests between France and Africa, Frenchmen and Africans, they also demanded equality of treatment in every material as well as cultural realm. Ultimately, they sincerely expected for the whole population a standard of living equivalent to that of France. They demanded as moral rights aid of all types, equality of working conditions, equal opportunities for the people of the same educational level, etc.

Nevertheless, advocates of Negritude continued to emphasize those elements that bound together France and Africa. From a basic weapon of conflict, the racial aspects of Negritude had evolved into a theory of synthesis and unity. "Language" became another basic component of Negritude that evolved in a similar fashion.

Language is a factor almost as important as race in the matter of communication, community, culture and conflict. Leon Laleau, a Haitian poet, wrote in Senghor's *Anthologie de la Nouvelle Poésie Nègre et Malgache* of 1948:

> Do you feel this suffering
> and this despair equal to no other
> Of being trapped with the words of France,
> This heart which is come to me from Senegal? [33]

Artists have always felt uncomfortable writing in a foreign language. The foreign artist involved in colonial relationships is doubly entitled to feel "trapped" when he is forced to abandon his mother tongue for that of the "mother country."

On the other hand, however, sharing a language with the "mother country" involves an African elite which also shares Western values and tends to seek status among foreign peer groups rather than uniting with local masses. Sharing the same language in the case of a developed and an underdeveloped country—a country so poor it could not afford its own printing plant, university or technological institution, for example— means that the poorer country will read the richer country's books, be influenced by its ideas, share at least its technological history. Foreign technicians in positions of power and influence will be exchanged with visiting students, trainees, politicians and others.

Senghor argued in the thirties that "There is no civilization

without a literature which expresses this civilization and illumi-
nates its values like the jeweler does the jewels of a crown. And
without a written literature, there was no civilization which
could go beyond being a simple ethnographic curiosity." However, he went on to argue that it was impossible to conceive of an
indigenous literature which was not written in an indigenous language. He was willing to admit that a black literature in the
French language was technically feasible, as in the case of Haiti.
But such a literature "wouldn't know how to express 'our soul.'
There is a certain flavor, a certain odor, a certain accent, a certain
black timbre, which couldn't be expressed on European instruments." [34]

Not going so far as to advocate the elimination of French or
the substitution of a local language, Senghor advocated a bilingualism which would be the "integral expression of the New
Negro." Scientific works, among others, would be written in
French, while the indigenous language would be used for poetry,
theater, tales, "the literary genius which expressed the genius of
the race." [35]

However, in 1963 he explicitly rejected this position.[36] He
no longer believes that a written language is necessary to raise a
civilization beyond "an ethnographic curiosity," or that only an
indigenous language can express the genius of a race. He not only
dropped his advocacy of self-expression in an indigenous tongue
but became a foremost exponent of the utility and aesthetic necessity of French.

Senghor frankly acknowledges an absence of choice as the
most important reason for the use of French by African writers:

> I repeat, we did not choose. It was our situation as a
> colonized people which imposed the language of the
> colonizers upon us, or rather their policy of assimila-
> tion.[37]

He goes on, however, to state that, if they had had a choice, they
still would have chosen French. In the eighteenth century,
French was accepted as the universal language of culture. If more

people speak English, Chinese and Russian today, and French is the official language of fewer countries, nevertheless French is the supreme language for communication: "a language of politeness and honesty, a language of beauty and clarity." [38]

Most important, according to Senghor, French has made it possible

> . . . to communicate to our brothers and to the world the unheard-of message which only we could write. It has allowed us to bring to *Universal Civilization* a contribution without which the civilization of the twentieth century could not have been universal.[39]

Thus, in the use of language even more than in the question of race, Senghor came full circle from a position of great hostility to one of complete acceptance.

African Critics of Senghor's "Accommodation" This apparent attitude of accommodation during the great African period of nationalism has produced bitter diatribes by Africans against Negritude in general and Senghor in particular. The radical critics of Negritude direct their attack specifically at the Negritude of this middle period and its bridges with France.

Thus, W. E. Abraham dismisses Senghor as a simple apologist for France who has become so much a tool of the French that he doesn't even write African poetry:

> Senghor does not in my opinion write as an African poet. What he does is to write French poetry which is interlaid with odd African allusions. Any Frenchman can do that. I think that it is important that always he talks of "forgiveness" and "bridges." He sees himself, not as an African writer writing in Africa and for Africans, motivated, pushed, inspired by the complex present African situation (which, in his country, I dare say, would include French influence). He writes, in my opinion, as an apologist of France speaking to Africa, who understands an African language and an African

63

idiom and can use African mannerisms in his rhythm
and cadence. This is what I think Senghor does. There
is nothing particularly African about his poetry.[40]

If Abraham does not here present a reasoned critique or take the
historical evolution of Negritude into consideration, Frantz
Fanon, in *Les Damnés de la Terre*, and other works, does.

Frantz Fanon presents the most radical and far-reaching critique of Senghor's Negritude. Viewing culture in Marxist terms
as superstructure, he argues that there will never be such a thing
as a single black culture until there is a single black state. Culture
which is not rooted in social relations is "mystification, signifying
nothing." [41]

Today's political reality is the nation-state. Culture must
therefore, he goes on to argue, be above all national. This is not
to say that African intellectuals and nations do not share certain
problems and that consequently their cultures will not have certain common characteristics. But it is the *political* and the existential which always has primacy. Thus Fanon writes that while
no common "destiny" can be shared between the national *cultures* of Senegal and Guinea, for example, a common destiny exists between the Senegalese and nations which are also dominated by the same French colonialism. "It is," Fanon argues,
"around the peoples' struggles that African-Negro culture takes
on substance, and not around songs, poems, or folklore." [42]

Senghor, Fanon went on, was a member of the Society of
African Culture, and sought to discuss African culture with him
and other Algerians; yet Senghor, during the whole war for national independence, supported French policy in Algeria. This
was a fundamental contradiction in terms. African cultural unity
could be achieved only by upholding unconditionally the
"peoples' struggle for freedom." No one can be honest in desir-
ing the spread of African culture if he does not give practical
support to the creation of the conditions necessary to the existence of that culture—that is, immediate liberation of the whole
continent from colonialism.

> All the proofs of a wonderful Songhai civilization will
> not change the fact that today the Songhais are under-
> fed and illiterate, thrown between sky and water with
> empty heads and empty eyes.[43]

"You will," Fanon goes on, "never make colonialism blush
for shame by spreading out little-known cultural treasures under
its eyes." [44] Therefore, the duty of the African leader is to rise
above his social origins and personal problems to arouse his
people in a national struggle against the colonial power. Fanon
assumed that these leaders were bourgeois in origin, well educated and removed from the people. He criticized Senghor not
for being estranged from the people, but for not realizing the
extent of his estrangement. Without this self-consciousness, no
type of development was possible.

In the final analysis, it is not literature that awakens the
masses, but violence. Fanon, one must keep in mind, wrote in
the context of the Algerian war, not as a student in prewar Paris.
Everything Senghor wanted to accomplish through his doctrine
of Negritude, Fanon thought was achieved through violence.
Fanon's most distinctive contribution to African thought is this
analysis and justification of violence that promotes affirmation of
self, negation of colonialism and colonialist values, the binding
together of leaders and masses and the establishment of responsible institutions.

Fanon's argument for the use of violence goes far beyond
the arguments of self-defense or national liberation or freedom.
Only a pragmatic test will prove whether violence rehabilitates
or destroys personality, and whether it creates a vigilant effective
citizenry to guarantee responsible government. One would imag-
ine great psychological variations in the effects of having killed.
Fanon's own evidence from case studies of combat neuroses
would suggest the reverse of his thesis of "liberation." Little evidence in the underdeveloped world, including post-independence
Algeria, supports Fanon's contention that violence will yield a
more democratic system.

Fanon's analysis nevertheless remains a most powerful political critique of Negritude. Ezekiel Mphalele, on the other hand,
focuses upon the cultural, racial and social aspects of Negritude.

Ezekiel Mphalele objects to an oversimplification and ro-
manticizing of African life and history. Negritude, he argues,
tells only half, and often only a falsified half, of the story of Africa. In a talk that he gave at a conference in Dakar on African
literature, in April 1963, he said:

> Who is so stupid as to deny the historical fact of Negri-
> tude as both a protest and a positive assertion of Afri-
> can cultural values? All this is valid. What I do not ac-
> cept is the way in which too much of the poetry in-
> spired by it romanticizes Africa—as a symbol of inno-
> cence, purity and artless primitiveness. I feel insulted
> when some people imply that Africa is not also a vio-
> lent continent. I am a violent person, and proud of it,
> because it is often a healthy human state of mind; some
> day I'm going to plunder, rape, set things on fire; I'm go-
> ing to cut someone's throat; I'm going to subvert a gov-
> ernment; I'm going to organize a *coup d'état*; yes, I'm
> going to oppress my own people; I'm going to hunt
> down the rich fat black men who bully the small weak
> black men and destroy them; I'm going to become a
> capitalist, and woe to all who cross my path or who
> want to be my servants or chauffeurs and so on; I'm
> going to lead a breakaway church—there is money in it;
> I'm going to attack the black bourgeoisie while I culti-
> vate a garden, rear dogs and parrots; listen to jazz and
> classics, read "culture" and so on. Yes, I'm also going to
> organize a strike. Don't you know that sometimes I kill
> to the rhythm of drums and cut the sinews of a baby to
> cure it of paralysis? . . .[45]

These would hardly be events calculated to appeal to a Western
audience. Mphalele's is scarcely the image of the African de-
picted by the black African elite in Paris which sought to estab-

lish itself as "civilized."

Mphalele argues that only the assimilated elite asserts the importance of being black:

> Must the educated African from abroad come back to re-colonize us? Must he walk about with his mouth open, startled by the beauty of African women, by the black man's "heightened sensitivity"? It's all so embarrassing! [46]

As an artist, Mphalele rejects this renewed interest as superficial, "facile protest" that makes bad poetry. The masses are "naturally unaffected" by this poetry. Their lives remain essentially the same, a sameness shared throughout black Africa. While the architects of Negritude employ the symbols of African culture, they have not succeeded in capturing the substance of this culture. Worse, in establishing a principle of art, Negritude constitutes a self-enslavement, an "autocolonization." Mphalele refuses to be categorized into a "Negro-African style," to write to a certain beat or about certain themes. Such things are the peculiar concern of the French assimilated Africans:

> It is significant that it is not the African in British-settled territories—a product of "indirect rule" and one that has been left in his cultural habitat—who readily reaches out for his traditional past. It is rather the assimilated African, who has absorbed French culture, who is now passionately waiting to recapture his past. In his poetry, he extols his ancestors, ancestral masks, African wood carving and bronze art, and tries to recover the moorings of his oral literature; he clearly feels he has come to a dead-end in European culture, and is still not really accepted as an organic part of French society, for all the assimilation he has been through. As a result, French-speaking African nationalists have become a personification of this strong revulsion, even though some of them have married French women.[47]

As noted above, these radical critics of Senghor focus their criticism on the Negritude of the period of independence. It seemed to them, concentrating on an analysis of the works of this time, that Senghor abandoned the real political and social issue of the era—nationalism—in order to create stronger ties to the French. After independence, however, the philosophy of Negritude takes a turn, as Senghor attempts to adapt it to the pressing realities of nation-building and economic development.

III. NEGRITUDE IN THE PERIOD OF NATIONAL CONSTRUCTION— THE POST-INDEPENDENCE PERIOD OF NATIONAL DEVELOPMENT

Two main aspects of Senghor's thought are significant in this most recent period in the development of Negritude as an ideology. First, influenced by Teilhard de Chardin, he increasingly places both Negritude and French culture in the context of their contributions to the "Civilization of the Universal" (this refers to the ultimate civilization which incorporates the special and unique aspects of all cultures).[48] This change in racial perspective involves a change also from a forced accommodation with colonialism to a justification and rationalization of it. Secondly, particularly after 1963, Senghor has become more concerned with the daily necessities of development, and has attempted to forge from Negritude a pragmatic ideology for nation-building and rapid growth.

The "Civilization of the Universal" Some of the ethnologists and scholars who denied the scientific basis for racial superiority, or the existence of a pure race, also made a prediction that had a profound impact on Senghor. They predicted that the "Negro" race, numbering only two hundred million, would disappear through cross-breeding. Senghor, stating that these scientists gave consolation at the same time, went on to quote Teilhard de Chardin, who wrote in 1939 that the "foyers of human development" always seemed to coincide with the points of meeting and synthesis of several races.[49]

Senghor saw in this approach of Chardin's a justification of Negritude. Synthesis, not assimilation, formed great civilizations.

Each civilization has some unique element. This element must be articulated before it can be brought as a contribution to the Great Civilization of the final Universal Synthesis. Senghor goes on to say:

> If it was then legitimate to cultivate the values of Negritude, to awaken in ourselves dormant energies, it should be for the purpose of bringing us into the current of cultural intermingling . . . into the current of panhumanist convergence; to the edification of the Civilization of the Universal.
>
> Biological intermingling occurs by itself . . . encouraged by the very laws of Life—against all the policies of apartheid. It is different in the cultural domaine. Our freedom remains whole to accept or refuse cooperation, to provoke or not to provoke a synthesis.[50]

He has welcomed the awakening of the "Third World" not simply in terms of the emancipation of its peoples, but for the potential contribution to universal civilization they can make.[51] Participation of the new nations in world politics means that the day draws closer when the Universal Civilization will be a reality. All are affected. The advent of this time will not only mean the intellectually and culturally richest civilization the world has ever known, but there will also be material abundance when all the untapped creative potential of the world is harnessed.

Colonialism has actually aided in the hastening of the "Civilization of the Universal." Senghor asserts that:

> Since the beginning of the century, the gap between peoples and nations has been narrowed progressively as a result of three factors: the extension of European colonization, the intensification of inter-continental relationships, and the independence of former colonies. The cumulative action of these three factors has thrown the races closer together, showing them their brothers in a new light, and the complementary values of their

different civilization. It is in this context that we must
study Negritude.[52]

Not only modern communications, but the common experience
of colonialism, have facilitated increasingly universal contacts.
Senghor emphasizes the benefits of colonialization and urges the
importance of encouraging this cultural intermingling, so that all
peoples can help in the creation of the Civilization of the Universal. Interestingly, he indicates how Negritude has changed its
position in regard to France, as its authors have come to see the
contribution that French civilization was making to the same
Civilization of the Universal.

> As far as the policy of France, even though we had
> often vituperated against it, it finally ends up with a
> positive balance obliging us to actually assimilate Euro-
> pean civilization. This has stimulated Negritude. To-
> day, there is no longer opposition but complementarity.
> Henceforth, the militants of Negritude, as I have often
> said, must assimilate and not be assimilated by benefit-
> ing from European values in order to reveal the dor-
> mant values of Negritude and bring them as a contri-
> bution to the Civilization of the Universal.[53]

Negritude and Development   If Senghor has been more abstract and general in his discussion of the Civilization of the Universal, and more generous in discussing the contributions of other
non-black cultures, at home he has turned his thinking to the
most concrete and specific work necessary to economic development. Senghor did not really become fully involved with day-to-
day production problems until after the fall of the former Prime
Minister, Mamadou Dia, in 1963. Dia, until then had been
more concerned with the organization of the economy than Senghor, who spent a considerable part of his time on Senegal's business abroad.

Negritude in this phase of economic development has become increasingly instrumental: an ideology concerned with pro-

duction, with motivating people to harder effort. In a recent discussion of the necessity of planning, Senghor noted that planning depended on science and technology: "the most modern scientific and technological discoveries, in sum on rationality." "Rationality" today, he continued, "is not *truth*, which is the domaine of philosophy, but efficiency, which is essential for underdeveloped countries. It is a question of an instrumental rationality and technology." [54]

Being concerned with technology and productive rationality (in other words, with thought as an instrument of production) does not mean forgetting ultimate purposes. However, one must distinguish between immediate objectives and ultimate ends:

> But let us make no mistake, objectives are not ends. The global objective is the society of abundance, of well-being. As far as the end, the end of ends, if we wish to be faithful to the genius of our race, to the Negritude which is existentially disinterested, if we only wish to be faithful to our human vocation, this final end can only be the society of culture; of supreme being. [55]

Senghor then goes on to affirm that to relegate "cultural problems" to the end of the plan is to risk their being forgotten. It would also be to risk taking out of the plan something which was a *sine qua non* of success.

> The image alone of material abundance is not a powerful enough lever of action. A mechanical world of automobiles, refrigerators, air-conditioners, television sets, a world without theatre, cinema, sport, without music or dance, books or records, a world without imagination or play, that is, without art—such a world would be a dead world which wouldn't be worth the trouble to be lived. It wouldn't be able to attract any serious effort for its realization. . . . And the most captivating games are the games of art which are those of the soul.

71

Bread and Circuses. The expression is more expressive than one believes.[56]

However, two distinct questions persist: (1) is materialism a powerful enough spur for the individual and social advancement; and (2) is a society built on this basis morally worthwhile?

For the first time Senghor develops the distinction between ultimate goals and immediate ends, and this seems to be a factor in this confusion. Now Senghor's primary concern is increasing economic development. For this purpose he is preoccupied with rationality, not Reason; with technology, not pure science. A division between goals and ends pushes any serious intellectual consideration of abstract philosophical ideas into the background —despite protestations to the contrary. Thus what begins as a defense of the vision of ultimate purposes turns out to be an examination of these ideals for their immediate instrumental utility—as a further prod for motivating people to increased production.

This new practical Negritude—a hint of the direction in which it can develop—attempts to link the African tradition of communalism with the cooperative movement. Thus, Senghor says:

> My government is committed to perfect the cooperative organization which symbolizes the autonomy and the liberation of the peasant world, while at the same time exalts one of the essential virtues of Negritude— *Communal life and work.*[57] (Emphasis added.)

Perhaps a more immediate practical result will be seen in a revised educational system. Traditionally, under the French, both students and educational authorities prized law, social studies and the humanities more highly than science and engineering and other technical fields.

In Senegal a further problem has been to keep control on accelerated urban migration. Sending a child to school guaranteed that he would never settle in a rural community. The countryside lost its most talented youth. Education previously has had little relevance to rural life. From the design of the school-house, to the teacher who counted himself in exile, to the peda-gogy developed in France, to the curriculum which never treated agricultural subjects, education was an intrusion. In the past, this system was meant primarily to turn out cheap white-collar work-ers for the colonial regime. Now, with independence, this had to be changed. Senghor tells us:

> . . . the African school in general and the Senegalese school in particular must from now on respond to the needs of independent nations trying to develop. The school must not uproot the student from his milieu, but on the contrary must prepare him to fully play his role in his society. This is why the African school will integrate the African values of civilization and will bear the stamp of Negritude.
>
> It is a question of a Negritude open and forward-looking. Because it is rooted in the past, our school will better prepare the future. We must then—because such is the imperative for development—form more engineers than philosophers, more economists than poets. This is the truth of the twentieth century. There will be found in addition, some philosophers to explain this development, and some poets to praise it.[58]

There will still be philosophers and poets, but they (like abstract philosophy and poetry) are increasingly relegated to a more leisurely era in the future. In the future it will be necessary to continue more closely to ally the philosophy of Negritude and the tasks of nation-building.

In a speech to a rural audience in the Mosque at Kaffrine, in 1961, Senghor said:

> The Americans are American and White before being for free enterprise, and the Russians are White and Eu-ropeans before being Communists, and it is the same

thing for the Chinese. One will not construct the national independence of Senegal without the pride of our Negritude, and I intend by Negritude, not the color of the skin, although we have no shame of our skin. I intend by Negritude the permanent values of our civilization, the communal spirit, the spirit of enterprise, the respect of cultural values, of spiritual values, the sense of the concrete, the sense of the facts.[59]

While explicitly rejecting an appeal based on race, Senghor nevertheless raises the issue of color and nationalism and links them together as more important than formal ideology or the way in which economic systems are organized.

In doing this, Senghor is perhaps following the prescription of Sartre when Sartre explained why workers did not produce poetry:

> . . . it is the present circumstances of the class struggle which turn the worker from poetic expression. Oppressed by technical forces, he wishes to be a technician, because he knows that these technical forces will be the instrument of his liberation. If he must be able to some day control and direct vast enterprises, he knows that it will come about only through economic and scientific knowledge. He has of that which the poets have named Nature a profound and practical knowledge, but this comes to him more through his hands than through his eyes. Nature is for him Matter, a passive resistance, a taciturn and inert opposition which he works with his tools. And Matter does not sing. At the same time, the present phase of the class struggle demands of him a continuous and positive line of action: political calculation, an exact foresight, discipline, organization of the masses. To dream here would be treason. Nationalism, materialism, positivism: these great themes of his daily battle are the least propitious for the spontaneous creation of poetic myth.[60]

Conclusion

Negritude originated in the quest of young black intellectuals for a *separate* personal identity; and it soon emerged into an ideology which linked this identity securely to the colonial mother country. Its original character was abstract, psychological and philosophical; its most recent impulse is pragmatic and action-oriented.[61] Until now, Negritude in Senegal has been neither an ideology of, nor for, the masses. The audiences to which it spoke were either the members of the various French establishments, or black intellectuals. An examination of the relationship of Negritude to the ideology of Senegalese socialism can illuminate the possibilities for a successful ideological appeal to the masses.

NOTES TO CHAPTER II

1. For example, Jean-Paul Sartre would have us believe that the authors of Negritude were scarcely aware of the existence of a European audience because they were so intent upon their creation of a radically unique black world. In his introduction to Senghor's anthology of black writers, which was responsible for much of the original recognition of Negritude as an important literary and social phenomenon, Sartre stated (p. 11):

   All those, colonial and accomplice, who open this book will have the sensation of reading as though over another's shoulder, words that were not intended for them. *It is to black men that the black poets address themselves; it is for them that they speak of black men* [Emphasis added]. [*Black Orpheus, op. cit.*, p. 11]

   Together, Abiola Irele, in "Negritude or Black Cultural Nationalism," and Walter A. E. Skurnick's "Léopold Sédar Senghor and African Socialism" in the *Journal of Modern African Studies*, Vol. 3, No. 3 (1965), pp. 321–371, give an indication of the importance attached to the doctrine of Negritude and the importance of Senghor's thought, as well as a basic synthesis of the generally accepted Western interpretation. Abiola Irele claims that Negritude is "the only really significant expression of cultural nationalism associated with Africa" (p. 321). Walter A. E. Skurnick argues that Negritude was "rooted in the destruction of an idea: absorption by French civilization"; that this was necessary in the "search for dignity" (p. 349).
   Among the other interpreters of this school of Negritude see also: L. V. Thomas, *Les Idéologies Négro-Africaines d'Aujourd'hui*, mimeo, N.D., N.P., as well as his "Le Socialisme de L. S. Senghor et l'Ame Africaine," *Afrique Documents*, No. 75, Dakar, 1964; Victor C. Ferkiss, *Africa's Search for Iden-*

tity (George Braziller, New York, 1966); Claude Wauthier, *L'Afrique des Africains: Inventaire de la Négritude* (Editions du Seuil, Paris, 1964); Georges Balandier, "Senghor et la Négritude," *Dakar-Matin,* January 19, 1965; Colin Legum, *Pan-Africanism: A Short Political Guide* (Frederick A. Praeger, New York, 1962); especially Chap. 1, "The Roots of Pan-Africanism," Chap. 4, "Culture and Politics" and Chap. 7, "Modern Political Ideas."

Janheinz Jahn in *Muntu: An Outline of the New African Culture* (Grove Press, Inc., New York, 1961) saw the "Neo-African poet" as the noble embodiment of the collective aspirations of his people, and Negritude as "Liberation . . . from the European paradigm" (p. 206).

Thomas Melone describes the intensity of the search for a uniquely black mission of the "Negro wrenched out of his natural order and precipitated into a hostile universe. . . ." *De la Négritude dans la Littérature Negro-Africaine* (Présence Africaine, Paris, 1962).

Lilyan Kesteloot, although not primarily interested in politics, sought to demonstrate that the black African writing in French formed a vast and authentic literary movement. In *Les Ecrivains Noir de Langue Française: Naissance d'une Littérature* (Université Libre de Bruxelles, Belgium, 1963) she seeks to demonstrate that they are the representatives of a cultural renaissance which is neither French nor even Western.

2. *Discours Prononcé à l'Université d'Oxford,* October 26, 1961 (mimeo, N.D., N.P.), reprinted in part in William H. Friedland and Carl G. Rosberg, Jr., eds., *African Socialism* (Hoover Institute Publications, Stanford University Press, Stanford, 1964). All references are to the original mimeographed French text.

3. As an indication of how French critics received Senghor's published works, see the extensive selections from the reviews reprinted in Armand Guibert, *Léopold Sédar Senghor, L'Homme et l'Œuvre* (Présence Africaine, Paris, 1962) and M. and S. Battestini, eds., *Littérature Africaine 3: L. S. Senghor, Poète Sénégalais* (Fernand Nathan, Paris, 1964).

4. For an example of liberal French Establishment opinion, see Robert Delavignette (a former African High Commissioner, Directeur des Affairs Politiques, Ministère de la France d'Outre-Mer, former Directeur de l'Ecole Nationale de la France d'Outre-Mer), who concluded his study *Freedom and Authority in French West Africa* (Oxford University Press, London, 1950—a translation of *Service Africain* [Gallimard, Paris, 1946]) with a direct address to Senghor, whom he cites by name:

> . . . I would hesitate to invoke him were it not that in the face of what threatens us we must assert our common right to live—he the black man and I the white—in freedom and as comrades. What threatens us? The racialism of today, more enervating to the spirit than the most exhausting African climate, is to anemic Europeans. . . . In drawing attention to Léopold Senghor, I am not trying to justify a system: I don't have to produce him in evidence, for he is not a product of anything—he is a man. [P. 148]

Yet, Delavignette continues, Senghor's fellows

> . . . equally worthy, are still illiterate. . . . Effective administration combined with humanity, these are the lines on which action must proceed in order that the new world of Africa may live, in its local chiefs, its provincial institutions, its peasant communities, and so that it may beget men like you, Senghor. [P. 151]

5. In his introduction to *Les Techniciens de la Colonisation (XIX–XX Siècles)* (Presses Universitaires de France, Paris, 1947), Charles-André Julien ana-

lyzes the social and educational background of the high-level colonial administrators and finds them almost without exception to be from families of high social status and men of intellectual leaning who often occupied their leisure with studies of philosophy, history, archeology, ethnography, linguistics, etc. (pp. 4–7 *passim*).

For a better understanding of the nature of the colonial establishment, see also *Les Constructeurs de la France d'Outre-Mer*, a collection of the writings of French overseas administrators edited by C.-A. Julien and Robert Delavignette. Faidherbe, "the Creator of Modern Senegal," is particularly interesting where he promises to an African elite "opportunities in service with France in which neither caste nor color will be a barrier and only individual abilities will count." "Discours Prononcé à Saint-Louis le 14 Juillet 1860 à l'Occasion de la Distribution des Prix," *op. cit.*, p. 249.

6. Mercer Cook maintains that the widespread belief in French racial liberalism is overstated. In "The Last Laugh," in *Africa as Seen by American Negroes* (Présence Africaine, Paris, N.D.), pp. 199–203, he shows that there has been a racist image prevalent in French culture from the classical down to the present writers.

   Senghor in the French National Assembly was forced on numerous occasions to defend blacks against statements that they were racially inferior. See, for example, "Interventions de 27 Novembre, 1950," reprinted in *Receuil des Interventions Faites à l'Assemblée Nationale Française par le Président Léopold Sédar Senghor de 1946 à 1958 en Sa Qualité de Député du Sénégal* (mimeo, Dakar, N.D.), hereafter referred to as *Interventions*.

7. Senghor, "Le Problème Culturel en A.O.F.," *Paris-Dakar*, Nos. 489–492, September 7–11, 1937, rep. in Senghor, *Liberté I: Négritude et Humanisme* (Editions du Seuil, Paris, 1964), pp. 11–21. This volume contains reprints of many of the most important statements and articles made by Senghor on Negritude.

8. Lilyan Kesteloot, *Les Ecrivains Noirs de Langue Française: Naissance d'une Littérature*.

9. Eugène Guernier, *L'Apport de l'Afrique à la Pensée Humaine* (Payot, Paris, 1952).

10. *Ibid.*, p. 234.

11. Thomas Melone asserted in this respect that "Negritude is a state as solitude is a state of a person alone" (*op. cit.*, p. 24).

12. Senghor, "Discours . . . d'Oxford," *op. cit.*

13. *Ibid.*

14. *Ibid.*

15. Most of Senghor's poetry, including his previous anthologies, have been collected in a single volume, *Poèmes* (Editions du Seuil, Paris, 1964). See, for example, the poem "Femme Noire, Femme Nue," originally published in *Chants d'Ombre* (Editions du Seuil, Paris, 1945), in *Poèmes*, p. 16. For a good translation, see John Reed and Clive Wake, eds., *Léopold Sédar Senghor, Prose and Poetry* (Oxford University Press, London, 1965), pp. 105–106.

16. Senghor, "Discours . . . d'Oxford," *op. cit.*

17. *Ibid.*

18. *Ibid.*

19. *Ibid.*

20. *Dakar-Matin*, January 26, 1965.

21. Senghor, *Afrique Action* (Tunisia), March 31, 1961, quoted in Thomas Melone, *op. cit.*, p. 37.

22. Senghor, "Discours . . . d'Oxford," *op. cit.* In 1951 Senghor told the French National Assembly that it was a remarkable fact that, more than once, electoral colleges in French African territories with African majorities

had elected Europeans to the local assemblies, the Council of the Republic and Assembly and the French Union. Even more remarkable, in the course of various demonstrations and violent incidents that had taken place in various African cities, no European businessman, *colon* or administrator was molested. "Election des Députés," session of The French National Assembly, April 21, 1951, *Interventions, op. cit.*

23. See, for example, the historical analysis of colonialism by C.-A. Julien, "From the French Empire to the French Union," *International Affairs*, Vol. XXVI, No. 4 (October 1950).

24. Senghor, "Le Problème Culturel en A.O.F." *op. cit.*, p. 12.

25. *Ibid.*, p. 19.

26. *Ibid.*, p. 13.

27. Senghor, *Discours d'Ouverture du Colloque sur la Littérature Africaine d'Expression Française* (mimeo, N.P., March 26, 1963).

28. Jean-Paul Sartre, *Black Orpheus, op. cit.*, p. 60.

29. Frantz Fanon, *Peau Noire, Masques Blancs* (Editions du Seuil, Paris, 1952), pp. 127–128.

30. Paul Niger, "Je n'aime pas l'Afrique," *Anthologie de la Nouvelle Poésie Nègre et Malgache de Langue Française* (1948), quoted in Kesteloot, *op. cit.*, p. 253.

31. See also Martin Kilson in "African Political Change and the Modernization Process," *The Journal of Modern African Studies*, Vol. I, No. 4, p. 432.

32. Sartre, *op. cit.*, p. 14.

33. Quoted in Claude Wauthier, *op. cit.* See his Chap. 1, "Lingua Franca," for a brief discussion of African intellectuals writing in a foreign language.

34. Senghor, "Le problème Culturel en A.O.F.," *op. cit.*, p. 19.

35. *Ibid.*, p. 19.

36. In re-edition of the 1937 speech for *Liberté I: Négritude et Humanisme, op. cit.*, p. 19.

37. Senghor, March 26, 1963, in *Présence Africaine*, p. 10.

38. *Ibid.* See also Senghor, "Le Français, Langue de Culture," *Esprit*, November 1962.

39. *Ibid.*, p. 10.

40. Lewis Nkosi, "Some Conversations with African Writers," *Africa Report*, Vol. 9, No. 1 (July 1964), p. 17; see also W. E. Abraham, *The Mind of Africa* (University of Chicago Press, Chicago, 1962), *passim*.

41. Frantz Fanon, *The Damned* (Présence Africaine, Paris, 1963), p. 189. Originally published by François Maspero (Paris, 1961) under the title *Les Damnés de la Terre.*

42. *Ibid.*, p. 189.

43. *Ibid.*, p. 169.

44. *Ibid.*, p. 179.

45. Quoted in Ezekiel Mphalele, "The Fabric of African Culture," *Foreign Affairs*, July 1964, pp. 624–625.

46. Ezekiel Mphalele, *The African Image* (Frederick A. Praeger, New York, 1962), p. 23.

47. *Ibid.*, pp. 25, 26.

48. Teilhard de Chardin was a French Jesuit priest who had great difficulties with the Catholic hierarchy during his lifetime because of his ideas on materialism and evolution. For an assessment by Senghor of his significance, see L. S. Senghor, *Pierre Teilhard de Chardin et la Politique Africaine* (Editions du Seuil, Paris, 1962).

Still another aspect of Negritude in the post-independence period is Senghor's effort to build closer connections with the peoples of North Africa. See his *Les Fondements de l'Africanité ou Négritude et Arabité* (Présence Africaine, Paris, 1967), where he argues that Egypt and sub-Saharan Africa

have a common black origin.
49. Senghor, "Discours . . . d'Oxford," *op. cit.*
50. *Ibid.*
51. See, e.g., Senghor, *Discours Devant l'Académie Brésilienne des Lettres à Rio de Janeiro*, September 20, 1964, reprinted in *L'Unité Africaine*, No. 66, September 24, 1964. See also collected speeches of this trip, *op. cit.*
In *Présence Africaine*, March 1963, Senghor stated that:

> Others, from Rimbaud to Breton, have said it before me that European civilization which was presented to us as *the* Civilization was not yet worthy of the name, since it was a mutilated civilization deprived of the dormant energies of Asia and Africa. In fact, it could not be called *humanism*, since it excluded from participation in the Universal two-thirds of Humanity—the Third World.

52. Senghor, *Présence Africaine*, March 1963.
53. Senghor, "Discours . . . d'Oxford," *op. cit.*
54. Senghor, *Planification et Tension Morale, op. cit.*
55. *Ibid.*, p. 8.
56. *Ibid.*, p. 8.
57. Senghor, *Discours à l'Assemblée Nationale*, Dakar, April 19, 1963 (mimeo).
58. *Ibid.*
59. Senghor, *Discours à Kaffrine*, January 22, 1961 (mimeo, N.D., N.P.).
60. Sartre, *op. cit.*, pp. 12–13.
61. As part of Senghor's increasing concern with concrete realities and the specifics of the Senegalese situation, one may note his 1967 statement: "When I was younger, I would gladly have come forward as the spokesman for all Africa, or at least for Negritude. By now, experience has taught me the diversity of Negroes and of Africas, and it would be presumptuous of me to speak in the name of either" ("Negritude and the Germans," *Africa Report*, February 1967, p. 46).

79

III

France and Senegal: The Appeal of Colonialism for Dependent Countries

QUOTING A MARXIST journalist who said that the misery of Senegal was to have had three hundred years of a French presence, Senghor affirmed that this was true, but he went on to say that, to be complete, one must add: "and its good fortune."[1]

A rather peculiar situation existed in the Senegalese-French colonial case. While in fact the situation involved an encounter between foreign states, in theory *both* African and French leaders held Senegalese politics to be only an extension of the domestic concerns of France. This ideological perspective increased the difficulty for Senegalese leaders of maintaining strong attachments with their African constituencies and potential mass support. In addition, while local councils had existed, their powers had always been severely limited. The Senegalese had one major source of representation, and that in a foreign political arena— the French National Assembly. Senegal had no popularly elected national or territorial political assembly with significant authority until 1957; previously, French institutions decided matters of both domestic and foreign concern.

These factors, combined with Senegalese colonial ideology, help explain the lack of nationalistic fervor in Senegal in comparison to the English-speaking colonial experience. Most of Senegal's leaders had an image of the imperialist power and the colonial relationship much more benign than that of their English-speaking homologues. They did not speak of "inalienable rights to self-government," the necessity of "national liberation" movements, the "conquest of political power" or "the masses." They considered the political party important, but certainly not sacrosanct; in any case, they never felt it to be an instrument for "positive action" in dealing with the colonial power. They cooperated with "national liberation movements" in other parts of Africa to only a limited degree; and in the case of Algeria, Senegal sided materially with France.[2]

Accepting the dichotomy Fanon finds in nationalist movements between reformists (inclined to compromise with the colonial power) and revolutionaries (who demanded immediate independence) leaves no doubt that Senghor would fall into the first category.[3]

Pierre Bonnafé asserts that "the ambition of L. S. Senghor is summed up as: an association connected with an assimilation—respectful of its African originality—within a French Empire."[4] While this characterization is essentially appropriate, one must distinguish again between Senghor's attitudes in various historical periods and note the basic ambivalences in his positions.

In 1937, during the most "radical" phase of his career, Senghor explained that solidarity between Africa and France was a necessity because:

> We are engaged in the same destiny. There are for us formidable competitors in economic battles, as well as in political competition. If we wish to survive, the necessity of an adaptation, of an assimilation, cannot escape us. Our *milieu* is no longer only West-African, it is also French, it is international; it is Afro-French.[5]

Almost from the beginning, Senghor emphasized political unity with France, even when he was most strident in affirming African cultural independence. Uninterested in moral recriminations against the past actions of colonialism, Senghor states what he calls the "colonial fact": that colonialism did exist whether or not one liked it, and one must begin from there to determine the course for the future. Writing in 1945, Senghor posed two questions which he considered crucial in regard to colonialism: "What is *France* making of her colonies? What ought *she* to make of her indigenous populations?" [6] (Emphasis added.)

In formulating the problem in this way, Senghor seems to place the initiative of reform and action in the hands of the French, rather than envision a policy of self-determination by the colonized peoples.

He went on to argue that colonialism is not simply a fact, but an historical fact; that over time various doctrines of colonization have been attempted, particularly those of association and assimilation. France did not, however, bring civilization to the uncultured, but brought her particular civilization into contact with another of at least equal merit. Africans should therefore learn and absorb the good in European civilization (they should assimilate) but not allow *themselves* to be absorbed into this foreign culture and lose their true identity. Hence, Senghor's felicitous phrase (which European businessmen posted as a slogan in the Kaolack Chamber of Commerce), "Assimilate, don't be assimilated."

And no wonder, for look what colonialism had brought:

> The latest colonization, that of Europe over the world, was the work of the Renaissance. It stemmed from a social surge; it was stimulated and achieved by the confrontation of revolutionary ideas and techniques. It sprang from the humbling of the feudal landed gentry by monarchical centralization, and especially from the emergence in cities and communes of an intellectual and commercial bourgeoisie. Under the urging of this rising class that would later wage the French Revolution, the mind was freed and invented new techniques.

It pushed God back toward heaven, *de-sacralized* the world and opened it fully to the European's feverish quest. . . . It exported not only merchants and soldiers; with professors, physicians, engineers, administrators, and missionaries, it also exported ideas and techniques. It not only destroyed, it built; it not only killed, it cured and educated; it gave birth to a new world, an entire world of our brothers, men of other races and continents.[7]

Although not an unqualified ode of praise to colonialism, this balanced picture of benefits creates an image justifying further French-African cooperation.

Immediately after the war in 1945, even as he argued for internal reform of the French Imperial system to provide greater political and material benefits to the overseas populations, Senghor maintained the necessity of fidelity to the Empire:

Is not the Empire today a grouping of humanity in search of a common ideal, a common purpose in life? The colonies tell the *métropole* that they can find this common way of life in its own tradition, that it is their traditions which will unite the French Empire.[8]

He asserted that the time had come for Africa to make her contribution to France and the world, and be joined with France as a full partner. Increasingly, the "Imperial Community" would replace the "Imperial Empire." [9]

Despite his "balanced appraisal" of imperialism, Senghor understood its exploitative aspects. He has not only distinguished slavery from colonialism, but also the economic from the political aspects of colonialism . . . a distinction particularly marked from the immediate postwar period through the tripartite government in France. Analyzing the rejection of the first proposed constitution for the Fourth Republic in April 1946 (which was very liberal in its provisions on the overseas territories), Senghor was quite generous in blaming the "capitalist forces of overseas—the great commercial firms and large *colons*." He went on to say:

> Autonomy is not an end for us, but a means. In other terms, we wish less to get rid of the metropolitan tutelage than of the tyranny of international capitalism. We think that an autonomy which would simply return us to the feudal regime of castes would not resolve the problem, although this regime was less oppressive for man than the colonial-capitalist system. We are not rebels, but revolutionaries. We wish to construct a better world, better than the colonial world of yesterday, better also than our world before the European conquest. We will do it under the inspiration of scientific socialism and ancient African collectivism.[10]

Despite his assertion that "we are not rebels but revolutionaries," Senghor neither dwelt upon the inequalities of the capitalist forces nor advocated action against any particular institution. The science upon which Senghor later based his socialism was not Marx's but that of a Jesuit priest, Teilhard de Chardin. One finds few, if any, references to the "great capitalist forces and large *colons*," "scientific socialism" and "revolution" in Senghor's later writings. Generally, Senghor sees capitalist exploitation as only the smallest part of the colonial relationship. He felt political and—above all—cultural ties to be much more important.

Indeed, he treats the colonial problem primarily as a racial and cultural problem in most of his writings. Commenting on the Bandung Conference, Senghor drew the analogy between that conference and the 1847 London League of Communists when they published the Communist Manifesto:

> Analysis reveals a similar alienation in both instances. The proletariat of the nineteenth century was estranged from humanity; the colonized people of the

twentieth century, the colored peoples, are estranged even more seriously. To economic alienations, others are added: political, social, and cultural. The result is physical and moral suffering. . . . In both instances, revolt and struggle serve to "abolish present conditions" and "transform the world." . . . Where colored peoples are concerned, it is accurate to speak of a "revolt against the West."

However, since the situations are not identical, although similar, the aims of the revolutions are not exactly the same. In Europe, it is a question of eliminating inequalities arising from the formation of classes. In Africa, it is a question of eliminating inequalities arising from the colonial conquest, from political domination.[11]

Linking together colonialism and racial oppression could constitute the basis of a radical critique of imperial policy. Senghor, however, goes on to soften this analysis:

Though we must start from our situation, from our alienation, it would not be fair to insist upon it, although its after effects are still present. For the situation as we have just briefly analyzed it *no longer really exists.* It has already been rendered *passé* by the Constitution of 1958. We are now fully autonomous and more than autonomous. We have freedom to choose.[12]

Thus, for Senghor, no bitterness can endure. He here treats colonial injustices and racial oppression as problems of the past, to be viewed in historical perspective. Further, he implies that with autonomy, race becomes again primarily a problem of culture rather than of politics or economics: a problem of alienation to be solved with the new "freedom to choose."

Indeed, he blames the analysis of colonialism based on class struggle for some of the mistakes of the past.

Our error was not that we fought with the weapons of colonialism—most African politicians, though not all, unfortunately, are anticolonialist—but with the weapons of Europe. *To fight colonialism we borrowed the weapons of the European proletariat, who told us that their struggle and our own were identical.* Similar, perhaps, but not identical, for our situations are not the same. . . . In fact, the European proletarians are held in dependent status as individuals grouped in a class, not as a race or a people. As for us, we have been colonized, to be sure, as underdeveloped, defenseless individuals, but also as *Negroes* or Arab-Berbers—in other words, as people of a different race and different culture. . . . We were "primitive" and ugly to boot; it was necessary to expose us to progress, to the "light of civilization." Naturally, progress and civilization could only be European.[13]

Given this analysis, Senghor turned away from reliance on Marxism and theories of class struggle, to Negritude and theories of culture. Two major consequences flowed logically: first of all, a de-emphasis of political solutions, implying that they ignore the fundamental problem; and secondly, an elitism resulting from the definition of the *beau idéal* as the "man of culture" (a distinct minority in an underdeveloped area). Senghor always regarded nationalism—which involves both politics and masses—with a bit of distaste.

Senghor was most likely to have called for immediate revolution during the time of his student youth, but then he immersed himself in the problems of Negritude and the French-African cultural scene. Later, after World War II, his developing African audience consisted of Senegal's elites which (like his French audience) would tolerate criticism of the system but wanted no radical break with France. The *marabouts*, for example, had reached an accommodation with the French, who were now their staunchest allies. Similarly, the lower civil service (clerks and minor functionaries) enjoyed its association with a superior status group and soon joined France's most avid supporters. The higher civil service and liberal professions, trained in and by France, had no objection to association with France so long as the pace of "Africanization" opened up good positions and responsibility within the hierarchy. Senegalese politicians were already represented and enmeshed in the constitutions and political life of France. Veterans, with their pensions and remembrances of glory, were among the most patriotic of French partisans. Labor's interest was more in bread-and-butter issues than political matters. When Senegal finally did become independent, its poverty dictated a continuing tight association with France.

A combination of personal instinct, character and tastes operating within a particular colonial milieu thus affected Senghor's attitudes and policies toward colonialism. Personality, environment and various social groups which formed the foundation of his political support combined to produce the ideology that became Senegalese socialism. Thus, far from rising in revolution against the colonial system, Senghor articulated its merits and advocated cooperation within the "community" framework. His criticisms of colonialism were directed not so much against the principles of French rule—particularly those that embodied the ideals of 1789—as against the fact that these "immortal principles" were not applied "completely and without hypocrisy." [14]

In the French National Assembly: Citizenship and Democracy Within the French Union

In his speeches in the National Assembly from 1946 to 1958, Senghor again reveals that remarkable characteristic, consistency, in constantly pursuing two themes: the contributions of France to the social, economic and cultural development of Africa; and the African's need for (and right to) further material and technical assistance. He holds that French values morally obligate France to guarantee less privileged peoples social justice. In the course of these debates, Senghor's only justification for the acceptance of this aid is need. Later, he develops the theme of the Africans' unique contribution to the Civilization of the Universal. Throughout, he manages to identify completely and simultaneously with both Africa and France. He is in the National Assembly a "man of the dialogue" and at the same time a propagandist for Africa and an apologist for France.

From the first, Senghor articulated the concept of democracy in the National Assembly. ". . . What is Democracy," he said, "if not, as the etymology of the word indicated, government founded on the sovereignty of the people. Democracy means that all the men and all the women who form the people be . . . members of the sovereign"—i.e., citizens. "Further, it means that all its members concur in the designation of the deputies to whom will be delegated the popular sovereignty." [15] When the French Union was constituted in 1946, Senghor asked that, as their first task, the members of the Constitutional Assembly proclaim that the new constitution be democratic in the above sense. He asserted that the overseas territories belonged as much as did France to the French Republic. In a truly democratic republic, there could be no separate citizenship for the residents of France and the various indigenous peoples in the overseas territories, as long as these territories did not have autonomous status.[16] Since the overseas territories were part of the French Republic, their inhabitants could only be French citizens. Any other solution—one depending on the individual's personal status, for example—would result in injustices and absurdities. At the time that Senghor wrote, Moslems were excluded from the rights of French citizenship, which were automatically granted to all Catholics. Within a single family (as within Senghor's own) there were both Catholics and Moslems. Such legislation was obviously divisive and discriminatory.

These laws had a primarily racial basis. Members of the Constitutional Committee complained about cannibals and savages, anarchy and barbarity. Berating these pretended defenders of civilization, regretting their mistrust and ignorance, Senghor argued against the idea of a *single* civilization. There were many civilizations, each of which accentuated a particular aspect of the human condition. Maintaining that technical progress is not necessarily a sign of civilization, Senghor quoted the Catholic philosopher Georges Bernanos: "The civilization of Bikini [of the atom bomb] is a counter-civilization." With all its glories, Senghor pointed out, Western civilization is still the civilization of the gas chamber and the crematorium. Assuming the offensive against the detractors of African society, Senghor argued that unquestionably Africans would not colonize and destroy French civilization; neither should France attempt to destroy Africa's original civilization. Rather, the *métropole* must learn how best to enrich itself through the richly endowed humanity that Africa brings as her offering. Africa, on her side, can develop her own riches by taking advantage of that "spirit of technology" which created the grandeur of Europe.[17]

This mutual exchange between civilizations, in Senghor's view, would transcend the false debate which formerly characterized French policy as varying between association and assimilation. From his perspective, both France and Africa were each assimilating the other to create a higher civilization:

> It is in this manner that together we will create a new civilization whose center will be in Paris, a new humanism which will be the measure of the universe and of man at one and the same time.[18]

Continuing this same theme, Senghor argued:

> In what sense are we to understand the civilizing mission of France? We think that no nation is more proper than she to fulfill this role, which consists in awakening and stimulating those dozing civilizations which, while young, are not primitive. . . .

Senghor's praise again is not wholly unqualified, for he goes on to say:

If we willingly praise the work of education that France has undertaken in the old colonies, we cannot in contrast prevent ourselves from deploring that the local authorities of French West Africa have not been at the height of their mission, far from it.[19]

On the whole, Senghor accepts as just the civilizing mission of France. He pronounces it legitimate—an admission which would be anathema to any nationalist leader from English-speaking Africa of Nkrumah's generation. Senghor is able to acknowledge the civilizing mission of France *culturally* insofar as France is technologically more sophisticated, more advanced or more developed scientifically. Furthermore, if this particular science happens to be associated with one particular race, so be it. To say that a race has one peculiar aptitude or genius is not to deny that other races may have other types of genius.

In later writings drawing upon the works of Chardin, Senghor argues again that the world is evolving toward the Civilization of the Universal to which every nation, race and civilization will bring its unique contribution. If the gift of Africa is Negritude, the gift of France is this scientific style. The concept of a "civilizing mission" therefore has no relationship whatsoever in Senghor's mind with the British concept of the "white man's burden."

In 1946, when Senghor was preoccupied with the problem of the genius of civilization, the political future of dependent Africa remained uncertain. Nkrumah did not return to the Gold Coast until 1948—and then at the invitation of middle-class intellectuals of the United Gold Coast Convention party, who advocated a cooperation with the colonial power not entirely dissimilar to that followed by Senghor. Independence may have been the ultimate goal in the British dependent territories, but in 1946 *nobody* was calling for "Self-Government Now!"

At the same time that Senghor spoke the praises of French civilization, he criticized in detail the local administrators' performance of their duties. Finding things to criticize in the French administration was not difficult. In his maiden speech to the Assembly, he began, appropriately enough, with the policy of education in Black Africa. His use of specific grievances included the prescribed use of indigenous languages; the utilitarian approach to education, a concern with the training only of minor functionaries, and the inculcation in them of attitudes of good behavior for their masters.[20]

Moreover, not only were the examinations and tests for the baccalaureate more difficult in the colonies than in the *métropole*—an unjustifiable discrimination—but the government wished to limit teaching as much as possible to the primary levels and only to "practical" subjects. After giving numerous other illustrations of discrimination against Africans, Senghor further pointed out that the administration opposed by all means possible the formation of indigenous elites, and that the administration, composed of the colonial bourgeoisie, wished to perpetuate itself at the expense of the local people.

Inherently, however, in Senghor's terms nothing prevented the amelioration of this situation from within the political system by increasing the percentage of the budget going to schools, expanding the opportunities for secondary education and eliminating obstructionists in the administration. Rationalization of the system, not radical change, constituted the proper objective. During this most radical period of France's postwar colonial history, Senghor worked to strengthen and rationalize the colonial system rather than toward its demise. He directed his specific actions and complaints along these same lines of internal reform. For example, on several occasions he attempted to rectify disparities in salaries, family allowances and holidays between African and metropolitan civil servants.[21] He demanded that France reduce her imports from outside the Union in order to give additional business to her dependencies,[22] and he advanced arguments for a Euro-African community "based on the association and equal development of two complementary continents" rather than one in which the African products would be admitted only on disadvantaged terms.[23] He worked also for electoral reform, trying to get larger numbers of representatives elected to all official bodies by the overseas territories,[24] demanding a single electoral college and asking for the extension of the suffrage to new categories of voters.[25]

Quite stridently, Senghor demanded increased aid for economic and social development. He asked for more doctors and teachers[26] and demanded that the credit of the Fond d'Investissement pour le Développement Economique et Social (F.I.D.E.S.) not be reduced.[27] Reminding the National Assembly that Africa was essentially agricultural, he noted that agriculture must be modernized to increase production. He called for the digging of new wells, the creation of industries of transformation and new investments.[28] Demanding the stabilization of prices for African primary commodities,[29] Senghor also spoke out about peasant distress when buying power fell off sharply.[30]

Although Senghor argued that "logically and in terms of social obligation" the National Assembly should have begun by "freeing the peasants and salaried workers who compose 90 percent of the population," he played an important part in a law that was passed in 1950 guaranteeing a minimum salary, the right to organize into trade unions, the forty-hour week, the complete suppression of all forced labor, professional training opportunities and various other fringe benefits including the right of a labor organization not to have to turn over its membership lists to a government official.[31]

Senghor's tenure in the National Assembly coincided with the wars of national liberation in France's colonies, and he took positions on the violent conflict of the Rassemblement Démocratique Africain (R.D.A.) with the French in Africa, as well as on the wars of national liberation in Indochina, Tunisia and Algeria.

Apropos the R.D.A. insurgency in the Ivory Coast, condemned by many Western observers as "Communist" in nature, Senghor observed:

I am not a communist. I accept being "bourgeois" as I am reproached by my adversaries. I affirm from this perspective, that in the Ivory Coast, there is a problem, under color of an anti-communist battle of electoral chicanery. I affirm without fear of being contradicted by the facts, that in French Black Africa there are no separatists; there are only men who wish to be free and who refuse to sacrifice their dignity to fear or ethnic interest, to political, i.e. electoral scheming, not to say contrivances.[32]

In Tunisia, on the other hand, his advice was sharp and clear: "The interest of Tunisia is to keep close ties with France." [33] With respect to Indochina, even though he felt that in 1950 both Bao Dai and Ho Chi Minh had allied themselves with "blocs," he said: "We think that with or without Bao Dai the major task of France in Indochina is to restore peace and liberty." [34] Throughout his career Senghor has called for an immediate end of the war in Indochina. He believed that the vital interests of France were not at stake, and that a solution to the conflict was not a military one. Doubting that Bao Dai was representative of the people, Senghor demanded negotiations with Ho Chi Minh. In theory, therefore, Senghor was in constant disagreement with the diverse Fourth Republic governments. In practice, however, when it came to actually voting for specific acts, he never ceased to vote for the war appropriations.[35]

He did this, he claimed, solely because he did not wish "to leave without defense the French soldiers of all colors who were fulfilling a hard duty." [36] Under these conditions, Senghor continued, "we are, in the terms of the Constitution, objectively the representatives of the French people, I say truly, of the French people." [37] Therefore, it would be impossible "for we who are French" not to support "our" men.[38] He later applied this same type of reasoning to the Algerian war, where, despite an intense desire to settle the problem through negotiation, the Senegalese representatives faithfully voted for war appropriations and sent troops recruited in their homeland to fight against North Africans.

In sum, Senghor desired for Senegal, as for all other states, peaceful evolutionary change within the French framework: an evolution led by sophisticated, technically and philosophically capable elites. He sympathized with basic desires for autonomy of indigenous social-protest movements, remarking that "To the men whom neither the two last world wars, nor the Asian revolutions, have taught anything . . . I would say that the best way to avoid a revolution is to make it one's self." [39] Yet, despite his "progressive" opinions, Senghor supported virtually all of France's major efforts to maintain her colonial relationship with the peoples of the underdeveloped nations of the world. Senghor called for the "true" application of the Constitution, for nothing was fundamentally wrong with the institutions of France; they only needed to be implemented according to their original spirit. Thus, Senghor's record in the French National Assembly demonstrated his beliefs that the interests of France could be reconciled with those of Senegal, that colonialism need not necessarily be exploitative in its noncapitalist relationships, and that harmonious relationships could be developed between *métropole* and overseas France.

Post-Independence Criticism of Colonialism

Senghor became more critical of colonialism after independence. Personal involvement with the responsibilities of economic development has changed his perspective. Now he views colonialism more in economic than cultural terms. Now he searches the colonial legacy for an inheritance of barriers to growth, and finds that, to a very large extent, it is the fault of colonialism that Senegal has not progressed.

Senghor distinguishes between the slave trade, which was debilitating, and colonization, which brought tremendous opportunities. "In truth," Senghor says, "the African retardation is due less to the soil and to the climate, less to colonization than to the slave trade." [40] Calculating that there were over two hundred million victims of slavery, he asks, "Tell me, what civilization would have been able to resist such a hemorrhage?" In 1962 Senghor could still list colonialism's benefits, but now, rather than an "increased consciousness of the world," he spoke more specifically about "the education disseminated, epidemics controlled, the agricultural and industrial enfranchisement put into place . . . a good beginning which allows an effective take-off of development." [41] But, he goes on, he wouldn't be "complete" if he didn't point out the negative side of colonialism in material and cultural terms.

"Materially," colonialism left behind an "economy of trade," the "colonial version of capitalism." The dominant country maintains the dominated country in a position of subservience by keeping it an agricultural producer (that is, an underdeveloped country) while "there is no development without industrialization." At the same time, there are no basic foodstuffs because production has been shifted to "cash crops" for export. This results in the "pauperization of the colonized." Lacking both goods of equipment and goods of consumption, the colony is forced to import them from the *métropole*. Worse still, the balance between the prices of goods manufactured in Europe and primary agricultural products is never in equilibrium: the former is constantly rising and the latter falling. [42]

To a certain extent the great powers have instituted the "economy of the gift" to make up for these faults, but this is not adequate. Senghor suggests that foreign aid is the result of the troubled consciences of the colonizers "for not having resolved the problem" (of underdevelopment), for not having been at the height of their responsibilities as men of the twentieth century. [43] The receiving nation cannot always determine how the "gift" should be spent. For the most part, these government funds are spent on purchases from private industry in the metropolitan country, making minimal the multiplier effect in the land of the supposed receiver.

Besides these economic failures of colonialism, there is something still worse: the destruction of the "moral tension" of the African civilization. "More than its money, machines, or technology, we need the European spirit of method and effort," and yet the colonizer has "distributed an abstract teaching, a general culture, and furnished to a few privileged individuals a bourgeois situation." [44] Admitting that the colonizers have created a certain amount of resources, they have nevertheless left Africa "without educated peasants, qualified workers, trained technicians in sufficient number and with a taste for hard, creative effort." [45] Elsewhere, Senghor states:

> For not three hundred, but 150 years, since the return of Senegal to France after the English conquest, the colonizer has caused us to specialize in fulfilling the functions of a producer of peanuts, soldiers, civil servants, and indeed of politicians. All things which were not exactly functions of economic growth. [46]

Continuing this theme of the mental legacy of colonialism, Senghor stated in 1963:

> . . . let us dare to say it, we are not yet decolonized. We continue to think, to speak, to act as if we were still colonized. In effect under the colonial regime, what were our modes of thinking, speaking and acting? In a word, what was our policy? It was *irresponsibility*. It was true of every party. Majority Party and Opposition. The responsibility of governing, assuring the balancing of the budget, combatting sickness, misery and ignorance, we left to the colonizer. . . . We were only preoccupied—every technical-professional category—with obtaining a little more of the "territorial" revenue, without being at all concerned with development, or even with economic growth, as if the public good was that of the colonizer, as if the prosperity of our country didn't concern us. [47]

Colonialism developed selfish habits of self-interest and a lack of concern for the "public" or "community" interest.

French governors indulged more often in demagoguery than in civic education—a trick Senegalese leaders must discard along with other habits of colonialists. Foremost among these characteristics acquired by the Senegalese elites is a "taste for bourgeois comfort at the same time as a penchant for leftist verbalism." [48]

In economic terms, even where France has apparently tried hardest, she has not brought unmixed blessings. Thus in an advertising supplement for Senegal that was addressed to a French audience and appeared in *Le Monde* in 1965, Senghor stated:

> Precisely because France tried to make Senegal the "pilot state" of French West Africa, today she is suffering more than her fair share of difficulties. Because Dakar was the capital of the former federation, today Senegal has over 10,000 civil servants that she really doesn't need, costing over 520 million annually that she really can not afford. Senegal benefited economically from the presence of French troops and the development of industries meant to service the entire federation. Now she must adjust to the loss of these revenues and the contraction of her markets with the closing of French bases and the disintegration of the Federation.[49]

Thus, over the years, Senghor changed his assessment of the contributions of colonialism. Originally he emphasized the contributions of French culture and the positive results of the synthesis of two unique civilizations. Now he is concerned with the obstacles to economic development of Senegal because of the foreign economic, social and psychological obstacles created by the imperial power in the past.

Neocolonialism is a problem which Senghor recognizes, but which doesn't overly worry him. On many occasions he has insisted that "real" independence cannot be obtained without economic independence. This means the ability of the formerly colonized to choose their own ways and means of development and economic growth. For an underdeveloped country, however, these ways and means are very limited. Whether it be called neocolonialism or something else, for Senghor the choice for the new nations lies only between different neocolonialisms.[50]

Increasingly, this fate is shared by most of the rest of the world, including the more developed states of Europe. For today the "old colonialism" is dead and has been superseded by the vigorous emergence of a neocolonialism of the great superpowers, the United States and the Soviet Union.[51] All that one can hope for, Senghor has concluded, is the least harmful of various neocolonialisms.[52]

NOTES TO CHAPTER III

1. "La France et Nous," *Le Sénégal, Etat Pilote de l'Afrique Occidentale Française*, advertising supplement to *Le Monde*, June 8, 1965, p. 9.

A *brief note on Interstitial Imperialism:* Although a matter of great debate, Senegal might well derive more in aid and other benefits from France, than she loses in unfavorable terms of trade and through various trade, import and price agreements. France's balance sheet can never be calculated simply in terms of Senegal alone, because of what might be labeled an interstitial imperialism. Modern technology and methods of business organization, in conjunction with the immensity and complexity of scales of operations, have completely changed the requirements for the exploitation and development of any market. A mechanism has been created to operate on a world-wide scale that involves not simply the business corporations that do the actual exporting and importing, but also hundreds of research and training institutes that provide specialized personnel for technical assistance. For example, there are colleges and universities that educate the elite of the associated areas for their part in development programs and metropolitan governmental agencies that play a vital role in creating the agencies and actual plans for development in the dependent nations. In large measure, these are part of the elements of the technocracy that governs in France probably more than in any other Western nation. What is new about this apparatus is its size, organization, sophistication and self-consciousness. It is also unique in terms of its organizational and productive efficiency, as well as the skills and training of the personnel involved. Calculations cannot, therefore, be made in terms of immediate accounting of any particular country, but only over the long run for the entire system. One must take into consideration not only the long-run development prospect of the client nations, and the prospects of future profitability, but also one must seek to guarantee the proper functioning of the exploitative machinery in France, which, like any other bureaucratic arrangement, can be expected to develop a life and rationale of its own.

This factor of ambiguity in determining the metropolitan-territorial material relationship would then be still another factor in supporting Senghor's desire to continue to maintain a close relationship with the former colonial power. On economic and political aspects of France's role in contemporary Africa, the following are of particular interest:

For an assessment of the role of the French in Senegal's economy, how the rate of development has changed, and the differential benefits of the colonial relation to France and Senegal, see Elliot P. Berg, "The Economic Basis of Political Choice in French West Africa," *American Political Science Review*, June 1960. An analysis of the recent trends of French aid to underdeveloped areas from 1963 to 1966 is made by Gilbert Mathieu, "Le Bilan de l'Effort Français en Faveur du Tiers Monde," *Le Monde Hebdomadaire*, March 10–16, 1966.

An important debate in France was opened by Raymond Cartier, who in a series of articles in *Paris-Match* denounced French aid to the Third World as wasted and spent on useless luxury projects while there was a desperate need for development capital in France and her provinces or for various social needs.

That France can still intervene vigorously in the affairs of its former territories is illustrated by its military aid to prevent the overthrow of the regime of President Leon M'Ba in February 1964, and by a speech made by France's Minister of Information, Alain Peyrefitte, at this time citing other instances of armed force in justification of this measure. He was reported as saying that French military intervention in Gabon was:

At the request of the legitimate government and required under the terms of the 1961 defense agreement. It is not possible for a few men carrying machine guns to be left free to seize a presidential palace at any time, he said, and noted that it was precisely because such a threat was foreseeable and foreseen that the new-born states signed accords with France to guard against such risks. The French Minister cited the following instances of French intervention in Africa since 1960 at the request of the legitimate governments concerned: (1) in Cameroun, 1960 and 1961, to help re-establish order; (2) in Congo-Brazzaville, 1960, to help the government quell inter-tribal warfare; (3) in Congo-Brazzaville and Gabon, September 1962, when a disputed soccer game resulted in ill-treatment of each other's nationals; (4) in Chad, "several interventions" between 1960 and 1963, the last being in March 1963; (5) in December 1964, "a show of force" in Niger to discourage a military uprising against President Hamani Diori; and (7) [sic] in Mauretania in 1961, once to assist the government in dealing with tribal agitation, and later (for reasons not given) in Nouakchott and Port Etienne. On the other hand, he explained, France did not intervene in the assassination of President Sylvanus Olympio of Togo in January 1963 because Togo had no mutual defense agreement with France at the time and, in any case, President Olympio was killed before counteraction could have been taken. In Congo-Brazzaville in August 1963, he said France offered to help but President Fulbert Youlou decided to resign. In Dahomey in October 1963, French troops did not intervene because President Hubert Maga gave up the presidency voluntarily. [*Africa Report*, March 1964, pp. 14–15]

2. Thomas Hodgkin's summation of the elements of nationalist theory that he claims are common to both English and French movements provides an interesting standard against which to compare Senegalese nationalism and attitudes toward the colonial power: "A Note on the Language of African Nationalism," in St. Antony's Papers, No. 10, *African Affairs, Number One*,

edited by Kenneth Kirkwood (Southern Illinois Press, Carbondale, 1961). See also by Hodgkins, *Nationalism in Colonial Africa* (New York University Press, New York, 1956), Part I, "Policies of the Powers," pp. 29–63; and *Background to AOF*, nine articles in *West Africa*, January 2, 1954, to March 6, 1954, in which he describes the complex of economic, social, cultural and political relations between colony and mother country dubbed "the Metropolitan Axis."

3. Fanon, *The Damned, op. cit.*, p. 122, *passim*.

4. Pierre Bonnafé, *Nationalismes Africains* (mimeo, Fondation Nationale des Sciences Politiques, Paris, October 1962), p. 27.

5. Senghor, *Liberté I, op. cit.*, p. 14.

6. Senghor, "Vues sur l'Afrique Noire, ou Assimiler, Non Etre Assimilé," *La Communauté Imperiale Française* (Editions Alsatia, Paris, 1945), reprinted in *Liberté I*, p. 40.

    See also Senghor's appreciation of de Gaulle as a "revolutionary of the twentieth century" who feels it his duty to "liberate peoples beyond individuals" in *Réception du Général de Gaulle à l'Assemblée Fédérale du Mali* (Imprimerie Nationale, Dakar, December 13, 1959), p. 7. Senghor speaks of de Gaulle as being one of the best of the French just as he speaks of the "we, the Senegalese elites" ("La France et Nous," *op. cit.*). In Senghor's view, colonial relations are essentially matters to be decided between metropolitan and African elites. This will benefit the entire African community. "Elite" to Senghor connotes an aristocracy committed by a position of privileged power to a doctrine of *noblesse oblige*. Senghor is confident that when members of the French elite, like de Gaulle, are called on for help, they, like the best members of any society, will respond to the appeal.

7. Senghor, "La Voie Africaine du Socialisme," Première Séminaire de la Jeunesse du P.F.A., May 1960, reprinted as "The African Road to Socialism," in Mercer Cook, *On African Socialism, op. cit.*, p. 81.

8. Senghor, "Vues sur l'Afrique Noire, ou Assimiler, Non Etre Assimilé," *op. cit.*, p. 69.

9. *Ibid.* See pp. 57–69 for suggestions for the reform of the colonial system. The most radical reform proposed was a reform of education to include a study of African tradition and values.

10. *Interventions, op. cit.*, June 1947.

11. Senghor, *Rapport sur la Doctrine et le Programme du Parti* (Parti de la Fédération Africaine) *Fait au Congrès Constitutif du P.F.A.*, July 1, 1959, reprinted as "Nationhood: Report on the Doctrine and Program of the Party of African Federation," in Cook, *op. cit.*

12. *Ibid.*

13. Senghor, "The African Road to Socialism," *op. cit.*, p. 68.

14. "Colloque sur la Littérature d'Expression Française de l'Université de Dakar," *Présence Africaine*, March 26, 1963, p. 10.

15. *Interventions, op. cit.*, September 18, 1946.

16. *Ibid.*

17. *Ibid.*

18. *Ibid.*

19. *Ibid.*, "Sur la Situation des Térritoires Français d'Outre-Mer," March 21, 1946.

20. *Ibid.*

21. *Ibid.*, December 30, 1949, August 8, 1951, February 21, 1956.

22. *Ibid.*, June 20, 1956.

23. *Ibid.*

24. *Ibid.*, July 26, 1950.

25. *Ibid.*, April 21, 1951.

26. *Ibid.*, March 21, 1946.

27. *Ibid.*, December 24, 1949, August 8, 1951.
28. *Ibid.*, January 17, 1952.
29. *Ibid.*, March 6, 1951.
30. *Ibid.*, January 3, 1952.
31. *Ibid.*, November 27, 1956. Senghor was also forced to argue that African labor was not inherently inferior and hence less productive than French or American labor. See also similar efforts for skilled workers. *Interventions, op. cit.*, August 8, 1951.
32. *Ibid.*, June 30, 1950.
33. *Ibid.*
34. *Ibid.*
35. *Ibid.*, October 27, 1954, and June 6, 1954.
36. *Ibid.*, January 3, 1952.
37. *Ibid.*
38. *Ibid.*, December 1, 1950.
39. *Ibid.*, November 27, 1950.
40. "Colloque sur les Politiques de Développement et les Diverses Voies Africaines vers le Socialisme: Les Données du Problème," December 3, 1962 (mimeo, N.P.).
41. *Ibid.*
42. *Ibid.*
43. "Allocution à l'Assemblée Eurafricaine," December 8, 1964 (mimeo, N.D., N.P.).
44. "Colloque sur les Politiques de Développement et les Diverses Voies Africaines vers le Socialisme," *op. cit.*
45. *Ibid.*
46. *Discours*, March 17, 1965 (mimeo, N.D., N.P.).
47. *Planification et Tension Morale, op. cit.*
48. "La France et Nous," *op. cit.* In his speech of March 17, 1965, *op. cit.*, Senghor lists additional French character traits left as an unfortunate legacy to Senegal, including "individualism" and "pushiness."
49. "La France et Nous," *op. cit.*
50. *Rapport sur la Doctrine et la Politique Générale ou Socialisme, Unité Africaine, Construction Nationale, IIIème Congrès de l'U.P.S., Thiès, 4–6 February 1962* (mimeo), p. 29.
51. *Ibid.*, p. 29.
52. While the concept of "francophonie" raised by President Bourguiba of Tunisia and Senghor in 1966 appeared to go back to a type of renewed Francophilia, in fact the contrary is true.

    In an interview in *Jeune Afrique*, Senghor stated frankly that the reason for the concept was that "francophonie" would help Senegal's economic development by creating tighter interests between the more technologically advanced French-speaking countries of Europe and North America—Canada, Belgium, Switzerland, Luxembourg—and the former French colonies of Africa. Thus, if France, for example, should refuse or be unable to send out teachers, Senegal could get them from Belgium or Switzerland. Interview with Mustapha Tlili, *Jeune Afrique*, No. 303, October 30, 1966, p. 41.

I V

Autonomy, Nationalism and Independence

To understand the nature of nationalism in Senegal is to understand the absence of mass involvement in politics at a crucial moment in the country's history. To the extent that development requires a *prise de conscience*, Senegal lost an opportunity; at best the beginnings of such an awakening were postponed. Elsewhere a new self-awakening arose out of the political struggle for independence. Senegal has yet to acquire this psychological prerequisite for development.

Senghor's views on nationalism differed radically from those English-speaking African leaders who sought immediate independence and freedom. His views were, of course, a logical extension of his theory of colonialism, which held that the search for nationhood and political and social fulfillment is an evolutionary process requiring the cooperation and assistance of France.

Though Senghor as a political leader did not opt for self-government until 1958, the initiative for political change did not rest solely with France. For "while waiting for France to decolonize, at least in Black Africa, we ourselves had begun to think out our situation in order to provide constructive solutions." [1] Describing the dynamics of French-speaking colonial nationalism in Africa, Senghor recollected in 1964 how, immediately after the liberation of France, African political parties affiliated or even integrated with metropolitan parties. This was natural because Africans needed support in the French parliament: "They lacked political experience; they lived in a climate of assimilation." Gradually, however, according to Senghor, they realized that no support could be entirely disinterested:

> . . . as protégés, they were at the same time pawns on the chessboard of the French parliamentary game. They learned that all the French political parties, even those on the Left, were national parties formed by national realities and oriented towards national interests, and they discovered that the French proletariat directly benefited from colonial exploitation.
>
> From this discovery . . . nationalist feeling was born among colonized people. I was about to forget the powerful leaven furnished Black Africa by the discovery and exaltation of Negritude, of Negro-African cultural values. One by one, the African parties drew away from the metropolitan parties. Affiliation replaced integration, and temporary coalition replaced affiliation when independence was not possible in the regular prescribed manner. No, the metropolitan French could not understand overseas reality—neither the situation nor the needs nor the values of Negro-Africans and Malagasy. Even when they did understand, they could not sacrifice the interests of the *métropole* to those of the overseas territories. To only the best of the French, and especially to General de Gaulle, belongs the honor of having had a perspective on the future, of having understood that these two groups of interests were not hostile, but complementary.[2]

Senghor claims to have publicly advocated independence as early as 1946. Interviewed in *Gavroche* on August 8 of that year, he assured

> . . . the whites of our unshakable determination to win our independence. . . . It would be both foolish

and dangerous for them to try to hold back the clock. We are ready, if need be, as a last resort, to conquer freedom by all means, not excluding violence. I do not believe that France, which has just eliminated Hitlerian racism, can blame us for this decision.[3]

This was during the time when he called himself a "revolutionary and not a rebel." Publicly recalling this statement in 1962, however, the only formally made specific demand he cited as made at that time was "a project for a Federal Republic." This he did before the Constitutional Committee of the Constituent Assembly (for the 1946 Constitution) and it only *implied* the *autonomy* of the various states.[4]

Autonomy, while a far-reaching demand within the context of early post-World War II French colonial policy, is, nevertheless, distinguishable from independence or immediate self-government. "Autonomy," in principle, involves some degree of French control and direction.

Independence could not be achieved overnight, for the "nation" might not be ready to receive it. The creation of a nation is a long-term proposition, and autonomy is but one step, although an important one toward that goal. For Senghor:

A nation is not realized in a day, like fruit it needs an inner ripening. The building of a state resembles that of a cathedral in the Middle Ages. It is a long-term enterprise, requiring centuries of effort and patience. It took France nearly 2000 years—up to Napoleon's time —to become a nation-state, and she was the first in Europe to do so.[5]

Senghor's attitude differs from that of the militant English-speaking African leaders not only in the substance of demands, but also in tempo and temperament.

Apropos of his tactics and style, Senghor once said, "It is not a question of victory but of success, of small successes. I like it this way. I prefer small successes to a Pyrrhic victory." [6] Because of his patience, Senghor felt that his position was constantly misinterpreted from all sides. "On the left they treat us like clerical reactionaries . . . and the moderates, they treat us like communists and revolutionaries." [7] This, however, did not profoundly alter his position.

As late as 1959, despite mounting pressures from within his own party, Senghor resisted acting without the consent of the French government. At the Congress of the *Parti de la Fédération Africaine* in August of 1959, pressures from militants demanding that Senegal opt for immediate independence apparently forced Senghor to intervene.

Altering his reasoning somewhat, Senghor told the party militants that the English-speaking African countries were prepared for independence while Senegal was not. In addition, he argued that:

As we develop economically and socially, as we train the cadres necessary for the state, and as we raise the standard of living along with the level of education, we shall amicably negotiate with the Community the transfer of authority. . . . In the end, we shall possess all the outward indications of sovereignty, of nominal independence. If we prove our *capacity* for autonomous organization and administration, *it is inconceivable that France will refuse to grant us* our nominal independence. Let us seek real independence, and the rest will be given to us.[8]

This argument preserves not only consent and cooperation with France, but the initiative of France as well. The Senegalese must prove themselves, and France will decide when they are ready.

Senghor further develops his argument when he distinguishes between "independence" and "immediate independence," territorial independence and the "de-territorialized" modern state in reference to Guinea's decision for independence in 1958. Quoting in part François Perroux's description, he said:

*Common terms that arouse deep emotional reactions
. . . such as sovereignty, independence, autonomy,
collective will, the will of the state—can no longer be
used interchangeably, despite the frequent tendency to
do so.* [Emphasis added.] A territorial sovereign state on
the pattern of Western institutions is strictly speaking
neither the necessary requisite nor, obviously, the sufficient requisite for a set of populations to determine itself, discover or re-discover the values of its own civilization, or increase its productivity and standard of
living. We speak of independence; we shall speak of it
again. It would be neither honest nor effective to talk of
"immediate independence." General de Gaulle offered
this to us on September 28, 1958. We did not take it.
Let us have the logic and the courage of our convictions.
We thought then, and continue to think, with François
Perroux, that "the real powers by which sovereignty is
exercised today are, for all nations, a function of effective alliances and coalitions." [9]

Each of the distinctions that Senghor makes is vital for his
theory of independence: sovereignty, independence, autonomy,
collective will, the will of the state all describe various stages and
aspects of this development of a nation. The attributes and requisites of a nation develop through stages, not simultaneously.
Every distinction, institution and added complexity that Senghor
discovers in the development of the nation-state further justifies
the theory that the unfolding of the nation-state is a process of
slow evolution, requiring the aid, cooperation and tutelage of the
métropole.

Senegal achieved complete independence in 1960 only after
France amended the Constitution to permit independent states
to remain in the Community. In his speech proclaiming the
union of Senegal and Sudan, Senghor defined independence as
follows:

National independence is the sacred, inalienable right of every people who feel themselves a nation, who are animated, like the Malian people, by a common desire for a common life. It is the right to dispose freely of one's self. . . . Only this liberty . . . allows populations divided by race, religion or social cleavage, to be associated into a people. . . . Because the national idea, the national will, is one of the great realities of the twentieth century, it has endured—let us have the courage to acknowledge—against all the proletarian revolutions.[10]

But at the same time as he sharply affirms the importance of independence, Senghor warns that . . . "National independence is the solitude of a people confronting itself in the nakedness of its existence. . . ."[11]

Before all French-speaking African states became independent, Senghor had always affirmed the possibility of self-determination within the French Community. The stirring words above plead for self-development, not necessarily independence. Independence goes a step beyond autonomy and Senghor is full of warnings about the dangers of solitude and isolation. Independence, he holds, "is the coming of age of a people from whom one has withdrawn its tutors."[12]

Actually, Senghor does not view independence as primarily a political act:

True independence is that of the spirit. A people is not really independent when, after its ascension to nominal independence, its leaders import, without modification, institutions—political, economic, social or cultural— that are the natural fruits of the geography and history of another race. I do not deny that every institution, every moral or technical value, is related to man, and thus has some universal validity. Nevertheless, it must be adapted to the realities of the native soil by retaining the spirit rather than the form. We would impoverish ourselves and probably despair of reducing our age-old backwardness as compared with Europe, if, on the pretext of anti-colonialist struggle, we refuse Europe's contributions.[13]

Senghor discusses foreign political, economic, social, cultural and technological institutions in the same context. He appears to be as worried about the threat of dominating foreign *culture* as he is about foreign political and social power. Thus he minimizes the distinctions between the political and economic features of the invading civilization on the one hand, and the cultural aspects on the other—between the exploitative and non-exploitative. Worrying equally about the subordination of "Africa" to French culture, and of Senegalese peasants to Bordeaux manufacturers, Senghor runs the risk of mistaking what, for most of his countrymen, are real and which are imaginary issues. If foreign culture is as great a threat as foreign political power, then understandably in this context Senghor's concern with Negritude becomes a legitimate substitute for nationalism.

Moreover, independence "is a question not of destroying, but of transcending the colonial fact."

Independence is not a refusal, it is a choice; a choice of goal and of means, as a function of our present situation. . . . It is now a matter of selecting, among European methods, the most effective ones for an exact analysis of our situation. It is a question of borrowing those of its institutions, values and techniques that are most likely to fecundate our traditional civilization.[14]

And yet it is a choice that must be made with others, for no nation in the modern world can stand alone.

The Theme of Interdependence

Senghor has consistently stressed the theme of interdependence. Independence, he argues, is never total, "not even for the Russians or Americans." [15] Neither does independence result from the stroke of a "juridical pen." It must be gained little by little by the patient effort of the nation involved. Apropos those countries of Africa still under colonial bondage, particularly the Portuguese colonies, Senghor warns:

To give total and immediate independence to all that remains of the colonies of Africa, without either preparation or transition, is to give the word and not the substance; it is to feed the Cold War; it is to make new Congos-Leopoldville. Because this would make the colonies of a single state into the colonies of a hundred states, the result would be truly only a recolonization and under the worst conditions. [16]

Although he insists that Senegal will battle for the liberation of Mozambique and Angola at the U.N., with as powerful means of diplomatic and economic pressures as are at its disposal, Senghor continues to deplore the use of violence:

. . . we continue to think that tests of force are not the best solution. Our Negro-African brothers will be the principle victims of violence. We must if we can, not be wasteful of the tears of women, the blood of men. We must allow them to prepare their independence through a period of autonomy and by negotiated agreements. [17]

The underdeveloped peoples of the world have time on their side and nationalism is only a passing phase of the world movement of history. Inspired by Teilhard de Chardin, he notes:

Much more manifestly than in the last century, there has appeared the irresistible march of Humanity to-

wards at the same time its "totalization" and "socialization," to use the terms of Pierre Teilhard de Chardin.
This is evidenced by science particularly in the development of the means of production. It isn't only men and
material goods that cross frontiers but even more, ideas,
techniques and mores; I mean civilization.[18]

The contributions of all the nations will end logically in a
universal civilization. "We do not believe that any one people,
one continent, one race, or one party, be it even international,
possesses by itself alone the Truth." Each possesses only a part of
the truth that she will bring as her contribution to the new universal community.[19]

For Africa, some form of federation would best express the
fact of interdependence. Senghor has been one of the foremost
exponents of federation for the states of former French Africa to
promote unity and prevent the emergence of isolated helpless
entities—what he has called "Balkanization." [20] He does not believe in the necessity of a unitary state, arguing that the United
States, Soviet Union, China, India, Canada, Brazil—the most
powerful nations today—are federal states. Indeed, he says, "the
weakness of France perhaps comes from her excessive centralization." [21]

Geography provides one of the sharpest arguments for a federal system: the grassland, prairie countries of Upper Volta,
Niger, Senegal and Sudan would complement the forest countries of the Ivory Coast and Dahomey. Furthermore, economically, federation would provide a greater domestic market, a more
viable unit for greater aid for development.[22]

In arguing for a federal rather than a unitary state, Senghor
advances the classic position that federalism results in decentralization, pluralism, safeguards against uniformity, and opportunities for experimentation:

Men cannot be handled like piles of dead wood. Above
all else, we shall take care not to succumb to one of the

temptations of the nation-state: the uniformization of people within the fatherland. The arch-enemy is the impoverishment of persons, their reduction to the status of robot-individuals, their loss of vitality and sap.

Wealth springs from the diversities of countries and persons, from the fact that they complement each other. We shall always remember a truth often expressed by Father Teilhard de Chardin: Races are not equal but complementary, which is a superior form of equality. Whence the superiority of the federal over the unitary state. I shall go even further. There is but one way to reduce the tyranny of the state, to ward off its diseases, as the socialist Proudhon said, and that way is through federalism—in other words, the decentralization and deconcentration of its economic and political institutions.[23]

Senghor believed in the necessity of federation, of a close association, in a unity bigger than that of the nation-state, to the extent that he actually appealed to "his people" to "resist pressing forward any claims as 'Senegalese' ":

Men and women of Senegal, for fifteen years I have often warned you against a certain sickness, introduced by colonialism, that I have called "Sénégalité." This was a superiority complex. Your role was not, is not, to lead, but to clarify. It is not to enter into the course of leadership; it is to unite in equality which is the condition *sine qua non* of cooperation.[24]

Senghor's activities and arguments for federation underlined his relative unconcern with nationalism and the nation-state. Federalism was another issue that directed Senghor away from developmental affairs of Senegal, and enmeshed him further in the affairs of France and other international relations. Later, with the approach of independence, he deplored this very

kind of attitude, blaming it on the French who (unlike the pragmatic British) failed to train Africans in the necessities of
"economic take-off."

Nation, Fatherland and State

Modern African leaders intent on achieving rapid nation-
wide development and popular participation in the new institutions of the state confront the problem of overcoming separatist
tendencies. Senghor, however, develops an ideological distinction between "nation" and "fatherland" which enables him to
justify the continued existence of various regional and parochial
loyalties instead of attempting to overcome them.

In 1945 when Senghor was mainly concerned to show that
the Africans were not primitives, that they possessed sophisticated political and social organizations, he used these terms quite
differently than he does today. Addressing himself to an essentially foreign or intellectual audience, he was preoccupied with
the development of a theory of culture. Although he successfully
demonstrated that so-called "primitive" tribes actually constituted the existence of "communities of language and culture" in
Africa, he had to account for the differences between these "ag-
glomerations" and modern European nations. It was at this time
that he first developed the distinction between "fatherland" and
"nation." A sense of self-consciousness was what distinguished
them. Tribes really were nations but without the sense of self-
identification as members of a nation that characterized Westerners. While in this first formulation, Senghor argued that the
nation preceded the fatherland, what is really significant is that
both were apparently conceived of as being territorially cotermi-
nous.[25]

Later, with the approach of independence, the crucial problem becomes one of national unity—the construction of a modern nation out of many disparate, separate entities. In the evolution of Senghor's theory of the distinction between nation and

fatherland, therefore, there is a redefinition of concepts. Fatherland comes to represent a lesser area than nation; a nation is formed out of a combination of a number of fatherlands in conjunction with the development of a self-conscious "common will for a life in common." [26]

In 1960 Senghor argued that the fatherland was the tribe and that many fatherlands had existed in Senegal for these fatherlands preceded the state. Slowly out of the various fatherlands (i.e., tribal and local entities, originally birth-communities) will come the nation—a new political form eventually able to sustain new, wider and unifying loyalties:

> The fatherland is the heritage handed down to us by our ancestors: a land, a blood, a language or at least a dialect, mores, customs, folklore, art—in a word, a culture rooted in a native soil and expressed by a race . . . West Africa, the fatherland, is the Serer country, the Malinke country, the Songhai country, the Mossi, the Baoule, or the Fon.
>
> The nation groups such fatherlands together in order to transcend them. Unlike them, it is not a natural determination and therefore an expression of the milieu, but a conscious will to construct or reconstruct.[27]

Senghor uses this distinction between nation and fatherland to accommodate his general theory of nationalism with the realities of Senegalese history and social structures.

Senghor is thus able to justify the various tribal and regional divisions and separatist tendencies that in other African countries were major problems to nationalizing leaders by the very invention of a resounding terminology; as well as by a sense of historical perspective which roots these problems in the dignity of hallowed time. Further, Senghor relates the grouping together of the various fatherlands into nations to his thesis of a community of communities.

In 1959 Senghor said of the nation that it:

. . . will unite these virtues of the fatherlands; most often, it will choose those virtues which, by reason of climate, history, or race, share a common denominator or a universal value. Once achieved, the nation forges a harmonious ensemble out of its different provinces: a single country for a single people, animated by one faith and striving toward the same goal. . . .

As can be inferred, the nation is superior to the fatherlands on the level of humanity, and even in terms of efficiency. It distills the values of the latter, sublimates them by transcending them. In this respect, it is *humanization*. For the proper characteristic of Man is to snatch himself from the earth, to rise above his roots and blossom in the sun, to escape in an act of *freedom* from his "natural determinations." It is by liberty that man conquers nature and reconstructs it on a universal scale, that man realizes himself as a god; this is freedom.[28]

In the "Community of Communities," individuals are neither isolated nor immediately under the authority of the state. Located within a larger community, the state in Senghor's ideal condition touches the individual only indirectly, after having acted through the leaders of the communities.

Nowhere else does Senghor talk about "man realizing himself as a god." Much more naturally could he speak of man realizing himself "in" or "through" God. Here he is carried away by the flight of this very Hegelian idea of the nation as *humanization*. Philosophically this conception conforms well with other aspects of his ideology—particularly since in discovering a classless, idealistic society, he stands Marx on his head. Senghor continues:

If the nation is a conscious determination at reconstruction, the state is its major means. The state . . . is incarnate in the institutions of government, parliament, public services. The government officials are its workers. It fulfills the nation's will and ensures its permanence. In domestic affairs, it mingles the fatherlands and shapes the individuals into the mold of the archetype. In external affairs, it defends the nations' integrity and preserves it from foreign intrigues. The two temptations of the state are assimilation and imperialism, for it is by nature a conqueror.[29]

It is the demands of independence that brings forth this concern with the "state" and "nation" in the evolution of Senghor's thought. Later, however, faced with the increased difficulties of development, Senghor develops another distinction between "state" and the "administrative" institutions because of conflicting interests and objectives. The state was to be the major instrument in the construction of the nation, but in the same way, the administration was to be the major tool for the economic development of the nation.

To summarize then, Senghor originally considered the national idea as secondary to the confrontation, rediscovery and reinvigoration of a new "African" culture and civilization. He believed in the necessity of tutelage by the *métropole* so that the "African" could assimilate—always being careful not to be assimilated—and to adopt the best aspects of Western rationality on his way to a higher synthesis. Before independence, Senghor considered the nation-state too fragile a unit in light of the need for "economic interdependencies." This need, coupled with presumed social, historical and cultural similarities, seemed to make the minimal viable political unit a federation of French-speaking African states within a French Community. Later, even as he became more involved with the development of the nation, Senghor could legitimize cooperation with traditional and regional leaders as well as assure them that independence would bring no radical change, by defining the nation as the "community of communities." Today he sees the nation-state as a temporary stepping-stone toward the Civilization of the Universal. However, he has increasingly emphasized the importance of the nation-state as the most significant unit for the attachment (even temporary) of political loyalties, in order to solve the problems of economic development.

In 1960, Senghor had proclaimed that "the national will, the national idea is one of the great realities of the twentieth century"; he shortly amended this to "The National idea is today *the* most solid reality of the twentieth century." In words reminiscent of Frantz Fanon, Senghor also stated, "Internationalism will be built only from the starting point of national realities, even from the realities of the fatherland." He makes it clear that by "Internationalism" he means "Civilization of the Universal." [30] Pointing out that neither Marx, Lenin, the coming of socialism, nor even of communism, could "relegate to the museum of history such aspirations as nationhood and independence, and such universal values as liberty, equality and fraternity," Senghor argues that even the Russians and Chinese, just because they are communist, are nonetheless Russians and Chinese: ". . . they have exhumed and exalted the permanent values of the national civilization of their race. . . ." [31]

This new emphasis on "national realities" is most significant in terms of Senegal's internal politics. As Senghor for the first time turned his full attention to the problem of economic development, he has attempted to link the idea of nationalism to this process. Returning to Kaffrine on a tour of the "bush" after an absence of two years, Senghor announced to his audience, "I tell myself, here is independence, here is true independence; it is the change of spirits and of hearts; it is the union of spirits and hearts for national construction." [32] And, in dedicating a new public building in the remote province of Western Senegal, Senghor declared to the assembled political and governmental officials:

> Today, the nation demands of us, not that we die for it, but that we roll up our sleeves, work, sweat a little; the true battle is not on the fields of carnage, the true battle is on the fields and in the workshops. Today it is a question of realizing, of proving that Senegal is not

a finished nation, of proving that Senegal is not an abstract nation. It is a question of proving that we are not simply orators, but that we are workers attached to the land and to work.[33]

Nationalism had finally come home to stay.

NOTES TO CHAPTER IV

1. "Author's Foreword," Cook, *On African Socialism, op. cit.*, p. 4.
2. *Ibid.*
3. Quoted in introduction to Cook, *op. cit.*, p. vii.
4. *Rapport sur la Doctrine et la Politique Générale en Socialisme, Unité Africaine, Construction Nationale, op. cit.*
5. Senghor, "Nationhood . . . ," *op. cit.*, p. 8.
6. *Interventions, op. cit.*, November 22, 1952.
7. *Ibid.*, August 10, 1951.
8. Senghor, "Nationhood . . . ," *op. cit.*, p. 2.
9. *Ibid.*, pp. 63–64.
10. "Proclamation de l'Indépendance du Mali," mimeo, N.P., Dakar, June 20, 1960, p. 8.
11. *Ibid.*, p. 7.
12. *Ibid.*, p. 7.
13. Senghor, "Nationhood . . . ," *op. cit.*, p. 8.
14. *Ibid.*
15. *Rapport sur la Doctrine et la Politique Générale, op. cit.*, p. 3.
16. *Ibid.*, p. 5.
17. *Ibid.*, p. 40.
18. "Troisième Message du Président de la République à l'Occasion des Fêtes de l'Indépendance du Sénégal, 4 Avril 1961," in *Messages de Monsieur Léopold Sédar Senghor, Président de la République au Peuple Sénégalais* (Direction des Services de Presse du Ministre de l'Information, République du Sénégal, Dakar, 1962), p. 20.
19. *Ibid.*
20. See on this point William J. Foltz, *From French West Africa to the Mali Federation* (Yale University Press, New Haven, 1965).
21. Senghor, "Nationhood . . . ," *op. cit.*, p. 13.
22. In terms of African unity, the following reason is also of some interest:

   The reconstruction of the old federation is also in the political interest of France; this is obvious to anyone who follows the extension of the Cold War to Black Africa. Guinea provides a typical example, as does—we daresay—the Ghana-Guinea Union. The Cold War is being waged not only between East and West, but also secretly among the members of NATO. (We know that the British Foreign Office did not look with disfavor upon the birth of this union.) We can be sure that the French-speaking states, troubled by domestic difficulties, run the risk of swinging, one by one, toward the Commonwealth or the people's democracies. What can Dahomey do, situated between Nigeria and Ghana? How can the poverty-stricken people of Niger resist the attraction of a rich and democratic Nigeria, inhabited, moreover, by 35 million people? [Senghor, "Nationhood . . . ," *op. cit.*, p. 15]

23. *Ibid.*, p. 13.

24. *Messages au Peuple Sénégalais, op. cit.*, "Premier Message du Président de la République, 6 Septembre, 1960," p. 6.

25. The following is the crucial passage in which he advances this thesis:

There are those who have denied that there were peoples and nations in Black Africa. I fear that they have given these words too modern a connotation; that they confuse them with "fatherland" which results from a *prise de conscience* of the nation, becoming a sort of laic cult; that they especially confuse them with the modern state that M. Lucien Fèbvre presents in the *Encyclopédie Française* as "centralized, based upon identical legislation for all, impartial administration for all, equal fiscal policy for all." But if the nation is a *social* fact as indicated by Professor Le Fur, composed of some of the following elements—only one of which may be a true indicator —race, language, religion, customs, and common traditions, "a will for a common life," one can say that the "will for a common life" was stronger at the level of the village and canton than the state. What was incontestable, in any event, was the feeling and then the attachment of a community of language and culture. Thus the Wolof did not generally use the scornful term *Lakakat*, Barbarian (literally: one who speaks in a foreign language) for the other Senegalese people—Toucouleur, Serer and Diola, whom they considered as their brothers of race and language. [*Liberté I, op. cit.*, pp. 46, 47]

26. Senghor, "The African Road to Socialism," *op. cit.*, p. 84.

27. Senghor, "Nationhood . . . ," *op. cit.*, p. 11.

28. Senghor, "Nationhood . . . ," *op. cit.*, p. 12. For a further elaboration of the definition of nation, see also "Deuxième Message du Chef de l'Etat au Peuple Sénégalais, 31 Decembre, 1960" in *Messages de Monsieur Léopold Sédar Senghor, op. cit.*, p. 9 and "Discours Devant l'Assemblée Fédérale. Mali," Dakar, April 6, 1959.

29. Senghor, "Nationhood . . . ," *op. cit.*, p. 12.

30. Senghor, "The African Road to Socialism," *op. cit.*, p. 90.

31. *Ibid.*

32. *Discours à Kaffrine*, January 22, 1961 (mimeo).

33. "Le Chef de l'Etat, à Inauguré la Nouvelle Maire de Kedougou," *L'Unité Africaine*, No. 154, April 15, 1965.

V

The Definition of Senegalese Socialism

WITH THE APPROACH of independence for many African states in the late 1950's, a new doctrine called African socialism began to gain currency among Africa's political leaders.[1] Senghor actively entered the debate about its meaning and relevance for the new Africa. Though the concept of African socialism was relatively new, leading Senegalese politicians had long engaged in the debates and politics of socialism in France.[2] They knew the developments of democratic socialism in Europe, its tendencies and problems. They considered its strong democratic and humanistic traditions part of their tradition as well. Senghor rejected both the Western capitalist and Eastern communist camps, and affirmed that he and his people were both African socialists and adherents of democratic socialism.[3]

As have many European social democrats, so has Senghor rejected Marxism, if in somewhat different terms. He has abandoned the concepts of the class struggle, nationalization of the means of production and reliance on the "working class." Further, to the extent that he does find meaning in the Marxist tradition, he is attracted to the humanitarianism of the "young Marx." Senghor, however, goes far beyond the mainstream of European social democracy in rejecting Marx's materialism and seeking final answers in Jesuitical science. In Catholicism he finds both a rationale for human activity and a final purpose

119

which he felt lacking in the writings of Marx.

While many others have trod the intellectual path followed by Senghor, none has simultaneously been chief of state or otherwise in so privileged a position to attempt the incorporation of theory into practice. Further, Senghor writes in the context of an underdeveloped area. The analysis, then, of the consequences of his special blend of Christianity and social democracy assumes special significance for the peculiar problems of a country demanding rapid development.

Sartre argues that Negritude is philosophically the precursor of socialism, for only with the establishment of an equal and secure identity could the black participate in a more universal socialist communalism.[4] Kesteloot, contesting this view, argues that in fact the Negro intellectuals of Paris in the thirties were Marxists and socialists first, and came to Negritude later. In her analysis, Negritude represented their finding "true" identities and a general rebellion against all Western values, including those of socialism.[5] *Be this as it may, however, like the doctrine of Negritude, Senegalese socialism, as historically formulated, has acted as more of a barrier than an aid to development.*

The theory of Senegalese socialism is part of a pattern of complexity in political coalitions, various administrations, social institutions, associations, ideas and even language. These complexities have acted to produce in Senegal a type of "Balkanization" which President Senghor feared at the interstate level. Not only do they make it difficult to stimulate popular enthusiasm, but they also result in confining politics to a relatively small number of people. One is either a political influential, a wheeler and dealer in groups and associations, or "out of it." To be at the very top of the pyramid requires the ability to wheel and deal in ideas such as Negritude, African socialism and community. Politics becomes the politics of intrigue, cabal, clans and personalities—the jockeying of position with a fixed circumference. There is change insofar as particular personalities may change, but not development in the political or the economic sense.[6]

To innovate, to introduce successfully new programs or policies, becomes difficult. The architects of Senegal set out to construct a uniquely black culture and civilization, and have increasingly found themselves slipping back into the footsteps of the old regime. The potential that does exist for innovation, rather than promising a new democracy and a new humanism, seems destined to lie in both nonliberal and anti-Marxist directions.

Historically, Negritude made more sense in France than in Africa. Ideologically and in practice, "Senegalese socialism" takes into account local realities, yet the pressure of these realities has proved so great that one may well wonder if anything either Senegalese or socialist can endure. Because it is a doctrine of such complexity, it adds to the already great difficulties of achieving a *rapprochement* between peasants and functionaries, planners and workers.

These problems are not unique to Senegal or Africa. Elsewhere, also, leaders in underdeveloped areas have been attracted to one or another variety of socialism as the answer.

Why Socialism?

Numerous authors have speculated on why socialism, developed in the West for highly industrialized societies, and dependent for its fulfillment on conditions of material abundance, has appealed so universally to the new nations.

First of all, one must consider the historical factors. As Fenner Brockway points out, most of the top contemporary African leaders were concluding their student days in Europe when socialism, riding the postwar wave of anti-fascism, achieved the height of its popularity. In 1945 the Labor Party was swept into power in England and a coalition of the Communist, Socialist, and Radical Christian parties governed France until 1947.[7] Earlier, the economic crisis of the 1930's undermined confidence in capitalism as a rational system for the organization of production and distribution. At the same time, fascism raised the specter of a personal menace because of the obvious racial implications of the Nazi persecution of the Jews. From 1922 Lenin tried to extend the idea of the proletariat to the colonial peoples, and the Communist Party International developed a strong interest in the fate of black people in general and the American Negro in particular.

Africans, however, did not require a Communist Party to reveal the close association between capitalism, colonialism and imperialism. They had a keen sense of economic exploitation, as well as manifold political grievances. Economic control frustrated African ambitions and created African resentments as much as did alien political control. Africans, many of whom were in no manner "nationalists," vociferously demanded Africanization of the civil service, business management, skilled trades and crafts.

By themselves, these factors might explain the support of socialism by African political leaders. Yet the strong adherence to socialism among key elites in many new countries experiencing the problems of economic growth has led analysts to search for broader explanations. Adam Ulam, in *The Unfinished Revolution*, has proposed one of the most interesting explanations of the appeals of Marxism in underdeveloped areas.[8]

Marxism, Ulam says, is attuned to the two greatest tendencies in the industrial age: worship of science and mechanization —and the limitless faith in their power to transform mankind— and the very opposite—protest against the soullessness and destructiveness of the machine age. Every society has its "Marxist period," according to Ulam, when the ideas of Marx are relevant even though Marx himself be unknown, because "Marxism to a remarkable degree reproduces the social psychology of the period of transition from a pre-industrial to an industrial society."[9] Ulam in effect applies to underdeveloped areas the sentiment of Durkheim that "Marxism is a cry of pain."[10]

Squeezed economically, forced to give up his land and work to a factory rhythm, the illiterate peasant is said to experience instinctively the feelings which Marxism formulated in theoretical language: a sense of alienation springing from his loss of property and status, antagonism to the authorities and mysterious forces that destroyed the conditions, old beliefs, and values that made the previous social existence possible (without apparently giving anything in return). Ulam looks upon Marxism as a "rationalization of instinctive anarchism," but goes on to point out the promise of Marxism, as well as its analysis of the evils of modernization—the promise of full emancipation from the evils of the present, in addition to future well-being.

Senghor's theory of socialism also attempts to fasten upon both the humanistic and technological problems of constructing a new society. He has clearly understood the appeal of Marxism which Ulam describes, insofar as he recognizes the need for a strong material base as a prerequisite for any satisfactory community. Senghor also rebels against the soullessness of the machine age. Further, he is responsive to Marx's condemnation of capitalism as a system resulting in the triple alienation of the worker from other workers, from his product and finally from himself. *Basically, however, Senghor responds to the problems of industrialism rather than of capitalism, the problems of the machine rather than of an exploiting class.*

In his perspective, *regardless of the economic system involved,* any society undergoing the transition from a subsistence to a market economy, and the transformations involved in economic development, experiences turmoil and discomfort. Therefore, Senghor need not see capitalism as the villain. The increasing abundance brought by technological progress will eliminate the social antagonisms once thought to be due to capitalism.

Further, the sense of alienation felt most strongly by Senghor stemmed primarily from his marginal position as a black intellectual in European society. Thus, ultimately he does not direct himself either to the "instinctive frustrations" of the illiterate peasant or to the problems of exploitation. His concern, rather, focuses on redressing the balance between the so-called "capitalist" and "proletarian"—i.e., the European and black— nations. This leaves him free to concentrate upon the most rapid development possible of the technological apparatus, as well as to protest against the soullessness of the machine age—and yet depend upon neither Marxist nor other radical solutions.

The nature of Senghor's socialism becomes clearer when it is compared not only to classical Marxism, but also to the kind of non-Marxist radical communitarianism of a leader like Jayaprakash Narayan (a former leader of both the Congress and Praja Socialist parties in India). Concluding his study of *Socialism in Southern Asia*, Saul Rose notes Narayan's triple contentions:

> . . . (1) that a political system based on class struggle or conflict of interests cannot create a socialist society which is essentially ethical; (2) that the human reconstruction necessary for a socialist society cannot be effected by the State, but can be achieved by a mass movement with a moral basis, such as *Bhoodan*; (3) that what is needed is not a movement for the capture of power, but a movement which requires participants to begin here and now to live the new way of life.[11]

Each of Narayan's points differs fundamentally from Senghor's socialism, even though at first glance they would appear to have more in common with each other than Senghor does with Western socialism.

Senghor believes one cannot hope for an ethical society as long as antagonistic and exploitative classes exist. He, however, *denies that classes exist in contemporary Senegal;* there are only "socio-technico status groups" whose interests do not conflict. This denial of classes makes Senghor's task easier, for he doesn't face the problem of creating a public interest and morality strong enough to overcome the more advanced, highly stratified social structure that Narayan recognizes in India. This also frees him morally to utilize the social conflicts that do exist as a political instrument in producing antagonistically balanced coalitions.

Moreover, Narayan's attitude toward the state as an instrument for development provides the greatest contrast between Narayan and Senghor (and, indeed, between Narayan and most leaders in underdeveloped areas). Increasingly, Senghor emphasizes the necessity for decentralization of planning, participation of the rural masses in all phases of development politics, their *prise de conscience*. Nevertheless, *key direction and control remain with the institutions of the state*. He utilizes the administration as the essential mechanism for change. Senghor does not think primarily in "mass" terms. Certainly he has no conception of a mass with a "moral basis." Persons are moral, societies are moral, but he cannot envision "human reconstruction" by a mass movement. Reconstruction without political power would be a contradiction in terms for him.

Senghor does seek a new way of life for the people of Senegal. Yet moral considerations are secondary in the sense that he seeks a new rationalistic outlook rather than an immediate personal code of ethical behavior. Ultimately the system may be morally directed, but in the interim he seeks a rational and technical way of life rather than an ethical one. Or, perhaps more precisely, he gears his new ethic to a rational technology.

In general, then, Senghor finds that the latest scientific innovations will solve the problems of industrialization in economic growth. His concern therefore focuses upon the technicians capable of attaining a tremendous increase of output, rather than on the overthrow of an outmoded exploiting class. For the problems of the soullessness of materialism Senghor finds solace in Catholic humanism and the promised advent of a Universal Civilization. In the end, therefore, personal salvation provides the solution to the problems of isolation and alienation, rather than the type of popular participation in the political arena that both Marx and leaders like Narayan find necessary for men to become truly free.

Because Senghor's ideology of socialism does not lead to any mass mobilization of the population in movements of protest, it does not constitute a threat to powerful interests in Senegal. His analyses of the class struggle, Marxist materialism, atheism and racism enable him to attract labor, young socialists, intellectuals and black chauvinists; at the same time he manages not to offend the business middle class, religious adherents, traditional leaders or Europeans. This factor assumed growing significance as Senegal approached self-government and found itself confronted with the actual functioning of government and the determination of its principles and objectives.

The Need to Confront Marx

In expositing his theory of socialism, Senghor begins with a confrontation with Marx—the Marx, as H. Stuart Hughes has written, "who less than fifteen years after his death had been transformed into an ideological institution and who could properly be called the midwife of twentieth century thought." [12]

In similar fashion, because of the importance of Marxism in intellectual history and in the politics of France and her dependencies, Senghor felt that he had to establish a position regarding this most important figure.[13] In this confrontation, although apparently carefully selecting and separating the valid from the fallacious in Marx, Senghor's inquiry resulted in the total rejection of Marx's philosophical and social system and the fashioning of an ideology not only personally satisfying but particularly well suited to the prevailing political realities of the Franco-Senegalese political situation.

Senghor maintained that one must start with Marx in order to learn something of method and history, and because there was much in Marx that had to be confronted:

> We are not Marxists . . . insofar as Marxism is presented as atheistic metaphysics, a total and totalitarian view of the world, a *Weltanschauung.* . . . We are *socialists.* We shall start from [Marx and Engels'] works as from those of the "Utopian socialists," . . . But we shall retain only the method and the ideas; the method, to help us analyze our situation; the ideas, to help us to solve our problems. . . .
>
> Whatever their limitations, their inadequacies, or

their errors, they more than all others revolutionized
the political and economic thought of the nineteenth
century.[14]

He argued that even while churchmen cannot accept his positive
values, they do not deny Marx's contributions, and that since the
liberation in France, Jesuits have published the most important
works on Marxism.

Senghor does not, however, bother to explain the historical
context and rationale of the Church's interest in Marx. At the
end of the war against fascism the communist parties constituted
the largest domestic political forces in France and Italy. Soviet
consolidation of power in Eastern Europe and the strengthening
of "socialism in one country" in the U.S.S.R. resulted in a widespread fear of Soviet expansionism. The Church had to admit a
basic appeal of communism to intellectuals and workers. It became generally alarmed at the inroads of an atheistic philosophy,
and particularly at the appeal of communism to people who were
among the Church's most fervent followers. Church writers
therefore approached Marxism openly and with a ready sense of
appreciation, because at bottom atheistic materialism constituted such a dangerous enemy. Rather surprisingly for an African
leader reputed for his philosophic socialism, Senghor also takes
this approach.

Senghor finds, among Marx's positive contributions, "the
philosophy of humanism, economic theory, dialectical method." [15] Senghor finds Marx's greatest contributions in what
Eric Fromm has called the "Younger Marx"—in Marx's analysis
of man's relationships with other men and with things:

> . . . The fact is that Marx came to economics through
> philosophy, detouring through Hegel, from whom he
> borrowed the theory of *alienation*, and Feurbach, who
> taught him the importance of *praxis*. His sociology is
> based on the general theory of alienation, which he de-
> velops through the particular theories of *value* and *cap-
> ital*.[16]

Elsewhere Senghor notes that Marx borrowed the idea of alienation as well as that of social justice indirectly from the theolo-
gians of the Middle Ages and the Church fathers.[17] Throughout
his analysis, while carefully expositing Marx's ideas, Senghor me-
ticulously shows where possible their derivation: how they were
originated and shaped in their development by *other* thinkers.
Taking as his departure point the conception of a "commodity,"
Senghor embarks upon the classical exposition of Marx's critique
of capitalist society. He analyzes the concepts of "use value,"
"exchange value" and "surplus value," the theories of alienation
and class struggle. It is in his discussion of "reification," however,
that one can most clearly discern the theoretical bridge between
classical socialism and Senghor's "African socialism."

"Reification" means that

> . . . In capitalist society mercantile relations gradually
> replace human relations; consciousness tends in its
> forms of thought and feeling to empty itself from the
> inside. Its manifestations—religion, ethics, art and lit-
> erature—lose their real autonomous character as they
> are invaded by the "ghostly realities" of the economy.
> . . . As Marx has shown us, the proletarian is the vic-
> tim of the greatest alienation. That is why he avoids
> labor and takes refuge in the satisfaction of animal
> needs. His sole superiority over the bourgeois is that he
> feels his estrangement. If, historically, he refused this
> alienation, it was always because of the initiative of less
> alienated bourgeois intellectuals, who showed him the
> road to liberation.

Relating the Marxian analysis of capitalist societies to the situation of colonial peoples, Senghor continues:

> So it is with colonized people who are the victims of a
> multiple alienation. The intellectuals—often European
> intellectuals—have awakened them and made them dis-
> cover their spiritual, human riches. In truth, and this

follows from Marxian analysis, *all Western civilization, all machine-civilization, all factory-civilization, is reified.* We shall see what role the colonized peoples must play in the struggle for *dereification.*[18] [Emphasis added.]

Here, as elsewhere, Senghor shows the distinct separation he feels to exist between the elites, whether they be French or African, and the masses who must be moved. Here also he links socialism and African socialism, not simply in his substitution of the colonial peoples for the proletariat, but more importantly, *in the rejection of all Western civilization as reified.*

Marx argued only that capitalist society was reified: that machinery by itself possessed a political and ethical neutrality in the sense of being free of any social values.[19] Senghor's apparent demonstration of a basic gap in Marx's analysis of society implicitly provides an additional reason for rejecting both the Marxian model of socialist society and capitalism. Negritude will provide the answer to the problems of machine civilization, for it will bring the warmth of a new type of reason and community to reestablish nonalienated relations between men, as well as between men and things. Additionally, as mankind evolves toward the Civilization of the Universal, it will find a new togetherness in a higher being.

What Senghor finds most significant, however, is more a question of values than of the inherent nature of machinery. Western civilization, he asserts, will perpetuate the reification of relations not because of its machinery but because of its egoism and materialism. Indeed, in the final analysis, Senghor does not frown upon modern machine-based technology; rather, he views it as essential to progress. Modern science thus becomes crucial for understanding Senghor's perspective on Marx.

Marxism, Science, and Humanism

Reinhard Bendix, in Social Science and Distrust of Reason,[20] has written that "today, we are all Marxists" in the sense that we have all become sensitized to categories of analysis previously ignored. In this way Senghor also accepts Marx. In part as a result of the confrontation with Marx by the social theorists of the turn of the century, Senghor has no problem in deciding between the scientific and nonscientific aspects of Marx's thought. Clearly, he feels that history has shown that Marx is no scientist. This issue has been settled.

Marx's method is that of dialectical materialism. Yet, insofar as "dialectical materialism" is dialectical, "it is nothing new." Heraclitus first affirmed the mutability and instability of things, their perpetual becoming, and "Hegel, from whom Marx borrowed dialectics, merely reflected on the subject and formulated it." [21] On the other hand, Senghor completely rejects the materialism of dialectical materialism on the grounds that it does not adequately acknowledge the historical role and significance of the nonmaterialistic. Further, Senghor accuses Marx of at times reverting to a "mechanistic materialism," seeming to "deny the active role of the subject in knowledge," becoming a "positivist," becoming increasingly "deterministic" and "subjective," "sacrificing theory to practice" and being wrong in his prophecies, and finally outmoded by wave mechanics, quantum theory, relativity and other discoveries of modern science that have shaken classical determinism.[22]

No matter, however, for, according to Senghor, Marx is really a humanist. This is really the "essence" of Marxism. Only today there is available a superior humanism which also happens to embody a superior science, and therefore "historically" has "outmoded" all other doctrines. This becomes an important point for Senghor, for it is crucial in his destruction of Marx.[23] Protesting that his scientific failure was not fatal for Marx's true importance, again and again Senghor underlines his contention that Marx was a philosopher rather than an economist, a humanist rather than a scientist:

> Humanism . . . rather than economics, is the basic character and positive contribution of Marxian thought. As we said earlier, Marx does not formulate laws from economic facts; he defines "the economic law of motion of modern society" which is a social tendency rather than a law. In his analysis, he advances by postulates and theories that explain the facts.[24]

On the other hand, while Senghor certainly has nothing against philosophy *per se*, he notes that ". . . the major contradiction in Marxism is that it presents itself as a science, whereas, despite its denials, it is based on an ethic." [25] Thus, Marxism attempts to present itself as something that it definitely is not. Marxism as a science is not valid. But more than that, since Marx's philosophy was grounded in his science and his science is not to be taken seriously, one can select or reject any elements of his humanism at will, for no longer does any underlying unity hold them together.

Along with its positive revolutionary contribution, Senghor contends, Marx's humanism presents a negative aspect:

> Its weakness is that it proceeds from a one-sided conception of man and universe. . . . Marx's ambition— and his paradox—has always been to express, throughout his entire work, the dignity of man and his spiritual needs without ever resorting to metaphysics or ethics or religion, not even philosophy. *He is a philosopher in spite of himself.* . . .
>
> In the name of whom or of what, after all, does Marx dare to affirm the dignity of man and man's right to appropriate all the products of his labor? In the name of whom, or of what, does he condemn night labor, child labor, and the African slave trade, unless it be in the name of a *certain quality or a transcendent*

something beyond man. Science notes facts and their relations; it explains, it does not demand. It cannot pass from a factual to a value judgment.[26]

Previously Senghor had argued that the passion with which Marx wrote lay at the bottom of his humanism, illuminating his entire philosophical system. This made Marx primarily a philosopher rather than an economist or scientist. Now Senghor goes on to distinguish between the "objective" and "subjective" conclusions of Marx. Insofar as a contention is merely "subjective," it is merely a personal opinion, hence easily discounted. Above all, Senghor rejects Marx's atheism, which he sees as "the fruit of the subjective tendency." One must not take Senghor's criticism of Marx's atheism lightly because:

. . . atheism is deep in Marx . . . it is basic to him. For Marx, the most complete alienation of man stems from religion, because religion separates man from nature, from society, and from himself in order to enclose him in an abstract world where he cannot realize his potential. In Marx's view, the religious act is the most absolute act of *dehumanization.*[27]

In formulating a personal philosophy or governmental program, Senghor argues that we must draw a distinction between immediate objectives and final ends. Marx worried only about immediate objectives; he absolutely refused to deal with this problem of ultimate purposes. Yet Senghor demands:

. . . on what is founded the obligation of duty? Progress of science and technology places between our hands the instruments of an incalculable power. For what should we use them? [28]

How can one, Senghor asks, "pass from being to duty except in the name of a transcendence of religious origin"? [29]

The explanation of Marx's atheism lies: (1) in the fact that Marx only knew the external practices of religion, since his father

was a Jew compelled to embrace Christianity; and (2) historically, Christianity of the moment of Marx's writing had sunk
into a deviation under the triumph of capitalism. Thus:

> . . . Marx's atheism can be considered as a *reaction of
> Christian origin against the historical deviations of
> Christianity*, which violated the essence of religion all
> the less because the idea of alienation was of religious
> origin. We find its equivalent in Islam. Later, we shall
> see a churchman use a similar dialectical approach to
> materialistic atheism.[30]

Alienation, which was originally considered by Senghor to
be the most important concept of Marx's entire humanist philosophy, is therefore found ultimately to be of Christian origin.
Marx, in a sense, is no more than a parenthesis—although a significant one—in the historical development of a *religious* exegesis of the nature of man.[31]

Elsewhere Senghor goes on to infer that Marx is responsible
for the loss of individualism and freedom, the anonymity and
"massness," of those who adhere to his banner. For Africans and
other peoples of emergent nations, he also points out Marx's
anti-nationalism:

> The Party has come to submerge the individual under
> the collectivity, the person under the class, to hide real-
> ity behind the screen of ideology. If we reflect on these
> various cases, we shall discover that . . . if the indi-
> vidual is forgotten, it is because Marx did not pay suffi-
> cient attention to the "natural determination,"
> namely, the Nation, which is not effaced by class.
>
> Marx underestimated the political and national
> idealism that, born in France upon the ruins of provin-
> cial fatherland, won over the world in the Revolution
> of 1789. "Justice," Marx writes, "humanity, liberty,
> equality, fraternity, independence . . . these relatively
> moral categories that sound so nice but in historical

and political questions prove absolutely nothing." I repeat: *independence*. If the creator of scientific socialism returned to this earth, he would perceive with amazement that these "chimeras," as he called them, and above all the concept of *Nation*, are living realities in the twentieth century.[32]

"In the name of history," Marx and Engels have gone so far as to show themselves not even "anticolonialists." Engels defended ancient slavery and Marx the British colonization of India.[33] Thus, the perverted humanism and evil science of Marxism have led to the point where the individual is corrupted, the nation betrayed, God forgotten and human society twisted beyond recognition. This is Senghor's final appreciation of Marx. In terms of Senegalese politics and sociological realities, Senghor is indeed fortunate to find himself such an intense religious believer. Atheism in Senegal involves social isolation, to say nothing of political suicide. Leaders of the Moslem brotherhoods greatly admire the intensity of Senghor's religious belief, even though he is Catholic. His religious philosophy has been a major cause for Senghor's attraction for them.[34]

Having rejected the philosophical and moral basis of Marxist socialism, Senghor not surprisingly proceeds to reject its key sociological concept—the class struggle.

The Class Struggle in African Society

One can distinguish between African socialist leaders on the basis of their belief in the existence of classes and class struggle in Africa.[35] But even within the category of those who reject the concept of "class" as inappropriate for Africa, important differences remain. For example, while both Sekou Touré and Senghor contest the Marxist notion of class conflict,[36] the differences between them are at least as significant as this similarity.

On the one hand, Touré believes that because of Guinea's

poverty all of her people belong to one class, that of the "dispossessed." The struggle for independence—"the first and the only true problem for the colonial peoples"—achieved an overriding unity of the Guinean people. Before that, "internal contradictions" existed. In the first place, the peasants—who constitute 80 percent of the population of Guinea—turned against feudalism, which, perverted by the colonial regime, had ceased to be the true expression of the thought of the nation's social units. "Created, supported, and used by the colonial regime," this "feudalism" fundamentally opposed the ideas of the people. The chiefs lived on the exploitation of the peasant masses, and they justified the colonialist practices with which their own interests were intimately linked.[37]

Touré also discusses the "nascent opposition" between the "intellectual elite" and the peasant masses. Western education, he claims, was designed to assimilate, depersonalize and create "complexes" among the Guinean elite, so that they would drive themselves "to become more French than the French themselves." Furthermore:

> . . . there were the advantages and security of the material surroundings of the intellectual elite, which were absolutely foreign to the life of the immense majority of the people and constituted a privileged situation in comparison with general conditions. *The satisfactions of the requirements of one group appeared immediately as a new obligation, a new burden on the others who constituted not only the majority of the population, but also the most disinherited stratum.*[38]

Far more than any other leading African leader, Touré castigates the "intellectual" civil servants and students—those with a life-style different from the peasant from whom they draw their revenue. The intellectuals themselves are "non-producers." [39]

Senghor, on the other hand, paints a far more idyllic image of both Africa's past and her present social structure. Senghor does not often employ the term "feudalism" in his general analysis of traditional society. Religious and traditional leaders in Senegal collaborated with the colonial authorities, but Senghor does not excoriate them, nor has he ever tried physically to eliminate them. On the contrary, they constitute important elements of his support. Similarly, he allies himself closely with the civil servants and other "intellectuals." While Senghor increasingly presses austerity demands upon them, in practice his reforms have not threatened their position or even materially altered their status. Senegal experienced no struggle for independence resulting in national unity. Senghor never developed a nationalist movement with profound mass support. Moreover, Touré, in his classless society, proposes to replace feudalism by linking individuals directly with the state, whereas Senghor advances the notion of a community of communities, in which man's primary attachments and loyalties are to smaller associations and more personal relationships.

Most important of all, the last thing in the world that Senghor desires, both in terms of his political alliances and his philosophy, is self-conscious classes. Such classes always involve the possibility of class conflict, even of violence. They would mobilize the population in a fashion cutting across all the ethnic, geographical, sectarian and parochial loyalties that help create the mosaic of complexity that is modern Senegal. This would mean a fundamental confrontation that would certainly shake the existing social structure. Senghor's image of contemporary and historical Senegal as a classless society certainly provides an "ideological" (in Mannheim's sense) comfort to the established interests.

Senghor doesn't consider social class as a problem internal to nations. He sees the major class relationships as those involved in the colonial relationship between *countries* rather than individuals, and the major problem as one of capitalist versus proletarian *nations*, rather than the domestic organization of productive forces. In the capitalist nation, all classes (including the proletariat) benefit from their colonial connections. In the dependent country, all elements suffer. Even should domestic classes exist, their differences would be as nothing in comparison to this. On this point, Senghor has written:

> The problem is in the first place to recover equality while regaining the liberty which was confiscated and alienated by the colonizer. This must be done not by instituting equality between individuals, through the suppression of classes, which is the objective of classical socialism, but by establishing equality between the colonizer and the colonized, between two peoples, two races, two civilizations. . . .[40]

Senghor has fundamentally changed the emphasis of his interpretation of metropolitan-colonial conflict between the immediate postwar period and the period following independence. In 1946 Senghor, not long freed from a German prisoner-of-war camp, allied himself politically with the tripartite government of postwar France. The war against fascism won, the atmosphere rebounded with optimism that a new government of the Left would bring social justice to France and a new unity based on equality to her overseas peoples. A new class, Senghor felt, born of the best elements of both worlds, seemed destined to save the colonies from the evils of international capitalism, as well as from a Nazi-like racism. But by 1951 Senghor had radically changed his views, declaring again the realities of colonial domination:

> Hence, the African reality was not, in the first half of the century, the domination of one class by another, but the domination of one people by another, one continent by another, let us dare to say it, by one race over another.[41]

And after independence there was no point in raising the specter of internal conflicts: international differences were so readily available, and domestically, at least, basic harmony could prevail.

Since Senghor's ideology dictated that the fundamental gap

was between rich and poor nations, it seemed to follow that the chief task of the poor nations was to catch up. Effort, therefore, should be concentrated not primarily on achieving internal social equality, but rather on the progress of the nation as a whole vis-à-vis European countries. Hence, as one East African commentator stated, "the ideal of maintaining equality between Africans themselves in a given country has sometimes come into conflict with the ideal of creating equality between Africans and others." [42]

Traditional socialist-Marxist theory would dictate a policy of preventing the emergence of an African bourgeoisie. However, most sub-Saharan African governments, with Senegal in the fore, have urged "not so much African socialism as the Africanization of capitalism." Why should Africans be left behind or discriminated against, in business or any other field? Why shouldn't the gap in commerce and trade be eliminated, just as in politics, the arts and the sciences? Ali Mazuri, writing about Kenya and the socialism of its government, states:

> In an ethnically pluralistic society, the first task of socialism, according to this school, is not to abolish class distinctions altogether, but to prevent class distinctions from coinciding with racial difference. The problems of class distinctions can be mitigated by social mobility. A person can move from one class to another. The very creation of an African bourgeoisie would be proof that social mobility can be engineered or manipulated by government policy. [43]

Even though no comparable European problem existed in Senegal, there is nevertheless the feeling that the entire country was an oppressed nation and must prove itself against the rich nations of the colonial powers. Racial pride and a desire to throw off past humiliations are certainly not absent from these calculations. Successful African big-business men can create as great a source of pride as poets. In terms of the future of socialism, the government claims it need have no fear, for this African bour-

138

geoisie is certainly its creature. Equality in poverty is meaning-less. To create the socialist prerequisites of abundance, governments inevitably must grant temporary concessions (which Marx saw as historically necessary in the West). Denial of the existence of classes makes it all the easier to tolerate this "deviation" —the creation of an African bourgeoisie. The net effect of Senghor's emphasis on international rather than domestic classes *actually sanctions* the existence of internal social inequalities. Social inequalities, however, do not necessarily result in social disorder or class conflict.

I. CLASS AND CASTE IN TRADITIONAL SOCIETY

An absence of conflict characterizes Senghor's theory of the African community, particularly when he discusses traditional society. Senghor stated flatly in 1961 that, "regardless of what certain abstract theories might say, there were no classes here before the European conquest." [44] The existence of not only classes but "castes" in Senegal (unlike most other parts of Africa) provides a major stumbling block to this assertion. Senghor's method of handling this problem, however, has altered subtly in the same way as did his theory of colonial relationships. In 1945 he explained caste and class in Senegal, using the Serer Kingdom of Sine as an example as follows:

> That which is most striking is its unity and harmony.
> . . . We can equally see its faults and insufficiencies;
> scorn of artisan work, *castes in place of classes* [emphasis added], servitude—as tempered as it was—
> finally, in a general manner, the absolute subordination
> of the person to the community. [45]

Senghor in 1945, then, saw castes as enough of a social problem to wish to replace them with something more manageable, such as classes. In post-independence Senegal, however, classes seem to him a much greater problem than castes. For castes in Senegal were not indigenous to the people, but of "Arab-Berber importation." Moreover, "the Negro-Africans have Negrofied the castes in giving them, along with a religious foundation, a functional role in the division of labor." [46] Increasingly romanticized, Senghor conceives castes primarily in terms of new functions in the division of labor. "Class," however, as an analytic term, retains the connotation of conflict and exploitation.

Senghor argues that there is no polarization of antagonistic classes on the basis of ownership of the means of production in Senegal or anywhere else, for that matter. Extending his argument to the developed countries, Senghor contends not only that do classes not exist in Africa, but that class is no longer a problem even in the capitalist countries. "The notion of class, thanks to the progress of democracy, no longer corresponds to sociological realities." "Technico-professional groups" have replaced classes in the West, and the interests of these new groups, rather than clashing, converge within the framework of national development. [47]

II. CLASS AND INDUSTRIAL DEVELOPMENT

In the West, from the time of the French Revolution, political democracy has favored the growth of social and economic democracy, which has in turn provoked an evolutionary change in the nature of capital. Capitalism, Senghor continues, has passed not only from the industrial phase to the financial, but from the monopolistic phase to that of planning. "Becoming more intelligent, it has known how to adapt." Under pressure from "the masses," the state has intervened in the internal affairs of capitalism to combat monopolies and appropriate an ever increasing share of profits for the public benefit. In doing this, the modern state has had a double objective, inspired by socialism: first, an increase in the national income and product through productive investment within the framework of a development plan; and, second, the realization of greater social justice in the distribution of the national revenues and product. [48]

Thus has the West slowly but surely evolved—even as foreseen by Engels as taking place under the influence of the labor movement[49]—until it has reached the stage of a certain balance of classes. The East has experienced a similar process under communism since the October Revolution, in the sense that upon the ruins of the old bourgeoisie new groups of technico-professionals emerged, whose privileges are founded on their knowledge and technology. These technico-professional groups tend to crystallize into classes, and this creates a source of difficulty for Soviet ideology, which maintains the nonexistence of classes under communism.[50] Further, the dictatorship of the proletariat, contrary to the teachings of Marx, has made the state an omnipotent, soulless monster, stifling the natural freedoms of the human being and drying up the sources of art, without which life is not worth living.[51] Europeans need not worry about the condition of African society, because Africa is founded on spiritual values, while European civilization is founded on "discursive reason, technology, and money—a thoroughly materialistic affair." [52]

Senghor argues that the difference between parliamentary and communist regimes today concerns not the existence or non-existence of capital, but how it is used. And, increasingly, both systems utilize capital in the same way. The North Americans and Soviets conquered space and the atom, not simply because of their scientific superiority but because of the superiority of their capital. Lenin was mistaken, Senghor continues, in calling imperialism the last stage of capitalism. The last stage is that of state capitalism, or what Senghor calls "Capitalism of the Worker-State," which orients capital or money (the major means of production) on the basis of a plan toward the principal social and economic "poles of development."

Having been redirected toward new orientations, capitalism also acquired new social structures demanded by novel scientific, technological and accounting requirements. Today capital needs, for its proper utilization, to be directed and coordinated by an elite of scholars and technicians, who are rewarded with special privileges for their services. Teams of technocrats have replaced ignorant proprietors. Both systems in the East and West become increasingly similar in a sort of bureaucratization dominated by a technology.[53]

As far as values are concerned, Senghor notes that American and Russian workers have the same dreams "of villas and automobiles, of television sets and washing machines." Senghor sees contemporary capitalism as essentially an economic system involved with the increase of production; it is no longer an exploitative apparatus, or a matter for grave moral concern. This analysis represents a basic change in Senghor's image of capitalism.

III.   CHANGING IMAGE, POLICY AND THEORY OF CAPITALISM

Immediately after the war, Senghor denounced Naziism as being simply capitalism disguised as racism. He stated that resistance to the spirit of this phenomenon was the only effort that was worthwhile.[54] Upon passage of a law in the French Assembly that set standards for government workers that would have to be matched by private interests, he further asserted:

> We say that the bosses possess powerful instruments of combat, that in case of conflict, if we were not watchful, the battle would be unequal, that our solicitude, to be fair, must first go to the salaried worker, to the humble if not the just.[55]

After independence, when Senegal was actually seeking to attract private capital for development purposes, Senghor stated that while there might *seem to be* a contradiction between "our socialistic ideal and the aid we request of capital," analysis reveals that "the contradiction is only superficial and that it can be resolved if indeed it really exists." [56]

Downgrading the importance of class has helped Senghor to achieve a reconciliation with capitalism. Today, he states, capitalism is no longer a danger; even investors make only minimal demands:

What investors ask of us is not that we abandon our original way of "socialism" which they know is not "communism" but *African* and *Humanist*. What they ask of us is that we clearly define the end, objectives and means of our African Way of Socialism.[57]

In fact, capitalism has changed its nature so radically that, in at least some instances, one might say that capitalism is really socialism. At the inauguration of a new industrial enterprise in Dakar during June of 1965 Senghor informed the president of the corporation that he, the apparently capitalist entrepreneur, was in fact a "socialist."

I wouldn't say that you are a socialist "without knowing it," like Monsieur Jourdain when he spoke prose, or like the planners who vituperate socialism. You have just said or at least let it be understood that you are against wastage and mistakes; you are in the new independent countries for a "progressive economy" which requires a "plan of development"; finally, you accept a "capitalism of the state." Socialism is not "Communism which wants to divide and share all goods"; this Marx repudiated in his *Philosophical Works*; it isn't even atheism to which we are impervious. Socialism, once more, is nothing other than the rational organization of the forces of production for the purpose of the freest possible development of all men. . . .[58]

Senegalese socialism is such, Senghor continues, that "we intend to deny neither the law of savings nor the one of profit." This is because all regimes, regardless of their ideology, require "auto-financing," as well as the primitive accumulation of capital through savings. Furthermore, as the communist states have discovered, profit is the most powerful incentive for increasing productivity. Efficiency is the major problem for an underdeveloped country, and in the long run it will lead to social justice.

Against this criterion of efficiency, one must re-examine all the old socialist slogans, which have really become nothing more than shibboleths. This is, for example, clearly the case with "nationalization." Senghor asks, nationalization for what?

> . . . one has to have something to nationalize. To nationalize the meager capital at our disposal . . . would mean "killing the goose that lays the golden eggs," preventing other urgently needed capital from being invested. Economists note that in order to nationalize, one must have the necessary cadres, which is not true in our case. Even in the best circumstances and in developed countries, nationalization does not always succeed. . . . Since capitalists train and employ African personnel, reinvest part of their profits, and pay taxes, capital is, for all practical purposes, nationalized.
>
> Does this mean that we shall adopt a policy of *laissez-faire?* No . . . the positive aim [of the development plan] is to organize production rationally . . . banks, commerce, industry—will be oriented toward the objectives of the plan and, to a certain extent, controlled. How? By a long-term moratorium on taxes. . . . In return, capital in this sector will be expected to accept social legislation and even cooperate in building the social infrastructure: schools, dispensaries, housing, cooperatives.[59]

As far as African merchants are concerned, traditional commerce must learn to adapt itself to the requirements of modern economy. This means scientific management, large values at reasonable prices, an adequate system of distribution and an end to usurious rates of interest. The government does not want "to kill commerce," but to help it renovate and reform. This is why the government is willing to help merchants with Cooperatives and consortiums as well as financing and other means. In the end, "that which we wish, once again, is not to satisfy our ideological preoccupation, but to assure the masses of the best price." [60]

Not only will the state allow both domestic and foreign capital to exist, but it will control them only indirectly.

Hence how could one possibly say that in the twentieth century the problem is either one of class inequalities or of capitalism? This is quite obviously not the problem in Europe and certainly not in Africa, where technico-professional groups are far from being crystallized into classes and even castes are on their way to disappearing.[61]

Thus, according to Senghor, modern capitalism in no way poses a threat to the objectives of Senegalese socialism. More than this, because of the classless nature of Senegal, capitalism can be integrated within the nation in a way that is mutually beneficial to all concerned. This can happen because African society is not simply a classless society; more positively, it is a *community* society.[62]

For Senghor, the key problem is to attain equalitarianism and progress within the context of a hierarchical and well-ordered society. Dependent for support upon traditional and religious leaders, Senghor at the same time must satisfy the material aspirations and demands for increased political participation of a growing mass following. His theory of African community goes far toward meeting these ideological necessities: it postulates a fellowship of persons essentially equal, but united under the aegis of the elders or those with special grace. Authority is supposed to stem from special virtues of leadership which enable the community to fulfill its inherent purposes; it does not stem from riches or control over the means of production. At the same time, the community is one of work as well as fellowship—bodies must also follow where souls are told to go.

The study of traditional culture, Senghor argues, shows that "Negro-African society is collectivist or, more exactly communal, because it is rather a *communism* of souls than an aggregate of individuals." [63] This distinction between "communal" and "collectivist" is fundamental. While the supposedly individualistic

145

West refers contemptuously to the collectivism of the East, from an African perspective all European societies are collectivistic, precisely *because* they are individualistic. East and West both are "an affair of an aggregate of individuals." [64] Senghor further states on this point:

> To return to the distinction between Negro-African and collectivist European society, I would say that the latter is an *assembly of individuals*. The collectivist society inevitably places the emphasis on the individual, on his original activity and his needs. In this respect, the debate between "to each according to his labor" and "to each according to his needs" is significant. Negro-African society puts more stress on the group than on the individual, more on *solidarity* than the activity and the needs of the individual, more on the communion of persons than on their autonomy. Ours is a *community* society. This does not mean that it ignores the individual, or that collectivist society ignores solidarity, but the latter bases this solidarity on the activities of individuals, whereas the community society bases it on the general activity of the group.[65]

Traditional African society, furthermore, was "strongly structured, made up of family cooperation in the framework of the village mutual." Religion played an important role in this society, for it "gave its members a single soul, a high ideal of solidarity in which all communed." [66] As a classless communism of souls, African society had already achieved socialism before the coming of the European. Tomorrow "our new mutuals and cooperatives, integrating all the peasants, will be similarly structured and animated by the same idea." [67]

IV. CLASS CONFLICT AND DEVELOPMENT IN THE POST-INDEPENDENCE PERIOD. THE PRIVILEGED VS. THE DISINHERITED

The absence of classes in African society, Senghor argues, does not mean that it is without hierarchy or division of labor:

146

It is a communitarian society where hierarchy—and the power which stems from it—is founded on spiritual and democratic values, on primogeniture and elections; where decisions about all commands are deliberated over in a *palabre*; where work is divided between the sexes, and among the technico-professional groups which are at base religious.[68]

African traditional society, therefore, knows no exploitation, and one must prevent it from developing.[69]

Since independence, faced with growing pressure for an increase in material advantages, Senghor increasingly has denounced various "technico-professional categories" for being out for themselves with no sense of collective responsibility. He maintains that all of the strikes, and practically all of the political activity of the past, functioned only to increase the income of the "privileged" (the salaried) and not the disinherited (the peasants and herdsmen).[70] Today:

. . . there are no classes at war, but only social groups struggling for influence. Tomorrow, they will be at war with one another unless we are careful, if we allow the intellectuals—liberals and professionals, civil servants, employees, and even laborers—to form a class that oppresses by misleading peasants, shepherds, and artisans.[71]

An irresponsible opposition which stirred up discontent could make this danger a reality by converting social groups into antagonistic classes. Also, the European presence tends to the same end through the danger of assimilation of European values.

Conclusion

On the basis of available historical, anthropological and sociological findings, one may well ask why most African leaders stress the lack or nonexistence of classes when they so apparently have existed. Among the various reasons for this assertion, the following stand out: First, even though classes may have existed and do exist, the underdeveloped character of Africa's political and economic life has given them a different importance. They may not always constitute the same political and economic force as they have in other areas of the world. In addition, modern productivity and productive techniques create, in combination with the tremendous growth of bureaucracy, new classes which seemingly overshadow the traditional interests.

Second, the colonial situation has caused the new African men of power to define themselves primarily against foreign invaders. This is true despite the fact that in some cases the traditional forces were allied with colonialism. Moreover, to a large extent under colonial regimes, the authority of the traditional ruling classes had been withering away.

Third, a de-emphasis of conflict in the post-independence situation functions to avoid open confrontations when the modernizing sector of the state is unsure of itself or lacks sufficient legitimacy to be certain of the outcome of its policies. State-controlled mechanisms of coercion are weakly developed in the early stages of independence. In a small country, the use of force often means intrafraternal conflict as well as the exacerbation of regional and tribal divisions, and may prove a difficult legacy for future tasks of nation-building.

Fourth, the nation must achieve not only unity but also development. The recognition of class exploitation may well work against economic development. In the Soviet experience, for example, not only did the state have to reduce the role of the Kulaks, but it had to convince the peasants that they should deliver their produce to the state-controlled markets. Even if African governments were able to eliminate the "Kulaks" (which, in view of simple technological costs, seems doubtful), this may not be the most efficient method of attaining agricultural expansion. Exploitation of the peasant on the basis of the Soviet and East European experience does not seem the appropriate method for African countries.

148

Growth probably can occur more rapidly through more indirect controls of centralized planning. Even if all calculations dictated the greater use of force, ideologically many African leaders would not willingly tolerate such violence or the achievement of rapid development at the sacrifice of the peasants.

Last, in terms of social control, the doctrine is directed particularly at the middle-level bureaucrats, as well as other mobile groups in the society who feel themselves dispossessed. Historically, this has always been a revolutionary element. Functionally, the doctrine of community attempts to prevent the development of class consciousness, of the transformation of a "class in itself" to a "class for itself."

A basic assumption of African leaders, therefore, is that the politics of pure class are highly unstable. Senghor believes that the more non-class cross-cutting cleavages there are—ethnic, religious or regional—within society, the greater the chances for compromise and stability.

Class cleavage, however, might well be the most easily compromised, divisive set of interests in the society, as well as a factor in the promotion of greater national unity. Sectional, religious and ethnic sentiments can be more disintegrative and lasting than class hostility—particularly if, as society developed, there were increasing upward mobility. At the same time, class cleavages can override other parochial loyalties and thus tend to promote, if a broader division, also a broader basis for unity.[72]

Senghor's theory implies that conflict in general is dysfunctional for societies, and that this is particularly true of class conflicts. Yet, one may argue, class conflict in underdeveloped countries can result in restructuring society in a way more efficacious for economic development—for example, by eliminating "feudal" or "neo-feudal" classes. Economic development seems to require that the new classes or groups be future-oriented, individualistic, materialistic and rational. They should be capable of spreading modernizing values throughout the society and awakening the masses in a *prise de conscience* to these new possibilities.

Historically, there have existed two roads to mass participation, each having different consequences for the social structure: either the existing parties and power-holders have brought lower-class citizens into the system, or the lower-class citizens have organized parties and power centers of their own in opposition to the inherited system. Obviously, this question crucially determines one's attitude toward class-consciousness and the restructuring of society. Senghor's doctrine of community and class conflict, regardless of any intrinsic merit, functions ideologically to maintain a policy of evolutionary moderation. Senghor's ideology of socialism (as do his theories of Negritude, nationalism and colonialism) ultimately assumes that there is no need for mass involvement in the political process.

NOTES TO CHAPTER V

1. The expression "national ways of socialism" was first used in 1949–1950 when Yugoslavia broke away from Stalinist Russia. Leo Hamon, in tracing the origin of the term "African Socialism," argued that alongside international socialism as it had existed historically there now appeared what he calls "a socialism of fatherlands." "La Voie Africaine du Socialisme," *Connaissance de l'Afrique,* No. 5 (July–August 1963).

2. Senghor did not become preoccupied with the actual programs and the practical application of socialist theory to create a socialist society until the advent of independence of the former states of A.O.F. in 1958. Significantly, he did not use the term "Senegalese socialism" until 1962 in *Théorie et Pratique du Socialisme Sénégalais* (Ministre de l'Information, Dakar, March 1964, translated and reprinted in Mercer Cook, *On African Socialism* [Frederick A. Praeger, New York, 1964]), a booklet published for the benefit of Senegalese political cadres.

3. Numerous attempts have been made to characterize variations in African socialism and to develop typologies. See especially William H. Friedland and Carl G. Rosberg, Jr., eds., *African Socialism,* which contains a series of articles discussing general problems of defining African socialism and analyzing socialist programs in specific countries, as well as a selected bibliography.

   See also Charles Andrian, "Patterns of African Socialist Thought," *African Forum,* Winter 1966, and "Democracy and Socialism: Ideologies of African Leaders," in Apter, *Ideology and Discontent, op. cit.,* pp. 155–205: Fenner Brockway, *African Socialism* (The Bodley Head, London, 1963), p. 17 and *passim;* René Dumont, "Choice and Classification of the Basic Aims of Agricultural Development in Africa" (IDEP Paper, ECA-Ma/OUS/1964, mimeo). A particularly interesting attempt at classification is that of John N. Hazard, "Negritude, Socialism, and the Law," *Columbia Law Review,* Vol. 65, May 1965, who compares Senegalese socialism to that of the Soviet Union. Hazard argues in analyzing Senegalese socialism that "the attitude of the leaders cannot be pushed aside in favor of concentration on current practice, for this is the very factor that makes credible the Senegalese claim to being socialist" (p. 808). Ernest Milcent argued in, *Au Carrefour des Options Africaines: Le Sénégal* (Editions du Centurion, Paris, 1965) that Senegal was somewhere between the "liberalism" of the Ivory Coast and Nigeria, and the more rigid socialism of Guinea and Mali. For a series of discussions on the possibility of a "third way," see Laurence W. Martin, ed., *Neutralism and Nonalignment: The New States in World Affairs* (Frederick A. Praeger, New York, 1962), particularly Vernon Aspaturian, "Revolutionary Change and the Strategy of the Status Quo," pp. 165–196.

For further references, see note 1 to Chap. 2 above, and bibliography.

4. Sartre, *op. cit., passim.*
5. Kesteloot, *op. cit.,* p. 184.
6. For an interesting recent discussion of the difficulties of defining "political development," see Leonard Binder, "National Integration and Political Development," *American Political Science Review* (September 1964), p. 622.
7. Brockway, *op. cit.,* pp. 45–46.
8. Adam Ulam, *The Unfinished Revolution* (Random House, New York, 1960).
9. *Ibid.*
10. See the discussion in H. Stuart Hughes, *Consciousness and Society, The Reorientation of European Social Thought 1890–1930* (Alfred A. Knopf, New York, 1958), pp. 75–78.
11. Saul Rose, *Socialism in Southern Asia* (Oxford University Press, New York, 1959), p. 267.
12. Hughes, *op. cit.,* p. 74.
13. Speaking of the intellectual legacy of Marx, Hughes pointed out that this legacy was both untidy and ambiguous. By the 1890's

> the size of the political parties that recognized him as their prophet and the seriousness of the economic investigation that he had initiated made him a massive force that demanded to be related in some way or other to the major traditions of European Social thought. . . . As the decade wore on, a number of "bourgeois" economists and social thinkers of the most varying intellectual orientation found themselves compelled to come to grips with his doctrines. Yet it was not entirely clear with what part of the Marxian heritage they should grapple. Were they to treat Marx in the abstract as a "scientific" social thinker, or more pragmatically as the initiator of an extraordinarily successful political movement? [Hughes, *op. cit.,* p. 67]

14. Senghor, "Nationhood . . . ," *op. cit.,* pp. 26–27.
15. *Ibid.,* p. 45.
16. *Ibid.,* p. 27.
17. *Ibid.,* p. 43.
18. *Ibid.,* p. 36.

19. Only recently has this view been systematically questioned in the West. See for example, Herbert Marcuse, *One Dimensional Man; Studies in the Ideology of Advanced Industrial Society* (Beacon Press, Boston, 1964).
20. Reinhard Bendix, *Social Science and Distrust of Reason* (University of California Press, Berkeley, 1951).
21. Senghor, "Nationhood . . . ," *op. cit.,* p. 28.
22. *Ibid.,* p. 44.
23. *Ibid.,* p. 26. Specifically, Senghor asserts, Marx's determinism—which results in both an underestimating of man's freedom and the potential of capitalism —is rooted in his "excessive simplification of the class struggle theory." Senghor goes on to argue that a simple glance at the facts *today* shows how

unscientific Marx really was, and that one may well note the changes in "economic, social, and political reality" that have taken place since the publication of *Capital* (*ibid.*, p. 32).

24. *Ibid.*, p. 34.
25. Senghor, "The African Road to Socialism," *op. cit.*, p. 83.
26. Senghor, "Nationhood . . . ," *op. cit.*, p. 37.
27. *Ibid.*, p. 36.
28. Senghor, "Rapport sur la Doctrine et la Politique Générale," *op. cit.*, p. 21.
29. Senghor, "The African Road to Socialism," *op. cit.*, p. 83.
30. Senghor, "Nationhood . . . ," *op. cit.*, p. 38.
31. Senghor, "The African Road to Socialism," *op. cit.*, p. 76.
32. Senghor, "Nationhood . . . ," *op. cit.*, p. 47.
33. Léopold Sédar Senghor, "Colloque sur les Politiques de Développement et les Diverses Voies Africaines vers le Socialisme," *op. cit.*, p. 13.
34. See, for example, the important speech given in the name of the Khalif General of the Mourides by his secretary, M. Dramé, at the Grand Magal of Touba on June 8, 1966, stating the Mourides' appreciation of President Senghor and emphasizing Senghor's personal religiosity, as well as his contributions to religion in Senegal. "C'était à Touba: Le Discours du Khalif," *L'Unité Africaine*, June 16, 1966.
35. Kwame Nkrumah, who *does* believe in classes and the existence of class struggle theory, states:

> All available evidence from the history of Africa, up to the end of the European colonization, shows that African society was neither classless nor devoid of a social hierarchy. Feudalism existed in some parts of Africa before colonialization and feudalism involves a deep and exploitative social stratification founded on land. . . .
>
>   . . . an idyllic African classless society (in which there were no rich and no poor) enjoying a drugged serenity is certainly a facile simplification; there is no historical or even anthropological evidence for any such society. I am afraid the realities of African society are somewhat more sordid. ["African Socialism Revisited," *African Forum*, Winter 1966, p. 5]

In apparent reference to Senghor's assertions that contemporary African society is also classless, Nkrumah states:

> A classless society that at the same time rejoices in a hierarchy of power (as distinct from authority) must be accounted a marvel of socio-political finesse. [*Ibid.*, p. 6]

36. See, for example, Georges Balandier, who argues that Senghor and Touré are alike in their rejection of the Marxist doctrine of class struggle. "De la Négritude au Socialisme," *Jeune Afrique*, No. 111, December 3–9, 1962, p. 29.
37. *La Lutte du Parti Démocratique de Guinée pour l'Emancipation Africaine* (Imprimerie Nationale, Conakry, 1959, reprinted in Sigmund, *op. cit.*, p. 156). See also, by Sekou Touré, *L'Action Politique du Parti Démocratique de Guinée* (Présence Africaine, Paris, 1959), where he extends his attack to customary feudal religious interests, who align their interests with those of colonialism (p. 54). In *Expérience Guinéenne et Unité Africaine* (Présence Africaine, Paris, 1962), Touré discusses the sociological basis of support of the R.D.A., the government's political party (pp. 22–25).
38. Touré, "La Lutte . . . ," *op. cit.*, p. 156 (emphasis added).
39. See also Touré, *Expérience Guinéenne et Unité Africaine*, *op. cit.*, p. 14, for a discussion of the "obstacles" in the proper functioning of Guinean politics.

The fact that he considers and treats Guinean students as members of a privileged class may explain some of their opposition to him, even though their opposition is phrased in a revolutionary vocabulary.

40. "Discours au Banquet Affecté par le Gouverneur Général, le Docteur Nnamdi Azikiwe," January 8, 1961 (mimeo, N.P.).
41. Senghor, "Discours Devant le Parlement du Ghana," February 15, 1961 (mimeo, N.P.).
42. Ali Mazuri, "Borrowed Theory and Original Practice in African Politics" (unpublished paper, mimeo, 1965), p. 4.
43. *Ibid.*, p. 6.
44. "Discours Devant le Parlement du Ghana," *op. cit.*
45. Senghor, "Vues sur l'Afrique Noire ou Assimiler, Non Etre Assimilés," *op. cit.*, pp. 49–53.
46. *Ibid.*, p. 49.
47. "Rapport sur la Doctrine et la Politique Générale," *op. cit.*, p. 8.
    Paul Mercier, a French sociologist, in "Un Essai d'Enquête par Questionnaire dans la Ville de Dakar" uses the term "catégorie socio-professionelle" and argues that these "social categories" in Africa only "tendentially" have the character of social classes because "the character of colonial society on the one hand, and the persistence of traditional values on the other, don't permit it." P. Mercier, L. Masse, A. Hauser, in *L'Agglomération Dakaroise: Quelques Aspects Sociologiques et Démographiques*, Études Sénégalaises No. 3 (IFAN, St.-Louis, 1954), p. 18.
48. "Rapport sur la Doctrine et la Politique Générale," *op. cit.*, p. 8.
49. *Ibid.*, p. 9.
50. *Ibid.*, p. 9.
51. Senghor, "Nationhood . . . ," *op. cit.*, p. 33.
52. "Rapport sur la Doctrine et la Politique Générale," *op. cit.*, p. 9.
53. *Ibid.*, p. 11.
54. *Interventions, op. cit.*, March 21, 1946.
55. *Ibid.*, November 27, 1950.
56. Senghor, "Nationhood . . . ," *op. cit.*, p. 58.
57. Senghor, *Planification et Tension Morale, op. cit.*
58. Senghor "Les Investisseurs Peuvent Continuer de Nous Faire Confiance; à l'Inauguration du Nouvel Ensemble Peyrissac," *L'Unité Africaine*, June 24, 1965.
59. Senghor, "Nationhood . . . ," *op. cit.*, pp. 58, 59. See also Senghor, "Allocution à la Chambre de Commerce et d'Industrie du Dahomey, July 2, 1962," *Chambre de Commerce Bulletin*, VI, mimeo, Dakar, 1962.
60. Senghor, "Discours à l'Assemblée Nationale," *op. cit.*, April 19, 1963.
61. Senghor, "Rapport sur la Doctrine et la Politique Générale," *op. cit.*, p. 11.
62. For a discussion of definitions of community, see Maurice R. Stein, *The Eclipse of Community* (Princeton University Press, Princeton, 1960). Stein's work, subtitled *An Interpretation of American Studies*, is in part a major synthesis of American community studies. It is of direct relevance at many points for a better appreciation of the theory of community in Africa. See especially Chap. 10, "Anthropological Perspectives on the Modern Community," pp. 230–250.
63. Senghor, "Nationhood . . . ," *op. cit.*, p. 49.
64. Senghor, "Discours . . . d'Oxford," *op. cit.*
65. Senghor, "The African Road to Socialism," *op. cit.*, pp. 93–94.
66. Senghor, "Nationhood . . . ," *op. cit.*, p. 49.
67. *Ibid.*, p. 49.
68. Senghor, "Discours . . . d'Oxford," *op. cit.*
69. *Ibid.* Senghor has also stated that today West African society

. . . comprises three large sectors: (1) members of the liberal professions—lawyers, doctors, pharmacists, notaries, to whom we may add the merchants; (2) the wage earners—government officials, employees, and laborers; and (3) the peasants, shepherds, fishermen, and artisans.

These groups are less differentiated than in European society. First, because of our general underdevelopment and our democratic system of scholarships, a person passes easily from one group to the other. Moreover, the physicians and dentists, if not the pharmacists, are almost all government employees. It will be good to maintain this situation. On the other hand, the federal state will have to control the activities of the bar and of the notarial services. As for the merchants, most of them are small shopkeepers who present no immediate social threat. The danger would be that instead of getting rich, they become poorer and poorer, because of foreign capital and their lack of organization. Here again it will be up to the state to encourage them to unite and cooperate. [Senghor, "The African Road to Socialism," *op. cit.*, p. 94]

70. Senghor, *Planification et Tension Morale, op. cit.*
71. Senghor, "The African Road to Socialism," *op. cit.*, p. 87.
72. See Robert R. Alford, *Party and Society* (Rand McNally & Company, Chicago, 1963), for an elaboration of this thesis in the context of the "Anglo-American Democracies."

VI

Development and Socialism

THE POLICY OF SENEGAL," Senghor asserts, "is based on development, development, and always development." [1] Development is "integral humanism":

> . . . it is the work of men, but of men animated by a promethean will to transform the real, to render it docile. It has Man for its final end: the whole man, himself integrated into his community of life and work . . . in this civilization of abundance that Socialism aims at.
> . . . Economic development certainly, but cultural development also. Because politics, even economics, is only an aspect of culture.[2]

Senghor argues that priority must go to physical development; but in the hierarchy of values, cultural and moral growth are what are most important—"the harmonious expansion of integral man and of all men integrated into Humanity." [3]

> Our ultimate end is to allow each Senegalese to be freed from his material worries in such a manner that he may be able to realize his person through the integral expansion of all his faculties, by the satisfaction of his cultural and spiritual needs.[4]

Thus, the task of the government "is to bring the Senegalese people maximum social progress with maximum freedom." [5]

While this can be accomplished only by "rapid economic growth," in and of itself economic growth is not development. Development, according to Senghor, is something greater.[6]

One finds, in the literature on developing societies, a tendency to use the terms "economic growth" and "economic development" interchangeably. For our purposes, economic growth refers to a process whereby an economy's real national product increases over a period of time. Success in this endeavor by itself, however, would not be sufficient by Senghor's objectives. For Senghor, economic *development* involves the development of "the whole man and all men." Development, therefore, does not mean merely an increase in aggregate output, but also denotes a rising standard of living for the total population. This view, at the minimum, requires that economic development be defined as a process whereby the real per capita income of a country increases.

A *statistical* rise in real per capita income is still not a sufficient criterion for development, because it is arrived at simply by dividing the total population into the total increase in real national income. By itself, this figure reveals nothing about the *distribution of the income*. As real per capita income rises, it is possible that the rich are getting richer and the poor are getting poorer. Therefore, even if real national income and per capita income rise, it is possible that there has been no economic development unless the resultant distributions of income are also according to planned expectations.

Some economists may object that economic development, defined this way, no longer denotes only a quantitative concept but also a qualitative one; that it is being confused with "economic progress" or "an increase in economic welfare." Although this is true, even "objectively," the prescriptive term is analytically the better one. For the leaders of Senegal themselves maintain that development has a "persuasive definition," implying that a particular distribution of income is desirable.[7] Senghor emphasizes this by insisting that to achieve his objectives, economic development must be achieved under a socialistic system.[8]

Senghor holds that socialism is increasingly a movement involved with economic development whose final goal is the creation of free men, physically, intellectually and spiritually integrated, triumphing over sickness, misery and ignorance. Thus socialism is only a method, not a dogma, to achieve this final objective.[9] Socialism provides a framework, an outline that must be filled in; it requires constant rethinking of specifics according to the historical conditions of the peoples concerned. Socialism requires more than political power; it calls for a new organization of the means of production and distribution. Senghor asserts that the people of Senegal are now in the process of accomplishing this. Because he regards socialism as a method, not a dogma, Senghor feels free to discard the traditional techniques of socialism—nationalization, for example.

Maintaining that economic growth is the common objective of capitalism and socialism, he holds that the only difference in this respect is that socialism wishes to achieve this objective through "spiritual tension"—that is, "the integral mobilization, spirit and heart of the rural and urban masses." [10]

Over the past four centuries, Senghor argues, a public conscience was born in Europe. The emergence of this "conscience" was the result of a long, sometimes bloody "dialogue" between the haves and the have-nots. The rich made concessions to the poor[11] and out of this economic and social evolution came a certain idea of man, "of a man whose nature forbids that he be exploited," and all sides in this controversy recognized this nature and reformed the institutions of their societies:

Today, in each of the countries of the European Economic Community, there is something of socialism. . . . under no matter which regime or majority. That they proclaim it or not isn't important. Socialism, among other reforms, involves the substitution of technico-professional groups for the crystallization of classes . . . free teaching and social security . . . planning and attacks against private property under Roman law.[12]

This is the path that African societies must also follow. Socialism is not laissez-faire or economic anarchy, but rational organization, "reason operating upon the real" [13]—"rational because an effort is made to harmonize production and distribution with the needs and necessities of Man and all men." [14]

If nationalization as a technique is outmoded (and Senghor has promised not to nationalize European enterprises),[15] capitalism also became outmoded when, with the increasing division of labor, all work became collective and these new relations of production demanded a new form of proprietorship.[16] Capitalism, as an economic system, works for the well-being of only a minority. Obliged to reform under pressure from labor and state intervention, capitalism is still interested only in granting the minimum concessions possible. Capitalism permits the exercise of political, cultural and spiritual liberties only theoretically and on their surface. They cannot be lived. Concrete liberty requires economic liberty, which cannot exist in a system wherein a minority can exploit the majority. Liberty, wrote Teilhard de Chardin, is "the chance offered to each man, through the suppression of obstacles and the provision of the appropriate means to trans-humanize one's self by going to the end of one's self." Capitalism, a system driven by the search for profits, cannot provide this opportunity.[17] Let there be no doubt, then, that socialism concerns "essentially the transformation of the economic relations between men, and the transformation of the economic structures themselves." [18]

Above all, "socialism is essentially politics, that is, an art of governing men of a given society by organizing their relations harmoniously." [19] Socialists must be capable not only of projecting an image of man for the future, but of dealing politically with men in the here and now.[20] Since the ultimate object of socialism is not simply a reorganization of the economy, as many Marxists now believe, scientific research, cooperation and rational planning for economic development become the first order of the day.[21] "Socialism for us," writes Senghor, "is nothing other than the rational organization of human society considered in its totality, according to the most scientific modern and effective methods." [22] Socialism is "the only way capable of combining the imperatives of development and those of democracy," because ultimately it can realize social justice through an equitable division of national riches. But, in the meantime, "it's necessary to produce before dividing up." [23] This is why, at this particular historical moment, Senghor says, "for me, socialism is of course, economic growth for development." [24]

> If in the developed countries the battle of socialism is situated at the level of the division of income, here in Africa it is a question of producing more and better. The Socialist ideal is not realized in misery precisely because socialism is abundance and well-being . . . optimally rationalized—because it is planned.[25]

African socialism therefore requires a social state that will give primacy to law, work and justice.[26] Thus, Senghor has a number of times reaffirmed his adherence to the principle of democratic socialism[27] and warned against the "deviations of bureaucratism, totalitarianism, opportunism and expansionism." [28]

Socialists always considered work a necessity to attain a state of abundance. Social justice is "the possibility offered to every citizen to fully benefit in the common good." [29] Because such an opportunity exists, those who benefit have the obligation to participate in the further construction of this open society; since everyone benefits, everyone must participate. Social justice demands that each be paid according to his work.[30]

Social justice requires intellectual and moral rigor, lucidity and courage, an objective analysis of the facts and austerity. This is what socialism is.[31] Socialism is simple honesty.[32] One cannot have the optimum development of the production of goods and

the equitable division of these goods without an implacable battle against waste and embezzling. There is "no major formula
including socialism that can replace work and national unity,"
but the work will not be forthcoming and there will be no "unity
of hearts and spirits in a renovated democracy" [33] if corruption
cannot be stopped. This is why socialism also requires and is a
moral tension, a constant struggle for improvement.[34] Rooted in
human laws, amenable to human control, the process of development will be taken in hand by socialist masses to construct the
new society.[35]

The Search for the Concrete

With Senghor's increasing personal involvement with the
concrete tasks of development, his concern with the specific
needs of economic growth has deepened and he has become less
concerned with socialism as a philosophical system. In 1960, deploring an excess of philosophy, he argued that:

> *The time for philosophizing has passed; the time for
> action has come.* We must gird up our loins and as-
> sume all our responsibilities as political militants here
> and now. These responsibilities can be summed up in a
> single sentence: *We must transform our quasi-nation
> into a nation, our underdeveloped country into a devel-
> oped country,* by raising the standard of living and cul-
> ture for all the citizens of our respective states.[36]

But even as he issued this call to action, Senghor failed to
focus on any specific political or economic barriers to development. Instead, at this time he continued to dwell on cultural
independence as a prerequisite for full political and economic
independence. Following the fall of Mamadou Dia in 1963,
however, he began to emphasize more strongly the specific needs
of development, although never entirely abandoning the theme
of culture as a conditioner of development. In a 1965 speech

Senghor clearly states this shift in his thinking—the de-emphasis of "culture" and its subordination to the prior necessities of development:

> We must keep ourselves, in effect, from reducing development to culture—not to mention literature—as one had a tendency to do in Senegal following the example of a certain French tendency. It is good to react against Econometrics, but without excess. Marx insisted, not without reason, on the fact that the creative activity of Man, more precisely, the artistic activity which is the ultimate end of Development . . . is only possible once one's animal needs are satisfied. The problem is first economic growth: it's necessary for us to feed, clothe, house, and care for the Senegalese.[37]

Senghor's new concern with the concrete tasks of economic growth also reflects an increasing tendency toward technicity. Today Senghor holds that even "the most blind" should be able to see that "development is not connected to an ideology, but to methods and techniques which are indispensable to all nations no matter what their ideology." [38] "Simply proclaiming the revolution serves no end; one must realize it in one's daily individual and collective action." [39] Indeed, it is less the shenanigans of their politicians than their policies of development which distinguishes the nations of the world from one another. While Senghor says, "I will not go so far as to proclaim the 'end of ideologies,' " he does say that "it is time to recognize their ineffectiveness in the second half of the twentieth century." Either strict adherence to the letter of ideology has killed its spirit, or the ideal itself has been betrayed or by-passed by a more important abstraction, such as that of "nation" or "culture." [40]

In any event, not ideology, not future cultural needs, not preoccupation of future problems of leisure, but satisfaction of material needs dominates. On a visit to the *département* of Kaffrine in February 1965, Senghor stated: "Certainly, since Independence, Senegal has changed. If today you have schools, roads, rural technicians, you are still lacking schools, dispensaries, roads, wells. . . . Our policy is ordered towards the satisfaction of your needs, of all your needs." [41] On trips into the interior, Senghor follows a routine of stopping and exchanging greetings with local notables. He is next informed if any new wells have been dug, roads built or dispensaries constructed. The village then presents him with a list of new demands, from schools to government subsidies for waterworks.

Senghor spends much of his time on these trips visiting new installations, no matter how small, down to the tiniest administrative building.[42] Quite often he listens for hours to technical reports of field agronomists on fertilizer programs and other methods used to increase production.[43] All of these activities are part of his new emphasis on concrete measures of development.

Need for an Inventory of Culture and Resources

Foremost among these concrete measures is drafting a plan. In the past Senghor maintained that before this could be done, the nation must take inventory of its cultural, political and economic resources.

> On a threefold level, we must prepare: (1) an inventory of our traditional civilization; (2) an inventory of the impact of colonialism and French civilization on our traditional civilization; and (3) an inventory of our economic resources, our needs, and potentialities. Our development plan must not be solely economic: it must be social in the broadest sense of the word. . . .[44]

Now, however, Senghor thinks more in terms of the specific requirements of development. Increasingly, he emphasizes concrete work. Material progress, he points out, requires immediate hard labor. Senegal is not a poor country, but development requires tremendous effort.[45]

"We are," Senghor asserts, "in the Third Day of Creation: The rest of the seventh day is still far." [46]

Senghor cites a long list of the faults of colonialism—the legacy of monoculture, the arbitrary delineation of boundaries, the taste for and tremendous imports of consumer goods that the country cannot afford;[47] but foremost among these faults he places the failure to inculcate an ethic of work. Thus, the main objective in planning must be the production and formation of a new type of man motivated by a new ethic. This calls for zeal and emotion. Development is "the work of men, but of men animated by a promethean will to transform the real and render it docile." [48]

What the nation needs is "the new Senegalese; a man prepared for *action*, turned towards action." [49] However, to be effective, any action must be united action made by and for the whole of the nation. This presupposes "the communion of intelligences and hearts" which can only be achieved through education. It is in this sense that Senghor now maintains that culture is important, for each man must begin from an understanding of his own situation in particular. Too many African intellectuals have been so influenced by European techniques and impressed with European values that they have become completely egocentric and out of contact with African realities.[50]

The great object of reconversion, of creating "the new Senegalese" (meaning the "trained, educated Senegalese, healthy in body as in mind" [51]) is "to kill in each Senegalese the old slave-man, to bring about the conversion of mentalities and behavior." [52] The "Old Nigger" must be killed in the sense that one must transform one's self before one can begin to transform the world:

> It is not countries, it is rather men who are underdeveloped, technically and culturally in their fundamental attitudes to life, because development and underdevelopment are less questions of machines or capital than of men.[53]

163

To progress, what is needed is a great deal of personal, *internal* effort:

> Development will not be parachuted down in some heavenly manner from the outside. Whatever may be the generosity of outside aid, it will not be able to replace our own internal, national effort. Foreign aid will remain sterile if it isn't met by a conscious will to progress, an effort of austerity and of work.[54]

In creating the new man, one has to take into account the various levels and capacities of men—"especially that of the peasant who does not have the head of a theoretician or even of a polytechnician" [55]—as well as variations in sophistication and type of education—"the average length of life of any given people is measured by the use of soap, by the effectiveness of the battle against flies and mosquitos." [56] Creating the "new man," however, "is not a question of forming 'well prepared *heads*,' of experienced technicians," but of conscientious citizens who have the will "to transform their collective situation," "the desire for creative innovation," and above all, the "sense of a general interest." [57]

In the past, Senghor has held that three objects of Senegal's plan were the formation of a new Senegalese man, the expansion of the means of communication and the production of goods for consumption. Today, his emphasis differs.[58] He no longer theorizes about the development of man in the abstract; instead, he posits as a principal goal of the plan the training of men capable of promoting economic growth. Now, men count primarily insofar as they can help to fulfill the plan's objectives. Development then is the prerequisite of Senghor's entire system. Success will be measured, in the end, by an increase in per capita annual income, distributed equally among the population. Despite all of his concern with changing the nature of Man, Senghor, at the end of 1964, said that the reform of mentalities won't serve any purpose if it doesn't result in increasing production.[59] Neither violent social change, mass mobilization of the population, nor any radical alteration of the *status quo* is the key to development. The key, according to Senghor, is scientific planning.[60]

Need for Planning

To give proper historical credit, Senghor maintains, Marx and Engels first saw the necessity of planning. For them, contradictions inherent in capitalism require planning—"the conscious organization of social production." [61]

These contradictions (manifested in the constant emiseration of the workers, the growing numbers of bankrupt bourgeois who fell into the ranks of the proletariat and periodic crises of overproduction) had two basic causes: the drive and motivating force of profit; and the failure, through ignorance, isolation, anarchy and competition of capitalists to foresee the long-term consequences of their individual actions. Thus Senghor comments:

> The general objective of efficient planning must be the suppression of that contradiction. It must have the effect both of developing maximum production and of distributing production equitably among the workers by developing consumption. . . .[62]

Senghor accepts the Marxian analysis that "an underdeveloped country cannot develop rapidly and efficiently without an economic and social plan" which emphasizes rapidity and efficiency. However, Senghor points out by the middle of the nineteenth century, when Marx was elaborating his theory of scientific socialism, the great countries of Europe had already developed. Moreover, they did so without a plan. Though stimulated to a certain extent by the state, development came mainly through the economic activities of the bourgeoisie. The Soviet accomplishment, however, then revealed that the development of the productive forces could also be accomplished under the impulsion of the state and party. The main advantage of planning, then, is that a scientific rationalization allows for an economy of means, men and time. A plan, therefore, is nothing more than:

> . . . a balanced ensemble of objectives and means which aims for a certain economic and social growth. It is a question of obtaining within a determined time and sector a calculated quantity of goods and services; agricultural and industrial products, schools and hospitals, housing and clothing, etc. . . .[63]

Unlike Marx, then, Senghor regards planning as essentially technical in nature, not necessarily incompatible with capitalism. The experiences of the *métropole* undoubtedly influenced Senghor in this assessment.

Nothing illustrates the compatibility of planning with a variety of economic and political systems as well as the history of planning in France. Under the tripartite government after World War II, planning began with the nationalization of a number of major industries as a step in the fulfillment of a Marxian-socialist image of a classless society. Within a few years, a great transformation occurred. Planning became essentially capitalist in nature. Government ownership of firms in certain areas of the economy, such as coal and the railroads, worked primarily to subsidize those capitalistic enterprises which were predominant in the economy. The profit-based sector was stimulated by granting artificially low prices. This could constitute further evidence of the essentially technical nature of planning. Despite Marx's prescription, Senghor could believe that a revolutionary change wasn't necessary to affect the ends of planning.

Marx had, however, argued the impossibility of revolutionary change unless the men and classes involved were "animated by a conscious and practical revolutionary will." With this, Senghor agrees:

It is evident that the plan is not only a sum of objectives to attain. The plan is also, perhaps especially, a mystique, a spirit. To be faithful to the plan is to introduce into national life, at all levels, in the fields, in the offices, in the workshops, this spirit of rigor, of continuity in effort without which one would have to speak not merely of delays, but of the nonexistence of a plan.[64]

Senghor's conception of planning, however, encounters the very basic problem of a contradiction between a scheme *avowedly technical* in nature that, at the same time, seeks to stimulate mass enthusiasm.

Marchés Tropicaux, a journal directed to those interested primarily in overseas commercial affairs, said that Senegal's development plan "does not consist of a vulgar mobilization of brawn directed to produce something by an all-knowing brain."[65] Senegal will avoid "vulgar mobilization" by "showing them (sic) that they are contributing to the general good and that a share of this is naturally theirs." Somehow distinguished from a "brain washing program," the plan does involve "a psychological drive to encourage expansion and to create and to inspire supervisors and farmers to want higher yields."[66]

Because the "masses" were not involved fully in programs of development, Senegal introduced (theoretically) a new method for drawing up the second plan. In 1960 the first plan was "elaborated at the summit," at the national level and almost entirely by foreign advisors.

The Senegalese government restricted itself to simply choosing between various proposed alternatives. In contrast, the second plan was to be constructed by a method defined as "dialogue"

". . . between Senegalese technicians and those of foreign technical assistance, between the Government and the National Assembly, between the national summit and the regional . . . base, between the technico-professional groups met in national committees and now in the Council of Planning.[67]

This method of planning—by "dialogue"—became possible only when there were enough statesmen, pollsters, investigators and other trained Senegalese personnel to formulate a national plan. The first plan "in spite of all the efforts of the propaganda deployed . . . was not, in spite of everything, directly felt as the *affair of all the Senegalese*." [68] In order for the plan to really *exist*, it must descend into the fields and workshops, to make "the people concerned interested in the Plan or, better yet, to have them effectively conceive and realize the plan for themselves." The method of achieving this dialogue involved a program of decentralization, of "regionalization," theoretically establishing committees of development and meetings from the village level upward, giving everyone an opportunity to express his needs, wants, desires and specific suggestions. [69] The great objective would thus be achieved when "each Senegalese peasant, each shepherd and each fisherman feels himself directly concerned and goes so far as to consider the plan as a thing which belongs to him personally and the success of which depends in the first place, and above all, on his own efforts." [70]

The Politics and Institutions of Socialism in Senegal: The Changing Nature of Animation Rurale

Regionalization and decentralization attempt to stimulate widespread participation in the effort for self-development. The original institution designed for this purpose, however, is "Animation Rurale," or the "Service of Animation." The evolution of this program reveals the tendency toward technicity in Senegal.

On "Animation" and "rural expansion," Senghor in April 1963, explained:

The service of Animation has been conceived from the beginning as the original tool of our national development. . . . Animation has for its essential task the imparting to all echelons the mystique of development;

the arousal amidst the population of new structures which coordinate, while integrating the actions of the base. It is only through this meeting of the technical-administrative apparatus and the popular structure; it is only through their concrete work that the objectives of the Plan of Development will be able to be realized.[71]

Moreover, Senghor once considered Animation as crucial to the establishment of Senegalese socialism:

The participation of all in the effort of national construction within the framework of renovated communication structures, . . . is the meaning of our socialist option.[72]

Animation had the function of putting into effect techniques adapted to Senegalese realities. Above all, however, its task was to form "animators"—people selected from among the most dynamic, enterprising and conscientious volunteers from each village. The volunteers received training in technological and managerial skills useful for development, as well as equally relevant political ideals and skills of self-help and communal progress. Then, they returned to their home villages as "pioneers of renewal" to spread their knowledge, helping the "man of the country" to discover himself as the essential motor of the nation's economy, and hence create a "revolution from the base."

Writing in April 1963 at the peak of his enthusiasm for Animation, Senghor cited figures revealing among other things, how over 4,000 animators were "formed" in 1962 (in training sessions for the most part of less than two weeks) and over 1,250 villages "touched": he went on to point to the concrete accomplishments of the men and women peasants who were trained by Animation. Volunteers labored on the construction of roads, schools, dispensaries, hydrolic works. They introduced education concerning farming with animal-pulled implements, the proper use of fertilizer, fungicides, selected seeds, etc. Moreover, beyond these measurable results, Animation wrought profound social, economic and especially psychological changes in the villages. It numbered among its accomplishments liberation from indebtedness, reinforcement of the cooperative movement, the practice of collective savings, the diffusion of education about sanitation and support for the modern school.[73] Explaining the importance of animation, Senghor held:

> The transformation of mentalities, the creation of new attitudes oriented towards progress has as its corollary the will to reorganize better than in the past. Suppressing religious and ethnic quarrels, the divisions inherited from the colonial past, the peasants discover their solidarity of destiny.
>
> The villages regroup to form cooperatives, to develop virgin zones, and to realize work that is of collective interest.
>
> In this way, the ground is prepared for the intervention of the technical services at the same time that their effectiveness is increased by tenfold. An authentic dialogue can then be inaugurated between the awakened peasants and the agents of the technical services, a dialogue which results in a program of action. In this way, there is dialectically created between peasants and technicians *socialist cells* of development. These cells gather together, at the base, all of the political, administrative and technical elements who work in the service of the rural world.[74]

"There is still more," Senghor states. "Animation also undertakes certain activities in the cities, particularly in Dakar." Within the urban areas, he argued, an "important mass of the active population . . . does not yet follow the general movement of the Nation. The problem is to bring these men and women to take conscience of their potentialities by helping them find a socio-economic framework for action." [75]

In sum, at its inception, Senghor considered Animation as a "revolutionary" instrument—the force stimulating the first widespread self-awakening and participation in political and social processes. At the same time, a growing individual self-consciousness would create new values and attitudes crucial for economic development. In this way Senghor wished to "resolve the contradictions between dictatorship and liberty," to make the "revolution" at the least cost possible. Animation worked by convincing instead of constraining; by educating militants of African socialism at the same time as creating modern peasants.[76]

Given the tremendous importance Senghor attached to Animation and his apparent pride in its past accomplishments, it is somewhat startling to find him only two years later announcing a fundamental change in the nature of Animation, saying that government decisions had to be popularized at the lowest levels, "no more in the former *boy scout* style, but under their technical aspects. We have begun with the reorientation of the First Plan, to make Animation pass from its psychological stage to its technical stage." [77]

To the extent that Animation took its tasks as the engine of socialist development seriously, it increasingly ran into difficulties with the established traditional, political and religious leadership. Stimulating even part of the peasantry into self-consciousness often led to an awareness of exploitation, trickery and the inadequacy of their leadership. Animation revealed to some of the rural poor that they had rights that were not being enforced or opportunities that were denied. Often, the civil servants campaigned openly and clashed violently with members of the government political party. Soon the service developed a reputation for being over-zealous in its operation, staffed by so-called "hot-headed, irresponsible troublemakers."

At the same time, deficiencies in the animator's training soon became apparent. The civil servants increasingly encountered technical as well as social obstacles in the implementation of specific programs. While theoretically the task of Animation was simply to lay the groundwork for the more technical services, in practice such a division of function proved difficult.

At the same time as Senghor began to stress the technical

side of Animation, in March 1964 an outside French agricultural engineering firm was called in for consultation on increasing agricultural, particularly peanut, production. This European technical agency then taught scientific methods to Senegalese farmers. The French advisors showed the peasants how to grow better and more peanuts. Senegal's planters felt that by using better seeds, planting deeper rows further apart with new tools and employing fertilizers and fungicides, the foreign technicians would raise peanut production by 25 percent in three years, as well as substantially increase the crops of millet.[78]

Thus, purely technical means could achieve economic development. What, therefore, was the necessity for an agency like Animation, as it was originally conceived? Animation was designed as a vehicle for social reform. To a large extent because of the dynamism of this agency's particular leadership, it pursued this endeavor zealously—causing intense social and political reactions. Partly as a result of pressure from these injured parties, partly because of increased belief in the efficacy of new scientific innovations, Animation became increasingly preoccupied with technological skills and operations. Yet, in this area, Animation could not compete with the advanced know-how of the foreign technical assistance agency. To the extent that any function whatsoever remained to Animation, it certainly had little in common with the service's original functions.

Ideologically, this change in the nature of Animation—once the major apparatus for development—accompanies the transformation in Senghor's conceptions of socialism, culture, etc., toward increased technicity, more pragmatism and less theorizing.

For an Organized and Animated State: The Cooperatives

Animation was conceived as the *mechanism* of socialist social change; the Cooperatives were to be its *institutional* expression and embodiment. Senghor has said that "It is the will of my government to extend the cooperative movement to all aspects of the rural milieu and to create there a sector entirely social-ized." [79]

The cooperative movement began under the French and continued as a form of mutual aid, primarily in the marketing of peanuts. It has grown to the point where over 1500 Cooperatives exist in modern Senegal and approximately 80 percent of the peanut crop is handled under their auspices. Senghor in 1964 pointed out that while figures such as these were encouraging, without the proper "formation" of their members there was the danger of "having cooperatives without cooperators, that is to say, without the cooperative spirit which is the socialist, communitarian spirit." Therefore Senegal must guide the evolution of the Cooperatives toward definitive forms of socialist life:

> . . . the more the cooperative movement will evolve, the more will its political dimensions be affirmed; once passed a certain threshold, cooperation is no longer only an effective technique for commercialization and production. More and more, it will appear as an essential organization of work and of life, giving to Socialist society its basic unit. It will cease to be a technocratic, bureaucratic mechanism . . . a simple tool of the technical and administrative services, but rather the reverse . . . giving to the peasant the feeling of belonging to a coherent, whole, to a world, the cooperative and socialist world. [80]

Other institutions were supposed to aid the Cooperatives to carry out their socialistic and productive purposes. Centers for Rural Expansion (C.E.R.), as previously indicated, included all the representatives of technical services. Since 1961 the name "Polyvalent" was added to show that the aid of the C.E.R.P.'s was not confined to agriculture alone, but included health, education and anything else that might in a general way be important for development.

In terms of reorganizing the means of distribution, the most important and potentially the most radical reform came in January 1960, with the establishment of the *Office de Commerciali-sation Agricole*, or Agricultural Marketing Board. Its original task was to replace the traditional system of trading with one at the same time more efficient and socialist in its essential purposes. In practice, the O.C.A. assumed three tasks: (1) a virtual monopoly in the marketing of peanuts; (2) the importation of the most important materials and products required for agriculture, such as fertilizers; and (3) importing of the most important foodstuffs such as rice.

Intermediary organizations such as *Centres Regionaux pour le Développement* (C.R.A.D.) acted as the link between the Cooperatives and the O.C.A. taking care of the Cooperatives' books and accounting, overseeing the collecting of peanuts, and the distribution of goods imported under the auspices of the O.C.A. Located in all seven regions, the original duty of the C.R.A.D.'s was to manage and encourage the Cooperatives. Soon, however, the seven C.R.A.D.'s became wholly immersed in the job management of the Cooperatives, forgetting almost wholly about "encouragement." [81] Considerable corruption occurred within the C.R.A.D.'s; they also attempted to use their material resources as political fiefs.

Embezzlement, among other things, impeded the O.C.A. and C.R.A.D.'s from fulfilling their role of distribution in the rural areas: "Too often," Senghor exclaimed, "alas, the peasant did not receive the material that was 'coming to him'; too often the material and products remained in the C.R.A.D., where often they weren't cared for properly. These were grave faults because they touched upon the instruments of material production." [82] Senghor hoped to solve this problem simply by establishing better measures of administrative control over proper inventory and delivery systems.

Another important problem concerned "a commercial vacuum in the bush." This came about when the O.C.A. took the peanut trade out of the hands of private traders, thus curtailing free enterprise at a time when the Cooperatives could not yet take their place. To fill this void, Senghor established in March

1965, the National Society of Distribution in Senegal (S.O.N.A.D.I.S.). S.O.N.A.D.I.S., working through the intermediary of the O.C.A., has united together traditional French commerce, industry and banks, with some five hundred African merchants.[83] The government in this way aided businessmen by joining them into consortiums.[84] Now, the Cooperatives being formed consisted not of the peasants, but of the African merchants. Once in the past a respected observer of the Senegalese scene, Leo Hamon, had noted:

> . . . each time that one confided to Animation Rurale the transformation of the countryside, each time that one tried to reduce the economy of the traders through the creations of the offices of commercialization . . . one advanced towards a certain socialization.[85]

By the middle of 1965 it had appeared that neither Animation nor the Cooperatives would be effective instruments in the short-run building of socialism. The O.C.A. appeared increasingly in harmony with the business interests it was supposed to supplement. By the middle of 1968 no sign of collectivization had occurred, and few steps in the direction of increased communalization had been taken. Economic devlopment had failed to bring prosperity to any significant segment of the farmers. The substitution of a consortium of African merchants for the Cooperatives of consumers appeared a foregone conclusion, since the Cooperatives themselves gave absolutely no sign of progressing beyond simple marketing organizations. The administration came to focus almost exclusively on technical functioning. Not broad questions of ideology, but necessities for cost-cutting, determined plans for their reorganization.

A deplorable lack of coordination and too large a degree of autonomy in the various state services and institutions hampered the attempts to restructure the countryside. Agents as well as policy-makers of each service had little contact with each other. They did not share resources or coordinate projects, and often not even governors of regions knew what was going on. In sum, Senghor explained, despite all the formal apparatus: "The state is not organized at the regional and local level." [86]

Responsibility for a broad coordination of policy rested with the Regional Committee for Development. However, it met only once a month and had only very limited powers. Unable to do more than raise a very restricted amount of funds for the regional budget, the committee also could not elaborate or change in detail the program before it. This resulted in too rigid a system of centralization that inhibited the development of responsibility. Everyone looked for decisions to "Le Building Administratif" in Dakar. Having no voice in decision-making and considering the state's property as not being his own, the civil servant did not bother to take care of it. An absence of a spirit of innovation, of creative imagination and a persistence of "the rich man's mentality" of self-indulgence characterized the whole structure. Finally, not being informed himself, the civil servant could not inform others. Hence, state organization suffered and the animation of the population failed.

All of these problems, however, became viewed as technical problems of good management and increased production. The pressure to cut costs (which stemmed from the threatened cut in the subsidization of the price of peanuts after Senegal affiliated with the European Common Market) particularly submerged ideological considerations. The balance sheet emerged as the prime consideration for the Cooperatives, the O.C.A., and other originally socialistic instruments of production, distribution and exchange.

Finally by the law of October 12, 1967, the Senegalese government replaced the C.R.A.D. by the *Office Nationale de Coopération et d'Assistance pour le Développement* (O.N.C.A.D.) and the O.C.A. was superseded by the *Office de Commercialisation du Sénégal* (O.C.A.S.). The purpose of these new organizations was to run the Cooperatives and the agricultural sector as efficiently and profitably as possible with no responsibility for ultimate ideological objectives.[87]

176

An Appeal to the Privileged and Economic Development

Although Senghor does not believe in the existence of classes in Senegal, this has not prevented him from differentiating among various social strata in appealing for economic development. Above all, he directs his message to what he calls the elites of the nation. To them, he has said:

> Our task is enormous. To fulfill it, we must draw up a development plan: even before that, we must arouse our people's faith in their destiny and galvanize all their energy and enthusiasm. It is necessary that the *elites* understand their role and accept their responsibility. Those in privileged positions must be willing to make the heaviest sacrifices.[88]

THE CIVIL SERVICE

Most important are members of the civil service. Senghor has pointed out that in France, government workers constitute 17 percent of the adult population and are paid 25 percent of the budget. In Senegal, they constitute one percent of the population, but are paid close to 50 percent of the budget.[89] To be more precise, from 1964 to 1966, the percentage of the budget devoted to personnel declined from 47.2 percent to 45.3 percent.[90] While he cited these figures to show an improvement of economy measures, in fact the figures reveal more about the importance of the cost of the civil servants to the country, and the difficulty of cutting down on an established bureaucracy. Senegal has over 30,000 civil servants for a population of three and a half million. *Officially*, it is stated that this is at least 10,000 more than is needed.[91] The cost of these civil servants is a tremendous burden, as Senghor has stated, upon the nation, and takes away millions better spent on investment programs for economic development. At the same time, the civil servants—because of their number, education, skills and organization—form a most potent political force.[92]

Furthermore, in terms of development, Senghor has pointed out that the President and the highest leaders of the country cannot both make and execute policy; they cannot be everywhere at the same time nor do all things simultaneously. It is up to the civil servants to carry out policy. Here is a great gap:

> The weakness of the Nation is neither at the level of the highest state official nor at the level of the peasants of the Bush, nor even with the skilled worker; it is at the level of the lower and intermediary civil servants, many of whom are not yet decolonized, those who are still not aware of the fact that independence requires an increased effort of work, discipline and also politeness.[93]

To illustrate this situation, one could cite the tremendous difficulties of the O.C.A. and C.R.A.D. in properly distributing goods to the countryside as largely a problem of unskilled and unmotivated civil servants.[94] Senghor has therefore called upon the civil servants for a change in their attitudes and he has promulgated austerity measures. Yet at the same time, he does nothing that would result in their permanent alienation.

Complaining that he has not always been understood—especially by the civil servants touched by measures of austerity—Senghor lists some of his steps of retrenchment: (1) the stabilization of the number of civil servants—with exceptions made for students and pupils of the national schools for intermediary cadres; (2) an almost complete suppression of first-class travel for civil servants; (3) virtual elimination of material advantages such as paid water, gas, electricity, domestic servants; and (4) the elimination of the right to an automobile and the right of free housing.[95]

Apparently the suppression of these last two "rights"—free housing and automobiles—created the greatest protest. Senghor maintained these were "privileges" not "rights." They resulted from a French administrative policy ultimately extended to Africans, but eliminated by independent African governments, with the exception of Senegal. Why not Senegal? Because, Senghor went on, "our elites are the most bourgeoisified and we still have a rich man's mentality while the country is certainly poor." Because of their privileged position, the civil servants must consent to make sacrifices for the economic take-off of the nation. *However, Senghor declared, the relative position of the civil servants should still be maintained.*[96]

In spite of austerity measures, Senegalese civil servants still maintain a position of favor in comparison to those of the majority of the other Francophone states and of France itself. The annual average income in Senegal is six times less than that in France. On a comparative basis, the Senegalese civil servant, in terms of the annual average national income, earns more than four times as much as his French counterpart. Even recognizing the high prices in Senegal and greater social and family obligations, one can hardly dispute the fact that the Senegalese civil servant does well. Furthermore, in applying the austerity decrees, the government evidences a certain amount of "suppleness." Thus, suppression of the right to an automobile applies only to those civil servants for whom a car is not an absolute necessity in the work. Even they have a chance to repurchase a used vehicle "at a reasonable price."

Some of the more obvious abuses were curtailed: e.g., "certain week-end scenes which were a provocation to the urban masses. One saw them at certain gas stations, lines of touring cars waiting to be served, not only filling their tanks, but also 'jerricans.' " [97] As far as the restrictions on housing are concerned, Senghor gave assurances that nobody wanted to put civil servants out into the streets. At the same time that free rent was suppressed, the government offered opportunities to acquire complete ownership of private houses. Over eight billion francs C.F.A. were to be made available in Dakar alone, over a five-year period, for such construction.[98] Moreover, before the government had ever taken any action pertaining to the civil service, it always sought the advice of the Superior Council of the Public Service, a consultative body wherein the civil servants are represented by members appointed by the National Union of the Workers of Senegal (U.N.T.S.).[99]

Finally, in arguing for a temporary freezing of salaries, Senghor declared, apparently as a matter of principle, that:

> The living standard of our government employees should be higher than that of our peasants, but we cannot do less than to fix a relationship between the living levels of our quasi-classes. As the peasants' standard of living rises, in the same proportion we would raise that of government employees and salaried workers in private employment.[100]

The civil servants are a major force in the society. As with the *marabouts*, nothing substantial in Senghor's ideology will alienate them. But given this situation, one wonders about the reactions of people in the rural areas to Senghor when he states: "Senegal is not only Dakar, nor the administration, but still and above all, the peasants and shepherds." [101]

PEASANTS

Even to the members on the lowest rung of the hierarchy of Senegal's society, "the true proletariat," the peasants and herdsmen, Senghor has promised abundance through an increase in their standard of living.[102] He has maintained that he will protect them from being "squeezed" by landlords and usurers, as well as for the purposes of economic development. To a large extent, however, one may well expect that the peasant will always be cheated regardless of the type of regime, because he is the most defenseless member of the community. Lack of education and organizational skills, inability to communicate or to understand the consequences of actions and activities outside the immediate family, paucity of information, geographic isolation, mind-dulling work, an absence of leisure and economic resources, all contribute to his powerlessness. The most common and easy way of exploiting the peasant is not to pass on any increases in gross national product brought about by economic growth.

The peasant also has a problem of land tenure. Senghor's analysis in this matter, however, seems to have changed. In an interview with Raya Dunayevskaya, he is reported to have said, "Our way of life is tied in with land tenure. . . . We hold the land in Common, thus we have no landless peasantry." [103] This position is consistent with Senghor's image of a classless society. On the other hand in 1966 he wrote:

> The peasant works the land, but his tenancy used to be precarious because he did not own it. The landlord required him to pay a rent which diminished by that much the revenue he received from his produce. [104]

A question arose, Senghor stated, concerning the social usefulness of the landlord. His government decided that the landlord didn't have any. Therefore, the Senegalese National Assembly passed the Law on the National Domaine in 1964. This law, described as a "veritable agrarian reform" transferred to the nation-state the powers of proprietorship over the soil that once belonged to the ancient kings for the usage of the peasants:

> It was a matter of making the land the property of the nation and of putting it at the disposal of the peasant without cost to him. [105]

As finally passed the law did not, however, apply to all lands registered as belonging to particular individuals. A grace period was accorded to people who occupied and in fact owned the land, but had no legal title to it. In practice, the implications of this law are not clear. Even in theory, no radical reforms were envisaged. However, significantly, the government did admit the necessity of some measures to protect the peasants and the existence of a problem of exploitation.

Social justice, Senghor has said, means taking care of the

peasants.[106] Peasants should have priority because they are the most disadvantaged element within the society as well as the most important. Therefore:

> . . . the socializing activity of the state will have its privileged terrain in the rural sector, where it's necessary to assume the protection and education of the peasants who have most suffered from the economy of trading. The state will not tolerate any private interference without control on its part.[107]

Increasing technicity in this area, the declaration of a continued privileged position for the civil service, as well as continued reliance on the power and position of the *marabouts,* casts doubt on the ability of the state to, either in the short or long run, create socialism in this area.

YOUTH

Senghor distinguishes between elite and nonelite, privileged and nonprivileged. Only a minority in Senegal have access to education and only the smallest percentage can go on to the University. Although these few form only a small part of the population and not yet a decisive social force, Senghor is nevertheless concerned about their demands. He must cope with their criticism and aspirations, since they constitute a highly intelligent, highly articulate, potential lever of opposition. Students are also important as future technical instruments of production. Thus, he has argued:

> . . . our first elite group is the *students.* At twenty, one is enthusiastic and idealistic. That is good. One pounces on books and studies furiously. That too is good. In the intelligence and generosity of our students we have a precious leaven and admirable potentialities. These potentials must be realized, must serve the common good. Our students must understand however . . . that knowledge without experience is but empty

smoke. As models, they may take the North African students, who have always trusted the political leaders of their respective countries. African students favored autonomy when their leaders were struggling for autonomy; they favored independence when and only when their leaders fought for independence. What counts is the *unanimity* of a people rather than a particular doctrine, however excellent it may be.[108]

So enmeshed have they become in politics that Senegalese students, moreover, do not seem to work hard at their studies. Only a few manage to earn the *agrégation* or gain admission to the *Grandes Ecoles* of France. For Senghor, it's all right for them to want to become involved with politics—even to become Marxist-Leninists if they desire. But the best politics, as well as the best policy, for them is to work to become highly trained technicians. The best way of being a Marxist-Leninist if they insist upon it, is not to repeat slogans like parrots but to develop their minds by applying themselves to the realities of Africa, which are not those of Russia, or even China.[109]

The student who does not learn how to conquer his laziness or his egoism, who does not learn how to obey the law, will never be a free man.[110] Fortunately, most students and most of the youth of Senegal understand this full well. However:

There is among the youth of Senegal, like everywhere in the world, some who are mentally or morally sick, some who are uprooted, who will give themselves up to vagabondage or juvenile delinquency.

None of this is important. What counts is that most young people of all religions, social groups and regions love their country and have a will for national unity. Therefore, their parents, formal training, religion and political parties must educate this youth to construct the nation.

It is not with those who are over 40 that one can prepare the Senegal of tomorrow, because all the bad habits of egoism have already been established. It is with the young people that one can only prepare the necessary virtues.[111]

The duty of youth is to acquire a complete education, a technical training to become citizen-producers, working hard, respecting the law, and therefore able to enjoy the fundamental liberation of all citizens.[112] In this way, youth will best contribute to the harmonious development of the new society.

APPEAL TO ELITES: LABOR LEADERS AND FUNCTIONARIES

Elites, according to Senghor, also include the labor leaders. Once they were "confused." It required time—to say nothing of pressure—before they came to realize that "their roll is not to replace the politician, but, over and above professional demands, to help the political leaders to carry out their program." [113] Labor leaders also might unfortunately help further precipitate the unfortunate tendency, "a real movement," toward the *formation* of classes if they act irresponsibly.

The "Negro-African" labor movement organized before the end of the war fought on both the political and economic levels. Having produced the best political minds in Black Africa, it played a vital role in the liberation of Black Africa. This historical role does not entitle it to any special privileges. Indeed, Senghor argues, "despite or because of these past services, trade unions must be reconverted to a new, a more precise idea, of its proper function and tasks." [114] When there were no political parties, the unions played an important political role. Beginning in 1957 with the autonomy of the territories proclaimed by the Loi Cadre, "it was no longer incumbent on the unions, but rather on the political parties, to assume the totality of national responsibilities." From that moment on, the unions should have reconverted themselves to their natural role of defending professional interests.[115]

Today, well-organized political parties represent the whole nation. Labor unions do not speak for the entire population.

They concern themselves primarily with the purchasing power of their members. According to Marx, the working class could not attain its economic rights without creating a social revolution. Political and economic demands were inseparable. The working class, because the most alienated, developed the greatest self-consciousness and the most justification to create radical political change in its interests. Under colonialism, a similar condition prevailed to the extent that the exploitation of African laborers by French capitalism justified them in the necessity of turning to political agitation to achieve economic benefits. This period, however, has vanished.

> Our Negro-African situation is not identical to the situation in France, where wage-earners are struggling to snatch a larger share of the national income from a bourgeois state. In Africa, we and you are the state. At least the overwhelming majority of top officials and civil servants are Africans. It is against themselves that the labor unions, particularly the government employees, are struggling. This is an unnatural contradiction.[116]

If in Europe the workers were the majority and the most disadvantaged of the population; in Africa they are a minority and privileged. A good many members of the union are government employees whose annual incomes can run about 360,000 francs C.F.A.; a wage earner in the private sector can make 180,000 C.F.A., whereas the average annual cash income of a peasant in the former French West Africa is 10,000 francs C.F.A. Obviously, therefore, "it could not serve the public interest to increase the disproportion between the living standards of the classes now in the process of formation." [117]

The trade unions must not simply change selfishly into an agency for grievances:

> As the best educated and therefore the most conscious group, the wage-earners must transcend their own

185

group interests and their strictly professional preoccupations. Placing themselves on a higher level, they will
embrace all the interests of all social groups, and, first,
those of the underprivileged: the peasants, fishermen,
and artisans.[118]

Since they constitute less than 10 percent of the working population, entrusting control of the nation's interests to the unions
would violate the principles of democracy, and threaten the very
existence of the state. Therefore, there is no choice, "the conclusion to be drawn from this reflection is that the unions will adopt
the general political program of the majority party and the government." [119]

The unions in Senegal should, therefore, no longer have any
right to exist as an important independent *political* force operating outside of the arena of government policy. The government
has also severely restricted the civil servants, students and other
social interests. They justify these restrictions in the name of
economic development. The power of the state has constantly
increased in Senegal and been introduced into new areas where
it had not entered previously. Inevitably, the problem of authoritarianism arises.

NOTES TO CHAPTER VI

1. Senghor, "Discours à Conakry," March 8, 1967 (mimeo, N.D.).
2. Senghor, "Discours à l'Assemblée Nationale," April 19, 1963, *op. cit.*
3. Senghor, "Présentation du Premier Gouvernement Senghor," December 19, 1962 (mimeo, N.P.).
4. Senghor, *Jeune Afrique*, No. 158, November 18–24, 1963.
5. Senghor, "Advertisement for the Republic of Senegal," *The New York Times*, January 31, 1966.
6. Senghor, "Discours à l'Assemblée Nationale," April 19, 1963, *op. cit.*
7. For a further discussion of the distinctions between economic growth and development, see Gerald M. Meier and Robert E. Baldwin, *Economic Development; Theory, History, Policy* (John Wiley and Sons, New York, 1957), pp. 2–10.
8. On the basis of President Senghor's own figures, it is obvious that there has been virtually no economic development in Senegal. In a recent assessment of the state of the economy, he stated:

> . . . one expected of the first four-year plan an annual rate of growth of gross internal production of 8%. In reality, we had registered from 1959 to 1964, a rate of 3.27% brought down to an annual income increase per capital of 0.9%. In other terms, the value of gross internal production went from 119 billion, 460 million in 1959, to 140 billion, 210 million in 1964. [*L'Unité Africaine*, June 17, 1965]

By the middle of 1966, there was no improvement and Senghor was still calculating growth in per capita income at less than one percent (*L'Unité Africaine*, June 7, 1966). These figures are based on a current estimated population growth of 2.3 percent per annum. However, in an earlier speech, Senghor gave the estimated population increase at between 2.3 and 3.3 percent. (*Les Mésures de Rigueur et d'Austérité: Allocution à la Nation Sénégalaise*, September 13, 1963 [Ministre de l'Information, République du Sénégal, Imprimerie A. Diop, Dakar]). In October 1964 he also said:

> If since Independence, the rate of the annual increase in the gross internal product is almost 4.75%, the annual income per head of inhabitants remains unchanged because of the population growth and the dislocation between the price of tropical products and those of European products. ["Les Objectifs de l'Année," 1964–65, October 1966 (mimeo, N.P.)]

There is no reason to assume that the lower estimate of population growth is the correct one, particularly in the light of Senghor's statement that even at a 4.75-percent gross increase, there was no change in per capita income. Further, taking into account the continuous fall in agricultural prices and the apparent continuation of the disparities in the distribution of increased national revenue, it is not unlikely that the standard of living of the majority of the peasants has even fallen, rather than been improved.

Two other considerations in arriving at an accurate figure are: In calculating real national income, one cannot, as Senghor apparently has done, simply proceed by comparing the gross national product of two separate years. First, the money expression of national income must be corrected by an appropriate price index of both consumer and capital goods. Second, the index of gross national product makes no allowances for capital replacement. To be accurate, as well as realistic, net national product (which includes final consumer goods and services, plus the net addition to capital goods) is the measure that should be used. Every year with the exception of 1962, Senghor has argued that there has been some increase in the gross national product (*L'Unité Africaine*, April 7, 1966). Therefore, it is impossible to say that there has been *no* economic growth; there just has been very little.

Among the other reasons for Senegal's limited development in Senghor's opinion are both geography and history. A paucity of mineral resources, lack of water, the intensity of the sun's heat, are all combined with colonial disabilities. Colonialism, he recapitulated, was a burden in many ways: (1) unrealistic, arbitrary establishment of territorial boundaries; (2) a veneer of unsuitable living habits of the colonizers; (3) economies designed only for the needs of the metropole; (4) lack of preparation for international competition; (5) decreasing aid from Europe; (6) elimination of protective tariffs and beneficial quotas; and (7) a dwindling market with the break-up of the former federation (*Marchés Tropicaux*, October 24, 1964).

The break-up of the Mali Federation also exacted a heavy toll on Senegal. Before August 1960, Senegal exported 50 percent of its sugar, 35 percent of its matches, 30 percent of its tobacco, 20 percent of its shoe manufacture, and 15 percent of its cement to a market that was lost in Mali. The Port of

Dakar lost over $32 million annual revenue. See further, Victor D. Du Bois, *Mali and Senegal and the Dakar-Niger Railroad*, American Universities Field Staff, West Africa Series, Vol. VI, No. 4 (June 1963).

The difficulty of attaining an increase in the rate of growth is further explained by Senghor as due to the lack of experience of the nation with planning and the lack of necessary cadres (*L'Unité Africaine*, June 17, 1965). All this, however, was no cause for despair, according to Senghor, for a great deal of progress was made: (1) in the creation of an administrative infrastructure —trained cadres of professors, administrators, economists, engineers, etc.; and (2) in the encadrement of the rural population into some form of cooperatives (*L'Unité Africaine*, December 31, 1964).

Whether these were actions that contributed to economic development and, beyond that, to the type of socialist civilization that was to produce the new Senegalese man, or whether these activities simply added new numbers to the already enormous civil service and helped the rich peasants better their lot at the expense of the poorer farmers, remains a fundamental and debatable question.

In *Politique, Nation et Développement Moderne: Rapport de Politique Générale, VIe Congrès de l'Union Progressiste Sénégalaise* (Imprimerie Nationale, Rufisque, 1968), pp. 25–51, Senghor argues that the total tonnage of exports from 1959 to 1965 has increased consistently, but that Senegal has suffered because of a decline in the international terms of trade, coupled with an increasing reluctance of the great powers to maintain previous levels of aid.

9. Senghor, *Planification et Tension Morale, op. cit.*
10. *Ibid.*
11. *L'Unité Africaine*, December 8, 1964.
12. *Ibid.*
13. Senghor, "Allocution Devant le Parlement Malgache," June 28, 1961 (mimeo, N.P.).
14. "Discours à Kaolack," January 21, 1961 (mimeo).
15. "Comité Directeur du P.F.A. Résolution, Déclaration du Président Senghor," September 23–24, 1959 (mimeo, N.D.).
16. Senghor, "Discours," April 4, 1965, *op. cit.*
17. Senghor, "Discours . . . d'Oxford," *op. cit.*
18. Senghor, "The African Road to Socialism," *op. cit.*, p. 102.
19. Senghor, "The Theory and Practice of Senegalese Socialism," in Cook, *op. cit.*, p. 108.
20. *Ibid.*, p. 109.
21. Senghor, "Comité Directeur du P.F.A. Résolution," *op. cit.*
22. "Colloque sur les Politiques de Développement," *op. cit.*
23. Senghor, "Message à la Nation," February 18, 1963 (mimeo, Dakar).
24. Senghor, "Présentation du Premier Gouvernement Senghor," December 19, 1962 (mimeo, Dakar).
25. Senghor, "Discours à l'Assemblée Nationale," April 19, 1963 (mimeo, Dakar).
26. Senghor, "Devant la Cour Suprême," *Afrique Nouvelle*, December 13–19, 1963.
27. Senghor, "Message Fraternel," *Populaire*, Paris, September 17, 1964.
28. Senghor, "Message à l'Internationale Socialiste à l'Occasion de la Commémoration de Son Centenaire," *L'Unité Africaine*, September 17, 1964.
29. Senghor, "Discours à l'Assemblée Nationale," April 19, 1963, *op. cit.*
30. Senghor, *Planification et Tension Morale, op. cit.*
31. Senghor, "Rapport sur la Doctrine et la Politique Générale," *op. cit.*
32. "Présentation du Premier Gouvernement Senghor," *op. cit.*
33. Senghor, "Message au Peuple Sénégalais," December 31, 1962 (mimeo, Dakar).

34. "Présentation du Premier Gouvernement Senghor," *op. cit.*
35. Senghor, "Message au Peuple Sénégalais," *L'Unité Africaine*, March 17, 1965.
36. Senghor, "The African Road to Socialism," *op. cit.*, p. 67.
37. "Préparation du Second Plan Quadriennal ou Pour une Attitude d'Accueil," Conseil National, January 3, 1965 (mimeo, N.P.).
38. Senghor, *Dakar-Matin*, November 2, 1964.
39. *Ibid.*
40. Senghor, "Discours au Parlement Brésilien," *Voyage Officiel aux Etat-Unis du Brésil*, September 19–25, 1964 (Commissariat à l'Information, Dakar, 1964), p. 39.
41. Senghor, "Discours à Kaffrine," *Dakar-Matin*, February 22, 1965.
42. The following letter is interesting because it shows how, on the one hand, the presentation of demands to the President has become a regular, institutionalized part of his voyages into the interior, and, on the other hand, how each village is supposed to have some specific accomplishments to report as evidence that they are participating in the tasks of national reconstruction. While the political officials of each village were supposed to have the honor and duty of reporting directly to the President, in numerous cases they were superceded by other local dignitaries, especially by *marabouts*. The tremendous power of the Khalife General of the Mourides is illustrated by the fact that his personal secretary spoke for a whole *cercle* during the course of a reception. Apparently, direct contact between the President of the Republic and village spokesmen in this case was either not desired or not thought necessary.

March 4, 1963
Diourbel

Republic of Senegal
Region of Diourbel

The Governor
Note for the attention of Monsieur Habib Thiam, Secretary of State for Planning.
Demands Presented by the Population in the course of the tour of the President of the Republic in the Circle of Bambey, Diourbel, and M'Backe, the 27–28 of February and the First of March 1963.

Circle of Bambey
Village of N'Dondol: Building of the Youth House Constructed by human investment.
Demands presented by the Youth Delegation.
Village of Gauane—installation of a new well pump and the construction of a new water works; improvement of the Bambey-Gauane road; demands presented by the Marabout El Hadj Cheikh Taco M'Backe, in the name of the population.
Village of Thieppe: Dispensary; Demands presented by the Chief of the village in the name of the population.
Village of K. Sambakane: water works; asphalting of the K. Samba-Kane-Khomboli road; construction of a maternity.
Demands presented by the Political responsible.

Circle of Diourbel
Village of N'Dindy—improved road, demands presented by the political responsible.
Village of N'Doulo—construction of an improved road, demands made by the political responsible.

189

Circle of M'Backe
Village of Taiba. Decoration for Chief of the Village. Best wishes expressed by the Political Responsible.

The other demands in the Circle of M'Backe were presented in the name of the Kalife, in a speech read by his personal secretary, Drame, in the course of a reception on the first of March.

Signed:
The Governor of the Region
Medouane Fall

43. See, for example, the account of Senghor's encounter with the agricultural inspectors in Foundiougne, *Dakar-Matin*, February 23, 1965.
44. Senghor, "Nationhood . . . ," *op. cit.*, pp. 48–49.
45. For one example of an elaboration of this theme, see *Dakar-Matin*, April 5, 1965.
46. Senghor, "Message," *Dakar-Matin*, April 5, 1965.
47. Senghor, "Discours," March 17, 1965 (mimeo, N.D., N.P.).
48. Senghor, "Discours à l'Assemblée Nationale," April 19, 1963, *op. cit.*, p. 20.
49. Senghor, "Rapport sur la Doctrine et la Politique Générale," *op. cit.*
50. *Ibid.*
51. *Ibid.*
52. Senghor, "Discours," *Dakar-Matin*, February 20, 1965.
53. Senghor, "Discours à l'Assemblée Nationale," April 19, 1963, *op. cit.*, p. 20.
54. *Ibid.*
55. Senghor, "Colloque sur les Politiques de Développement," *op. cit.*
56. *Ibid.*
57. *Ibid.*
58. Senghor, "Rapport sur la Doctrine et la Politique Générale," *op. cit.*, p. 46. Before he became deeply involved in the actual mechanics of development, Senghor once stated, "In a word Senegal's organized planning is more the development of Man than economic growth" ("Socialisme Africain et Développement de la Voie Sénégalaise," *Sénégal "AN2" par Lui-Même, Développement et Civilisation*, 4th quarter, 1962, p. 1).
59. Senghor, "Introduction," special issue, "The Senegalese Economy," *Marchés Tropicaux*, English ed., October 24, 1964.
60. A major controversy in planning involved the relative priorities to be given agriculture and industry. Agricultural development, according to Senghor, conditions all development. In his analysis, failure to understand the significance of agriculture in development accounts for the failure of the socialist countries in their agricultural policies. Within the agricultural sector, he argues, moreover, a balance must be sought between industrial and food crops. First, one must eat, but in order to develop, it is necessary to export. Development also requires industrialization, but industrialization as a complement to agricultural expansion. To begin with, there will need be an increased processing of the raw crops in the place of origin, instead of abroad. This will act as a spur to the creation of further factories and industry which will, in turn, create new jobs and hence constantly accelerate the process of development.

To be truly successful, Senghor continues, agriculture and industrial expansion will also require a commercial expansion. This involves not simply the search for new markets, but the reorganization of existing trade relations on the basis of international agreement. The danger here is that the prices of primary goods will continue to fall, while manufactures rise, thus wiping out any local gains attained through stringent *national* progress in real increased output of the total gross product (*"Colloque sur les Politiques de Développement," op. cit.*).

While a great deal has been written on the relative merits of strategies of development emphasizing agricultural or industrial priorities, for the case of Senegal of particular interest is the debate that took place in Dakar in December 1962 at the Colloquium on the Politics of Development and Different African Ways of Socialism. See the report of the Colloquium, *Développement et Socialisme* (Présence Africaine, Paris, 1963), and also accounts of the dispute on this point by Jorgen Schleimann and Abbot Kaplan in *The Journal of Modern African Studies*, Vol. 1, No. 2 (June 1963), pp. 242–250.

61. Senghor, "The Theory and Practice of Senegalese Socialism," in Cook, *op. cit.*, p. 129.
62. *Ibid.*, p. 129.
63. Senghor, *Planification et Tension Morale, op. cit.*
64. Senghor, "Discours à l'Assemblée Nationale," April 19, 1967, *op. cit.*
65. "The Senegalese Economy," special issue, *Marchés Tropicaux, op. cit.*
66. *Ibid.*
67. Senghor, "Discours," March 17, 1965, *op. cit.*
68. *Ibid.*
69. "Préparation du Second Plan Quadriennal," January 3, 1965, *op. cit.*
70. Senghor, "Message du Président de la République du Sénégal," *Paysan Noir*, No. 2, Dakar, January 1965.
71. Senghor, "Discours à l'Assemblée Nationale," April 19, 1963, *op. cit.*
72. *Ibid.*
73. *Ibid.*
74. *Ibid.*
75. *Ibid.*
76. Senghor, "Socialisme Africain et Développement de la Voie Sénégalaise," *op. cit.*, p. 5.
77. "Les Objectifs Essentiels du Deuxième Plan Quadriennal du Sénégal," Conseil National de l'U.P.S., April 25, 1965, in *Sénégal d'Aujourd'hui*, No. 21 (July 1965), p. 14.
78. "L'Animation dans le Développement Economique," *Sénégal d'Aujourd'hui*, No. 21 (July 1965), p. 19. On the activities of S.A.T.E.C. and conflict of roles with Animation and other Senegalese agencies, see Senghor, *Politique, Nation et Développement Moderne, op. cit.*, pp. 39–137 and *passim*. In addition to discussing the entire Senegalese development administrative structure and international balance-of-trade problem, Senghor also again discusses the need for a revitalized political party capable of unifying, educating and re-energizing the population.

When discussing the overlapping and conflicting responsibilities in the education of the "encadreurs" between Animation, the C.E.R., S.A.T.E.C., etc., Senghor understates the situation most felicitously by saying there is present "un soupçon d'anarchie" (*ibid.*, p. 104).

79. Senghor, "Discours à l'Assemblée National," April 19, 1967, *op. cit.*
80. *Ibid.*
81. *Ibid.*
82. *Ibid.*
83. Senghor, "Discours," March 3, 1965, *op. cit.*
84. President Senghor had said apropos the possible conflict between business and socialist-inspired Cooperatives:

As far as the cooperatives of consumption and the consortiums of African businessmen, both will be placed together in a situation of competition as in the socialist states of Scandinavia. Once more, what we want is not the satisfaction of ideological preoccupations, but to be able to assure the masses of the best service at the best prices. ["Discours à l'Assemblée Nationale," April 19, 1963]

85. Hamon, *op. cit.*, p. 7.
86. Senghor, *Planification et Tension Morale, op. cit.*
87. Senghor, *Politique, Nation et Développement Moderne, op. cit.*, pp. 98–107 and *passim*. See also Senghor's analysis of various items of legislation passed in 1966 designed to "energize the public services" (*ibid.*, pp. 127–130).
88. Senghor, "Nationhood . . . ," *op. cit.*, p. 56.
89. Senghor, "The African Road to Socialism," *op. cit.*, p. 95.
90. Senghor, "Discours," June 17, 1965 (mimeo, N.D., N.P.).
91. Senghor, "Message au Peuple Sénégalais," December 31, 1962, *op. cit.*
92. *Ibid.*
93. Senghor, "Rapport sur la Doctrine et la Politique Générale," *op. cit.*
94. Senghor, "Discours," March 17, 1965, *op. cit.*
95. *Les Mésures de Rigueur et d'Austerité: Allocution à la Nation Sénégalaise*, 13 *Septembre, 1963* (Ministre de l'Information, République du Sénégal, Imprimerie A. Diop, Dakar).
96. Senghor, *Planification et Tension Morale, op. cit.*
97. *Ibid.*
98. *Ibid.* See also Senghor, "Rapport sur la Doctrine et la Politique Générale," *op. cit.*
99. For a history of the many statutes affecting the organization and regulation of the civil service, see Senghor, "Discours à l'Assemblée Nationale," *op. cit.*, p. 48.
100. Senghor, "Nationhood . . . ," *op. cit.*, p. 95.
101. "La Troisième Journée du Président dans le Sine," *Dakar-Matin*, February 20, 1965.
102. Senghor, "Discours à Kaffrine," *op. cit.*
103. Raya Dunayevskaya, "Marxist-Humanism," *Présence Africaine*, English edition, 4th quarter, 1963, p. 63.
104. Senghor, "The African Road to Socialism," *op. cit.* In October 1966 Senghor stated that 97 percent of the land in Senegal belonged to 15 percent of the feudal elements (Mustapha Tlili, "Senghor Se Confie Souvenirs et Projets," *Jeune Afrique*, October 30, 1966, p. 46).
105. Senghor, "The African Road to Socialism," *op. cit.* See also "Allocution à Kaolack," January 21, 1961, *op. cit.*, in which he discusses problems of land reform at Kaffrine. Senghor discussed grants of food, fertilizers and other governmental aid to peasants.
106. Senghor, "Un Message de Léopold Senghor au Populaire," *Le Populaire de Paris*, March 10–11, 1964.
107. Senghor, "Discours à l'Assemblée Nationale," April 19, 1963, *op. cit.*
108. Senghor, "Nationhood . . . ," *op. cit.*, p. 56.
109. Senghor, *Planification et Tension Morale, op. cit.*
110. Senghor, "Message," *L'Unité Africaine*, April 7, 1966.
111. Senghor, "Discours," *Dakar-Matin*, April 5, 1965.
112. Senghor, "Message," April 7, 1966, *op. cit.*
113. Senghor, "Nationhood . . . ," *op. cit.*
114. *Ibid.*, p. 117.
115. *Ibid.*, p. 97.
116. *Ibid.*, p. 65.
117. *Ibid.*, p. 56.
118. *Ibid.*, p. 56.
119. *Ibid.*, p. 56. After a period of quiescence and not receiving a substantial pay raise since 1961, in June 1968 union members joined university, secondary and primary students in strikes and riots in Dakar. While these were allegedly precipitated by the example of the demonstrators in France, real

grievances rooted in Senegal's declining economic situation (see above) did exist. See Alfred Friendly, Jr.'s dispatches in *The New York Times*, "Senegal's Leader Shuffles Cabinet," June 7, 1968, and "Resentment Against Senegal's Regime Rises as Economic Woes Increase," June 11, 1968.

VII

Democracy and Economic Development

A COMMANDING ISSUE in contemporary Africa is whether the demands for rapid economic growth are compatible with democracy. Senghor's views on this fundamental issue have varied somewhat and have been influenced not only by the massive problem of development *per se* and the need for national unity, but also by considerations of temperament and philosophical outlook. Elitism is central to Senghor's political outlook. As does de Gaulle, he believes that the best men should govern and aid their less well-educated brethren. Moreover, one can discern a hint of condescension toward even the most sophisticated and cultured men in Senegal.

Senghor believes in the equality of all men, but only in the sense that man was created in the image of his creator. In the real world, Senghor simply asserts the necessity of government guarantees for basic equality of opportunity. Those who have been able to exploit available opportunities—the most gifted— must promote the welfare of others. Once government has equalized all life-chances, however, few other rights need be guaranteed. Senghor, therefore, views democracy more in terms of duties and restrictions than rights.

While he construes the meaning of democracy narrowly, Senghor insists upon two points. Democracy requires, first of all, free elections; and secondly, something approaching a universal suffrage. These requirements create equality, in the sense of enabling participation in the political community.

At the same time, Senghor has emphasized the need for a strong state. He sees the state as the expression of the nation; it is primarily a means to achieve the nation. "Political history teaches that the lack of state organization is a weakness that brings on the fatal disintegration of the nation; the history of the Fourth French Republic illustrates this." [1] Distinguishing between phases of nation-building, Senghor argues that in the initial phase of nation-building, "we must organize the public powers of the federal state and of the federated states to provide a structure to guarantee their authority and permanence." Only after achieving this stability and unity can the nation go on to the second phase—that of development, where the "individual must grow as his standards of living and culture are raised." [2]

Toward an African Democracy

In constructing the new nation, the Senegalese will develop an African style of democracy:

> Europeans, those of the East and those of the West, speak to us often of "Democracy," as if we didn't have our own conception which cedes nothing to that of Europe.
>
> African democracy is essentially founded on the *palabre*. The *palabre* is a dialogue, or better yet, a colloquium, where each has the right to speak, where everyone takes the floor to express his opinion. Formerly, even the dead were consulted. But once every opinion was expressed, the minority followed the majority to manifest their unanimity. This unanimous opinion was then vigorously applied without deviation. The severe offender had to atone and seek expiation in order to reintroduce order into the community and universe.

195

Otherwise, he was excluded. You can see this speaking democracy was as far from dictatorship as anarchy and laissez-faire. The problem now is to restore this democracy under a modern form.

Another trap of Europe consists in persuading us that what is important is not the People, the Nation-State, but the individual, with his needs, passions, tastes, and fantasies. As if liberty was to be confounded with license, as if the individual could realize himself outside of the group, and the group outside of the Nation.[3]

Senghor consistently distinguishes between the "individual" —an isolated, selfish, materialistic being—and the "person" who achieves his true spiritual essence, and hence his only fulfillment, from participating in a community. Democracy is a social arrangement guaranteeing the necessary freedom for this purpose. Liberty must be understood in this perspective.

What, Senghor has asked, is the purpose of liberty?

Neither lack of foresight, nor disorder, nor anarchy, nor apathy, are Liberty . . . Liberty is the possibility which was given us to realize together a prosperous Senegal, thanks to which each individual will be realized as a person . . . Liberty is in other terms, the clear vision of our human frailty, because it is social.[4]

Liberty must, therefore, be used to further the interests of the community, and not particular individual interests. What then of opposition?

In order to realize a prosperous Senegal, to accommodate liberty and to realize the true "person," Senghor in 1960 said that "the Senegalese who are for the middle way" wish to reconcile law and effectiveness. In terms of the political organization of the state, they favor not a single-party system, but a "united party," or a "dominant party" system. This ensures "practicing a strong democracy which respects the constitution and admits an opposition on the single condition that it be a national opposition."[5] A policy of democracy, he stated, both conforms to "our humanistic ideal" and "pays dividends."

Single-party states and the rise of authoritarianism became realities in Africa with independence. Many Western observers, Senghor noted, have asserted that black dictatorship provided evidence of the unfitness of Africans for self-government. For long Senegal maintained a rare exception in that it tolerated an opposition in a multi-party system. Senghor, therefore, in the past could boast that "already public opinion in Black Africa and France is grateful to us. This is excellent propaganda."[6] "The rights of the minority, of the opposition," he went on, "will therefore be respected. . . . They will find their natural and legal limits in the rights of the majority, the popular will, that is sovereign."[7]

Although Senghor tolerated a minority, he nonetheless required not only that it be national in scope, but also that it not constitute a major political threat. This was the essence of the *dominant* party system: a condition of permanent hegemony established by the ruling party. The opposition existed; it fulfilled a certain function of criticism, representation and information, but only so long as it did not threaten to alter its position of subordination.

In distinguishing between constructive and destructive criticism, Senghor has asserted that:

Criticism means critical spirit, not the spirit of criticism or systematic carping. In a democracy, criticism must be constructive and serve the general, not factional interest . . . one cannot grant the opposition more rights than the majority enjoys. . . . The governments will take all necessary steps to curb demagogic opposition. They will not tolerate violation of the law, appeals to illegality, or to violence, whether the pretexts be religious or racial. This is the democratic sense that we attach to the "dictatorship of the proletariat."[8]

Castigating the opposition on the Left, he maintained that "for them there is no independence without blood and ruins, without unemployment and misery."[9] In 1959 he attributed disturbances in the Casamance to "reactionary parties in France who wished to create a dissidence of the right against the U.P.S." He maintained that this rightist opposition was simply bought with foreign gold.[10] Indeed, on a number of occasions Senghor asserted that the destructive opposition owed loyalty to foreign interests.[11] Too often, he feels, opposition has not been in the national interest, but was simply a matter of conniving:

> That Samba would want to take the place of Mamadou is human, too human if it is not always disinterested. This is not grave in itself; what is grave is that for this purpose, he will put himself under the orders of foreigners ready to use all means including those that would result in eliminating his fatherland from the map of Africa.
>
> Against this illegal, anti-nationalist opposition, I will assume all my responsibilities that have been conferred upon me by the confidence of that Nation. . . . These measures will be implacable because they are just.[12]

Discussing the two types of opposition, in order to reject their criticism, Senghor has argued:

> Either the Opposition takes up in its general approach the program of the U.P.S., or she dishes out, without any critical spirit, false ideological slogans launched from abroad. To the first opposition, I will respond that it brings us nothing new; . . . As far as the second Opposition, which gives itself, pompously and stupidly, the epithet, "Marxist-Leninist," I must note that it is neither de-colonized or even independent, refusing to think for itself. I must especially point out that in the

states that they present to us as models, the economy stagnates when it does not regress.[13]

When Senghor swathes himself in the cloak of nationalism, he seems at least for the moment to lose all mercy. Conflict between him and his adversaries takes on an intensity unknown at less important levels of political differences.

Rather than opposition for the sake of opposition, or for personal gain, he maintained strongly that all parties and interests in the country should seek unity. "Union is the cement, better, it is the very tissue, of the Nation." This was also true of the government coalition. Dissent and factionalism were not the monopoly of the organized formal opposition. Senghor also stressed unity *within* the dominant party. The party must arrive at an internal synthesis reaching beyond factions. "My government," Senghor strongly asserts, "despite first appearances, will not be the government either of a class or a tendency." [14] The search for national unity, moreover, goes beyond unity of the government party to the legal opposition. Elaborating on a constant theme of his politics, Senghor held out the olive branch to any reasonable opposition, because "my profound conviction once more is that to govern is to convince, not to constrain." [15]

While "the Constitution admits the pluralism of parties, it doesn't recommend them," says Senghor, and neither did he. A nation building itself up cannot, except at its peril, afford the luxury of the sterile play of factions. "There is room for all the men of good will in a Dominant Party or in a Dominant Trade Union." [16] If it is to be allowed to exist, "the opposition must pursue the same goal as the majority party. This is to prevent social groups from hardening into antagonist classes. Its role is precisely to be the conscience of government and majority parties." [17] The best way for a conscientious opposition to guard against stimulating nascent antagonisms into full-fledged conflicts, would be to unite within a broadened unified party. Senghor, long before success met his determined efforts, cried that

199

never would the U.P.S. "despair of rallying the opposition to our national ideal. . . . Because our positions are just, we can rally the opposition to them." [18]

The Futility and Despair of Politics

As Senghor has become caught up in the day-to-day problems of achieving economic growth, he has tended to feel that "politics" (in the sense of a constant placating and balancing of interests) is a waste of time and, indeed, a threat to the development and stability of the state. According to Senghor, in the twentieth century "liberty is born out of development" and to the extent that there has not been any development, he appears to be losing patience and becoming increasingly authoritarian.[19] Mamadou Dia's attempted *coup d'état* apparently startled and upset Senghor. Speaking in April 1963, he said: "Well, it is time to tell you the truth that has been hidden from you for almost two years. This situation is more grave than I even suspected myself." [20] Previously, after the *coup's* failure, he had maintained that "we are behind six months in the realization of our Plan. This, for the simple reason that we have passed our time during this six months chatting instead of working, arguing among ourselves instead of uniting." [21] Four months later he remarked that "there is no development, especially not planned development; in the climate of chicanery and in the spirit of clans which have marked the outgoing year." [22]

As a result of this attitude, Senghor has, first, further attempted to centralize and concentrate political power; and secondly, turning away from politicians and the political party, he has increasingly buttressed himself with the growing power of the administration and its allied institutions. The rapid growth of development and other agencies evidenced these trends, as did reforms of local government that greatly increased the power of the regional governor (making him directly responsible for all the services in his area and accountable to the President as his personal agent).[23]

Further, in his attempt to achieve a well ordered and organized internal society, Senghor has restricted various interests, trying to make them adhere to a national program. Apropos of the students, for example, he stated:

> It's necessary for us to place an end to the anarchy which presides over the orientation of students and pupils; it's necessary to begin practicing a certain leadership having in view the real needs of the country rather than the caprices of adolescents.[24]

Turning to the civil service, he has said that in terms of an alliance with parties or personalities, the civil service is nonpolitical:

> I will not ask any civil servant to be a member of the U.P.S. no more than I would ask him to be "for Senghor." But I will require of all an unequivocating faithfulness to the program of my government that they are called upon to realize, as well as an honesty above reproach.[25]

As far as the trade unions are concerned, Senghor has made clear that the right to organize for the civil servants or other workers, is, for the present, nonexistent:

> The right to strike is guaranteed by the Constitution and is exercised within the framework of laws that regulate it—which already make this right far from absolute. Beyond this abstraction, however, the right to strike is also exercised within a sociological and political context of a country on the way of development. The strike must not be contrary either to development or to economic growth. It must not be used to acquire privileges in favor of the salaried workers of the public sector, who are already favored in comparison with the Nation as a whole.

As far as liberty of opinion, this doesn't mean that a civil servant has the right to insult his chiefs and sap the foundations of institutions. Entry into the civil service imposes upon him total loyalty. Lack of this loyalty constitutes a disciplinary breach that the State must suppress.[26]

While the civil servants must have certain minimum guarantees of security to assure their loyalty to the state, Senghor reserves for himself the ultimate right to discipline a civil servant. The importance of a well-functioning apparatus to achieve economic development justifies such strong measures. Civil servants must act in the public interest, not the interests of any individual or class. Internal organization and stability concerns not only domestic politics, but attracts capital fearful of its investments:

Senegal will be able to maintain its international credit only if by its internal policies it provides the example of a state that is democratic and organized. I said organized—even unto a domain as political as sports.[27]

Clearly, the emphasis is on organization.

The Centralization and Concentration of Power

A two-fold process has taken place. First, the nation-state has centralized power which was previously located abroad. Senegal shared power previously as a member of first the Federation of French West Africa and then of the Mali Federation. Second, within Senegal, power has been concentrated in the hands of the President as head of the government, country and administration. (Before 1963 executive power was shared by a President and Premier in a two-headed political unit.)

At the same time that he threatened to take strong measures to attain party unity and tremendously strengthened the executive, Senghor has insisted that in Senegal power is still shared and dispersed because the government consists of three branches:

> The problem was not only to reinforce the Executive by unifying it. The problem was equally to reinforce the Legislative by assuring its independence . . . by establishing a clearer separation of powers which alone would allow for an effective cooperation . . . by allowing it, like the executive, to more often have recourse to the instrument of arbitration which is the Supreme Court.[28]

Nevertheless, Senghor struck a new and predominant note at the time of the 1962 *coup* in asserting the importance of his role as chief of state:

> Under these grave circumstances when the destiny of the nation and the fate of democracy were at stake, my *duty* was clear. I could not fail: I did not fail. In my quality as Chief of State, *guardian of the Constitution*, and stemming from this *Supreme Arbitrator*, my duty was to take all the necessary measures to assure the regular functioning of the institutions, particularly the National Assembly, as ordered by Article 24 of the Constitution.[29]

For some time Senghor had insisted on the existence of a balance between the Executive and Legislative branches of government: both were elected by universal suffrage, both had real power in their respective domains to form a government with the means to govern opposite a Legislature with the means to legislate.[30] By the fall of 1964, however, as the problems of development continued to mount, Senghor was talking about a strong Presidential regime—as opposed to a parliamentary system—although he still denied that power was concentrated in the hands of a single man:

In the name of the imperatives of Development, we have instituted a Presidential regime. But we have deliberately turned our backs to the "African-president-king." We have not desired a regime which, while proclaiming a facade of a separation of powers, in fact installs a concentration of power in the hands of a single man.[31]

There is no denying the tremendous growth in the power of the office. Finally, in a speech exploring the meaning of "Negro-African democracy" at the University of Strasbourg in November 1964, Senghor gave a philosophical justification to the Presidential regime.

The presidential regime expresses the spirit of Negro-African philosophy which is based not on the individual but on the person. The President personifies the Nation as did the Monarch of former times his people. The masses are not mistaken who speak of the "reign" of Modibo Keita, Sekou Touré or Houphouet-Boigny, in whom they see, above all, the *elected of God through the People.* . . . In this world of the twentieth century, the two-headed divided power of the parliamentary regime cannot efficiently, rapidly resolve the numerous and complex problems which the state must face. The developed countries are being convinced of this through experience; the underdeveloped countries have already decided. From this perspective, the essence of Democracy would not be the division of power, *but the free election of the holder of power.*[32]

As far as the single party is concerned, Senghor rounds out his revised philosophy of democracy by first pointing out that while such an institution did not exist in Senegal, it often involves free discussions between various national interests. He did not deny that there was sometimes constraint, but pointed out that almost every time constraint was applied, the regime fell. Without a proper dialogue as in Guinea or Mali, the African single party could not exist. Westerners have compared the African single party with the Communist Party, but the European Communist Party is a bureaucratic party. "It is a club where only the elect can enter"; whereas in black Africa the single party is a mass party that every adult of either sex can freely enter—"after an initiation ceremony, just as formerly one had to enter the sacred forest." [33]

Personification of power, Senghor therefore considers an important ordering factor in Senegalese politics. This apparent change of attitude toward the concentration and possible personification of power has come precisely at a time when social conditions have changed radically: the state has created new instruments of coercion—the administration and especially the army; pressures for continued material rewards have continued unabated and unrealized; there is recognition of a failure to achieve any significant economic growth; and institutions such as the political party have failed to mobilize the population for development or national unity.

The Role of the Political Party in the State and in Economic Development

What specific roles must the dominant political party play in maintaining democracy and in economic development? First, there is the role of leadership.

> It belongs to the people—to the masses—to express their aspirations and their own needs. But they are, at first, confused. It is up to the "intellectuals" and an "awakened" worker is also an intellectual—to teach the masses how to express their aspirations and needs. This is the proper role of the leadership of the party.[34]

Continuing along this line of reasoning:

. . . our party must be the consciousness of the masses. Its role is twofold. In the first place, it must be the echo of the popular aspirations—not only their echo, but their scientific expression as well. . . . But the party must do more: It must guide the masses. The consciousness of the masses, who lack education and culture, still remains confused, lost in the fog of animal needs. It does not rise to the level of "political consciousness, a superior form of consciousness." This can only reach the masses from the outside, from the "intellectuals." [35]

Secondly, the party must direct and support Animation, even though it is a program of the government. In addition, the ministers and the deputies and the majority of the civil servants are members of the party. In the regional and local committees of development, as well as in meetings and councils of all levels, the party should organize days of study and discussion for the education and animation of its cadres.

Third, the party can also act as a means of control. Meeting regularly, the party at all levels should systematically go over the actions taken by the government to see if they conform to the directives given by the National Congress. Senghor in 1962 argued that:

. . . governments must apply the law firmly, and legislative assemblies must check on the action of the government. Yet, it is necessary that the Party—through its congress, executive committee, and board—have the final say in matters of control.[36]

While the statements would seem to indicate the over-all primacy of the party, in reality the role of the party is much more circumscribed and actually quite limited in practice. Even in theory Senghor goes on to argue that, while the party is foremost, it is primary only in its particular field. For example, the party cannot override the Constitution. Like every other political or governmental institution, the party must function within its framework. In addition, the party is neither above the state nor synonymous with it. From the beginning, therefore, the party, in Senghor's terms, is not conceived as an all-powerful, all-encompassing instrument for total social mobilization.

These limitations meant in Senegal that there was no threat to democracy from this particular institution. However, these very limitations in the power of the party also diminish its significance for economic development. Despite Senghor's sanguinity, one must observe that insofar as there was a threat to democracy it would stem from this failure to develop as well as ultimately from the new alternative bureaucratic and technocratic institution that emerged.

As far as the actual operations of the party are concerned, critics have attacked the U.P.S. for three basic failures: (1) it is neither structured nor animated; (2) it is not inspired by a "democratic centralism"; (3) and it is a foyer of nepotism.[37] In response to these criticisms, Senghor has argued that the U.P.S. is in fact structured. It has a national network of committees from the village level up to the National Central Committee. He did admit, however—and this was crucial—that these organizations were not "animated," that there was not enough popular participation and that they did not meet often enough or do enough. It was also true that in certain districts racked with conflicts between clans, the members of the party did not even pay their dues, but had them paid for them. "When this happens," Senghor allowed, party members "are no longer militants, but clients."[38]

As far as nepotism is concerned, nobody can deny the existences of abuses within the party. Nepotism is "an infantile sickness of all underdeveloped states," and one must combat it in every possible way.[39]

The ultimate purpose of the party, says Senghor, is development. The major instrument for this is the plan. Therefore, he takes seriously particularly those criticisms bearing on the lack of animation and the directly related failure of internal democracy.

The elected representatives in the past failed to go back to the people once they were elected. Decisions made from above replaced democratic debate within the party. Within the U.P.S. the conflict of clans reached from the bottom to the very summit.

Asleep for all practical purposes, the political officials did not set an example. They neglected to popularize the decisions of the national council, and the people remained uninformed and unmotivated to participate in any national or self-help activity.[40]

At first Senghor argued against any drastic reforms within the party. One could solve the problem simply by making the existing organizations of the party function properly, with more meetings and open debates.[41]

By the beginning of January 1965 he held that one should have the courage to admit that the role of the party in the elaboration and realization of the plan was, to say the least, "limited." [42] The party did, Senghor gravely suggested, contribute *something* to popularizing the idea of the plan; perhaps it was only natural that the party failed to spread the mystique of the plan because the first plan was, after all, almost entirely the work of foreign technicians.[43] The party must have to prove itself; to reform the party into an effective instrument for economic development.

Even after Senghor had asserted that the state had passed into a stage of the development—with the aid of newly trained experts, scientific agronomy and foreign assistance—of a technical *encadrement*, he continued to maintain that the party had a role to play: "It is within this new technical orientation that the action of the party must be discussed." [44] It must again become the Animator par excellence, but from now on an Animator trained in the most modern and effective techniques. When it came down to specifics, it meant only that a regional day of study would be held in each three-month period—with at least one financial or economic question on the agenda. Then, the government would take measures to popularize the technical solution advocated for each question or group of questions.

Senghor still hoped for the resuscitation of the party as an instrument for development. Increasingly, however, he counted not on the party, but on technical assistance (including the army) to achieve economic development and national unity.

In large measure, the political party failed in terms of the goals of economic development because of its very success in faithfully representing the nation's complex social mosaic, which is dominated by conservative interests.

In theory, the political party was to motivate the entire edifice of economic development. It was also to realize Senegal's democracy and the expression of all her interests. Unity and progress were its twin objectives. Rapidly, however, the organization of society came into variance with the disorganization of the party. Economic development requires scientific skills and the party had none to offer. More impressive credentials came to the fore, and the political party also fell victim to the trend toward technicity. The new structures of development required a new institution of great strength. In the future, the shape of democracy in Senegal had to fit into the new technicity which emerged in response to the needs of economic development.[45]

NOTES TO CHAPTER VII

1. Senghor, "Nationhood . . . ," *op. cit.*, p. 25.
2. *Ibid.*, p. 25.
3. Senghor, "Devant le Parlement du Ghana," February 15, 1961 (mimeo, N.P.).
4. Senghor, "Sixième Message au Peuple Sénégalais, April 3, 1962," reprinted in *Messages de Monsieur Léopold Sédar Senghor, op. cit.*
5. Senghor, "Conférence de Presse," August 23, 1960 (mimeo, N.P.).
6. Senghor, "Nationhood . . . ," *op. cit.*, p. 52.
7. *Ibid.*, p. 52.
8. *Ibid.*, p. 53.
9. Senghor, "Les Accords Franco-Maliens," *L'Unité Africaine*, April 30, 1963.
10. Senghor, *Guinée-Matin*, February 21, 1959.
11. See, for example, "Discours de Senghor à l'Assemblée Fédérale de Mali," *op. cit.*
12. Senghor, "Sixième Message au Peuple Sénégalais," *op. cit.*
13. Senghor, "Rapport sur la Doctrine et la Politique Générale," *op. cit.*, p. 78. Political parties that have been outlawed include one of the Left, the *Parti Africain de l'Indépendance*, a Marxist-Leninist grouping, and two of the Right, both led by Cheikh Anta Diop, the *Bloc des Masses Sénégalaises* and

the *Front Nationale Sénégalaise*, the latter supposedly outlawed when Dia-ist elements were threatening to gain control. See the chapter on Senegal in Ruth Schachter Morgenthau, *Political Parties in French-Speaking West Africa* (Oxford University Press, New York, 1964).

14. Senghor, "Présentation du Premier Gouvernement Senghor," December 19, 1962 (mimeo, N.P.). Yet in 1968 the problem of clans and tendencies appeared to be as strong as ever. See his *Politique, Nation et Développement Moderne, op. cit.,* p. 147 and *passim.*

15. *Ibid.*

16. Senghor, "Sixième Message," *op. cit.*

17. Senghor, "The Road to African Socialism," *op. cit.,* p. 88.

18. *Ibid.,* p. 88. Senghor's efforts were finally successful in the spring of 1966 when the Parti du Rassemblement Africain (P.R.A.), the only significant organized legal opposition in Senegal, finally merged with the U.P.S. See *West Africa* (London), June 25, 1966, p. 729.

19. Senghor, "Présentation du Premier Gouvernement Senghor," *op. cit.*

20. Senghor, "Message au Peuple Sénégalais à l'Occasion de la Célébration du Troisième Anniversaire de l'Indépendance," April 3, 1963 (Ministre de l'Information, Dakar).

21. Senghor, "Présentation du Premier Gouvernement Senghor," *op. cit.*

22. Senghor, "Discours à l'Assemblée Nationale," April 19, 1963, *op. cit.*

23. See Senghor, *Planification et Tension Morale, op. cit.,* p. 42 ff., for a discussion of the history and significance of the relevant legislation beginning with the first reform of January 13, 1960, defining the powers of the governor.

24. "Discours à l'Assemblée Nationale," April 19, 1963, *op. cit.*

25. *Ibid.*

26. *Ibid.*

27. *Ibid.*

28. Senghor, "Présentation du Premier Gouvernement Senghor," *op. cit.*

29. Senghor, "Message au Peuple Sénégalais," December 31, 1962, *op. cit.*

30. *Jeune Afrique,* August 24, 1963.

31. Senghor, *Voyage Officiel aux États-Unis du Brésil, op. cit.,* p. 35.

32. Senghor, "Négritude et Civilisation Gréco-Latine ou Démocratie et Socialisme," *L'Unité Africaine,* November 26, 1964.

33. *Ibid.*

34. *Planification et Tension Morale, op. cit.,* p. 46.

35. Senghor, "The Theory and Practice of Senegalese Socialism," in Cook, *op. cit.,* p. 160.

36. *Ibid.,* p. 159.

37. Senghor, "Rapport sur la Doctrine et la Politique Générale," *op. cit.,* p. 79.

38. *Ibid.,* p. 79.

39. *Ibid.,* p. 81.

40. *Ibid.,* p. 77.

41. Léopold Senghor, "Rapport sur le Formation des Cadres," Conseil National de l'U.P.S., October 21, 1962 (mimeo, N.D.).

42. "Préparation du Second Plan Quadriennal," *op. cit.*

43. *Ibid.*

44. *Ibid.*

45. Senghor's 1968 report to the Sixth Congress of the U.P.S. reveals evidence of a growing tension in both the theory and the practice of the political party. More clearly than in any of his previous writings, Senghor distinguishes between the nature and functions of mass and elitist parties and presents the strongest arguments thus far for the latter. "The future," Senghor maintains, "belongs to the active minorities" (*Politique, Nation et Développement Moderne, op. cit.,* p. 18, *passim,* especially pp. 9–24 and 145–156). While he concludes by asserting that the U.P.S. is and ought to be *both* a party of

the masses and elitist, Senghor has striven mightily to remake this loose coalition from the top down into a tightly centralized organization accountable to a national leadership and capable of carrying out a given policy of action. In this respect, the readmission of Abdoulaye Ly, Assane Seck, Amadou Moctar M'Bow, and the P.R.A. into the U.P.S. is particularly significant. Senghor called upon exactly these same people in 1956 for their organizational, intellectual and ideological skills *after* the B.D.S. had been tremendously successful at the polls in large part to revamp the party (see Chap. 1 above). Yet again, Senghor gives no sign that he will change the basis of his *social* support. In the present context, a *party* bureaucratic elite would probably become simply one more element in the complicated mosaic of Senegalese politics, albeit one most advantageous for the President as another force particularly useful in balancing a too rapid trend to the more "conservative" forces in the life of the country.

VIII

Technicity and the New Humanism

I N T H E M I D D L E of the eighteenth century a group called
the *Physiocrats*, or Economists, made the problems of public administration their special study. De Tocqueville notes of
them:

> The Economists saw no hope of effecting the revolu-
> tionary changes they had in mind with this obsolete
> machinery (provincial assemblies and parliaments)
> and the idea of recognizing the nation as sole arbiter of
> its own destinies and entrusting to it the execution of
> their plans was little to their taste. For how could a
> whole nation be persuaded to accept and to put
> through a program of reform so vast and so intricate?
> To their thinking, the simplest, most practical solution
> was to enlist the support of the royal power.[1]

Senegal's technicians, despite any other differences of circumstances or belief, share with the Economists this attitude of
social engineering. They have little time for the bickerings of
politicians; they desire to employ directly all the force of the
state to implement their decisions.

Senghor has defined technique as "applied science," the objective of which is "the transformation, not merely the disinterested knowledge, of the real." In the post-independence period,
what "transforms the real" counts most.[2] Senghor claims this to

be the period of an "end of ideology"; one might more aptly characterize it as the period of the "ideology of technology."

In 1962 Senghor argued for the supremacy of the political party—for its ultimate control over both the technocracy and the bureaucracy:

> The technocrats believe that all problems must be considered—and resolved—in the perspective of science and technique alone, and they forget that the conscious will of men is a *sine qua non* of the revolution. The bureaucrats forget that the efficiency of labor is measured neither by the amount of paper blackened nor even by membership in the government party, but by technical knowledge and rational working methods.[3]

A year later, after a more intensive experience with the problem of development and the Dia experience, Senghor asserted that there was too much politics. He maintains, for example, that today Anglophone Africans are in a far better economic position than the former French colonies. They are getting ready for their economic take-off because they have always been more pragmatic, have given less priority to the political over the economic, and have not pursued various ideologies. Senegal, on the other hand, has had a great deal of difficulty in realizing her plan and "all these faults can be summed up in the primacy given in practice to the political over the economic." [4]

Senghor felt that Dia had turned many of the governors and prefects away from their administrative and economic activities and into various factional political conflicts. Thus, after Dia's fall Senghor felt he must "*depoliticize* the Administration in order to repoliticize at the highest level, that of the public good, of Development." In this sense:

> Their [the civil servants] role ought to be 35% administrative, 60% economic and 5%—in the ordinary sense of the word—political. In the political domain

their role is not to interfere in the interim affairs of the parties, but to follow their activity in order to inform the Government.[5]

If Dia had meddled with the civil service, the problem obviously involved more than a few personalities. Basic differences between social interests were at stake. Conflict between civil servants, politicians and deputies, regional counselors, mayors and political responsibles, intensified to the point where it could no longer escape Senghor's notice. The politicians "complained that the forces of order and the civil servants did not accord them the proper respect and precedence to which they were entitled. While they weren't general, these complaints were in great part well founded." As Chief of State, Senghor therefore ordered the governors to take all necessary measures to remedy the situation.

While matters of personality and human relations undoubtedly accounted for a good deal of the difficulty in rapport, Senghor recognizes that there are broader considerations. The nub of the problem seemed to be that the governors and prefects, representing the Executive and charged with the duty of applying the laws, found that in order to be effective they had to receive the complaints of the people, who were legitimately represented by elected representatives and politicians. As a result, the politicians apparently felt that their areas of responsibility were being invaded and their power threatened. The increasing importance of planning added to their sense of malaise. Even though supposedly represented and involved in every stage of planning, politicians felt uncomfortable and out of their environment in a technical setting. Increasingly, therefore, they felt left out of important events—a situation undoubtedly exacerbated by the contemptuous attitude of many of the technicians.

Senghor, caught between these opposing forces, is clear in his preferences. Although he ordered the governors to be courteous, he tactfully suggested to the politicians that they phone or write their prefects instead of paying personal visits.[6]

If Senghor feels that technical programs are more effective

than non-scientific politicians, it follows that the value of personnel and agencies bears a direct relationship to their scientific ability; the more scientific a service, the more valuable—even if it were a *foreign* concern.

Senegalese agencies seemed lacking in the proper knowhow. The government therefore summoned a French agricultural engineering company—not simply to advise national agencies but to replace them. Senegal entered a new stage in the evolution toward technicity. As Senghor noted:

> Cooperation, indeed even Animation . . . was somewhat technological without trained technicians or the appropriate technical means. The agents of Cooperation were reduced to doing "boyscouting"; the animators to civil training and the politician, naturally, to a politician's politics.[7]

The *Centres d'Expansion Rurale* and *Animation Rurale* were reorganized under one director, as were the agencies of Cooperation. New equipment became available for the first time and new Senegalese technicians graduated from the National School of Applied Economy. Finally, Senghor exclaimed, we have "passed from theory to practice, from civil education to technical education." It is no longer a question of singing of the "healthy joys of the country," but of determining under what conditions, with what financial means and techniques, a given rate of productivity can be obtained in three years, in five years, and at what rate of annual income per agricultural worker.[8]

Critics, however, have complained that, coupled with other government policies, this increasing technicity limits the role of the Senegalese, especially the peasant, in determining his own development.

The History of Technicity: Technique
Replaces Politics

A number of deputies of Senghor's own party reproached him for a policy that "depoliticized" government action and "demobilized" the masses.[9] In response, he first noted that the depoliticization of government was a general worldwide phenomenon after the two wars. It was part of a process—occurring as much in the Third World as in Europe and North America—whereby national problems took precedence over ideological problems, and economic and social problems over those of politics. This process occurred because the majority of the people, including workers and peasants, realized that power is not an end but only a means to achieve an adequate standard of living. This self-awakening stood at the origins of socialism. Socialism, while granting priority to taking political power, accorded the most importance to the economic situation. Today, Senghor continues, this self-awakening is renewed in the underdeveloped countries. It explains the popularity of ideas like "planning" and "depoliticization of the masses," rather than the politics of parties or politicians. The *people* now aid in the process of depoliticization and *demand* technicity, according to the President-Poet.

Under the colonial regime, the only possible strategy was "politics first." The first objective was the seizure of power even at the expense of economic growth and social development. According to Senghor, the policy at that time supported the interests of the salaried workers, the privileged, rather than those of the peasants and proletarians. If this resulted in financial disequilibrium, so much the better because the colonizer had to pay for it. If it resulted in social disequilibrium, the contradictions and tensions provided the germs of revolution and liberation: "We were in the *Time of Demands* which prepared the *Time of Reconstruction*." [10] But today the peasants understand that the colonial regime has passed. They ask something more of their leaders. They want "remunerative work" and, through this, more merchandise in the stores, more housing, more schools, more dispensaries and maternities:

> It is to the extent that these demands are not satisfied that they will be disappointed and demobilized. . . . Whatever the case might be, the working and peasant masses without asking permission have transferred politics from the domain of the ideological dispute and the quarrels of class, to one of economic and social debate.[11]

The peasants were, therefore, developing a sense of self-consciousness, a *prise de conscience,* even if they weren't doing it according to the Marxist conception of class struggle. The main way in which a *prise de conscience* is to be developed is through the development of a technical *encadrement* or framework. Senegalese technicity and Senegalese socialism finally come together in this notion of *encadrement;* these new techniques enable an economic growth which for Senghor provides an almost final refutation of Marxism.

Everywhere in Francophone Africa, however, people are convinced of the necessity of this *encadrement* of the population. Cooperatives, for example, contribute to *encadrement.* In the history of socialist thought, the significance in discussing cooperatives, collectives or communes lay in their non-exploitativeness, their anti-capitalist or humanitarian ethic. *Encadrement* of the population in Senegal means the organization of units of production, the development of a *prise de conscience* of the peasants. This latter aspect of the *encadrement* means more than simply the sense of shared work or mutual self-help—this, traditional society has done already. But neither does a *prise de conscience* imply the development of self-consciousness in the Marxist sense of a class "in itself" becoming a class "for itself." Marxist class-consciousness signifies that the peasants have an interest distinct and opposed to other interests of society: a condition impossible in the "classless society" claimed by Senghor. *Prise de conscience,* rather, means acceptance of the idea that self-progress is possible. There is no concept of exploitation. The

Marxist notion of self-consciousness is the realization by the workers that wealth is for them and that they are legitimately entitled to what they have produced. This increase in wealth, however, will not come about directly through the new self-consciousness but through social revolution.

The theory of Senghor's socialism implicitly holds that wealth is increased directly as a result of the *prise de conscience* which creates an increased rate of production. Thus, the lot of the peasantry is improved neither by taking wealth from a dominant class nor by eliminating this class as a "fetter on the productive forces," but by economic development made possible by the universal realization that it is possible, as well as increased technical efficiency.

This self-consciousness, or *prise de conscience*, it therefore follows, develops neither through the process of emiseration and class struggle, nor through the actions of the vanguard of a revolutionary elite. Rather, it emerges from the efforts of technocrats acting through institutions primarily technical in inspiration. These technocrats need not form close attachments with the population, nor necessarily even be of the nationality of the particular country. The technocrats simply possess the best scientific training available for optimum allocation of scarce resources on a strict, cost-accounting type of procedure. In this perspective, the Cooperatives and the whole process of *encadrement* become simple instruments for the given objective of economic development. This technocrat-led effort takes the form of an *encadrement* of the population because today technology enables the effective manipulation and utilization of whole communities.

One tractor can do the work of a whole village. It is so expensive that no single farmer can afford it. In scope of increased productivity as well as in terms of cost, these innovations would completely overpower and dominate an entire community, at least temporarily. The West absorbed innovations gradually over a long period of time. Now, however, developing countries are going through a process of telescoping, or skipping of technological stages. No single farmer can afford a tool which costs one hundred times his annual income, and which out-produces by a thousandfold his present yield. Thus, some form of collective enterprise is rational. Under these historical circumstances, one would expect the content of the Cooperatives and this process of *encadrement* to be different than in the past.

One indication of the technological character of this process is the fact that whether or not the "instruments of production" remain in private hands depends on factors that operate after there is a *prise de conscience*. One would logically say that the process of *encadrement*, involving as it does great psychological and economic changes, would be the determining factor—that inevitably the introduction of scientific rationality and systematically expanded productivity would undermine the basis of traditional or feudal society and values. A distinction, however, must be made between traditional values and traditional social relations in the sense of a hierarchical ordering of social economic classes. Modernizers sometimes assume that "Newtonian" innovations will not only change people's ways of thinking but also undermine the real underlying economic, social and religious bases of power of traditional and religious ruling groups. In reality, there is a question as to whether the process of *encadrement* can be technologically neutral with its content determined by the political nature of the state. If the Senegalese *ancien regime* can adapt to the innovations of the new processes and sciences, it will mean the failure of those socialist planners and technocrats who believe that their objectives can be achieved by indirectly subverting traditional systems with programs of *Animation* and *Centres d'Expansion Rurales* without a direct political confrontation.

Traditional classes may very well be able to maintain their relative position of predominance and control by shifting the basis of their power. Rather than inertly watch the withering away of their ancient sources of strength, these groups would more likely attempt to absorb the innovation and restabilize their control. Increased productivity might then result simply in increased inequalities; technological innovations, in the creation of a more efficient ruling class.

Reliance on the Army as the Logical Culmination of Technicity

The army is one of the best technical organizations in Senegal, in the sense of its ability to perform tasks with expert, scientific knowledge and the optimum organization and mobilization of men and resources. Greater discipline, better training, no corruption, unlimited hours, distinguish the army from the civilian bureaucracy with which it shares basically the same rational, instrumental outlook and education.

At the same time that the civil bureaucracy and political party have demonstrated their inadequacies, the army has grown tremendously in strength because of increased Presidential attention and appropriations. In a situation where government cannot meet increased demands from all layers of the society, Senghor, not surprisingly, has placed greater and greater reliance upon the army. One can also, however, regard his growing dependency on the armed forces as the logical, if not final, tendency in Senegal toward technicity.

The army saved Senghor's government from Dia's attempted *coup d'état*. On that occasion Senghor told the people, "After God, it is above all to our Armed Forces that I must address the thanks of the Nation . . . the army has been an example for the Nation, an example of submission, of faithfulness to the law." [12] Of all the interests, organizations, societies, brotherhoods and bureaucracies in Senegal, Senghor can count only on the army. This army proved that it was not "an army of pronunciamentos" but "an army that only obeyed its Chief and the Law." [13]

Senegal, he asserts, is fortunate to have an army that is both democratic and above politics:

Composed of all strata of the nation, removed from the
battles of clan and politicians, thus transcending particular interests, existing only to serve the law, that is
the National Will, our Army presents to us the ex-
emplary image of the Nation.[14]

Senghor in 1963 felt that the army should stay essentially
the way it was: particularly, it should remain aloof from politics.
As for himself, he promised, "Never will I use it [the army] to
resolve a political problem." [15] Defining a "political problem,"
however, was obviously a very difficult and subjective matter.
When Senegal was in the midst of its greatest austerity campaign
and the budget was being tightened, Senghor increased appropriations for the army because "it was important that the elements
put into place for the security of the state have at their disposi-
tion sufficient means to function with effectiveness." [16]

By mid-1965 not only had the armed forces continued to
maintain the internal as well as external security of the state, but
also some officers of the army were appointed as prefects. At this
time, army officers served as chief administrative officers only in
districts on the frontier, where there was some possibility of military activity—particularly from Portuguese Guinea, whose forces
did in fact bomb and invade Senegalese villages.

By 1965 the Ministry of the Interior had placed army officers in charge of reorganizing and strengthening the Gendarmes,
Republican Guard and police, in order to increase their unity and
effectiveness. Among other projects, the army constructed and
administered a workshop-school for untrained youth to provide
them with technical skills, as part of its new effort for economic
development. "In truth," said Senghor, "from year to year, our
armed forces participate more and more in national construction
—I didn't say 'in the realization of the Plan,' which is only one
aspect, although major, of the problem. They participate in it,
certainly, by their work of engineering, but perhaps still more by
their permanent example of organization, of discipline, of work,
. . . of patriotism." [17] Though as late as April 1965 Senghor

still excluded the army from participation in the *realization* of the Plan, the following year he proudly hailed the role of the armed forces in its elaboration:

> . . . not only in the construction of bridges, roads, and dams, not only in the technical and professional formation of the young, but also in tasks as diverse as the administration of frontier departments and the direction of the Transport Company of Senegal. . . . Refusing to make it a marginal organization in the nation, we have wished to associate our national Army in all national affairs—in our worries and in our joys; in the examination of our problems, of our difficulties, and in the search for their solution.[18]

Never before in the history of Senegal had the army played such an important role. Never before had the state been so determinedly non-ideological and technologically oriented. Having failed to rally the peasants, the workers, the political party or any sizable interest group (except the leaders of the religious brotherhoods) to his wholehearted *personal* support, Senghor increasingly fell back on the army. The army, although a rather surprising vehicle for Senghor's anti-Marxist socialism, seemed the perfect organizational expression of the new technology. Philosophically, moreover, Senghor found a base for the new technology in Christian humanism.

The Divine Milieu: Technology, Totalization and Totalitarianism

If Senegal has entered a technocratic and scientific stage, Senghor also has found a theoretician-guide who provides philosophic justification for his views—the Catholic philosopher Pierre Teilhard de Chardin. Christian concerns have preoccupied Senghor since his youth, which explains much about his profound anti-Marxism. It helps in understanding his concepts of authority and history, his deep contentment and his optimism. It sheds light also on one of the sources of his isolation as well as on his guiding principles for the reorganization of Senegalese society.

It is difficult to overestimate the importance of Teilhard in Senghor's life and thought.[19] In rendering homage to Pierre Teilhard de Chardin on the anniversary of his death, Senghor began by saying: "The problem is how to explain how a man—if you wish, a Negro-African intellectual—has been in his search for the Truth, helped, saved, by Teilhard de Chardin." Senghor discovered Teilhard after World War II, when he was facing a crisis of belief. Teilhard helped him find his identity, and in addition "he restored my faith while at the same time allowing me to be an African socialist, a believing socialist." [20]

In his philosophy, Pierre Teilhard de Chardin desires the material advance of civilization, but only so that materialism may be ultimately transcended by a more vital spiritual unity. In these respects Teilhard's philosophy fulfills the needs that Ulam found to account for the success of Marxism in societies undergoing industrialization or rapid social change.[21] In Teilhard's thought one can find justification for the fascination of the potential of the machine and Newtonian science, as well as sympathy for the hatred of dehumanizing routine and alienated labor. He relates his solution to ultimate questions of origin, destiny and purpose. His philosophy culminates in a vision of Man's greater glory beyond earthly materialism. And all this he founds on a scientific understanding of the universe.

Teilhard resolved for Senghor the three great difficulties he had found in Marx and Engels: (1) the failure to explore properly the transition from matter to mind—and why mind should consist more of intelligence and discursive reason than love and intuitive reason; (2) the absence of God; and (3) the battle of classes which was at the center of dialectical materialism. Senghor would not have found so elegant a solution to these problems had Teilhard not been a scientist with a vast philosophical understanding of modern scientific discoveries. Senghor asserts that:

> Teilhard studies man not as a philosopher or theologian, but as a scientist, retaining only the facts, the phenomena. His volume, he explains, is "purely and exclusively . . . a scientific treatise. . . ." [22]

Senghor is able to reject Marxism because he has found what he feels is higher philosophy and religion, as well as a more knowledgeable and powerful science. All of Senghor's propositions have a scientific underpinning. Implicitly, he always compares Marxist science and the "higher" science. Science is of great importance to Senghor in his political maturity, for it holds out the promise of rapid, painless economic development. Science was also of great personal importance in his student youth when it disproved allegations of racial inferiority and revealed a mechanism of change that would result in the "synthesis of civilization." [23]

Teilhard's philosophy has provided Senghor with personal satisfaction and justification for his politics. As an ideology for development, however, it encounters two serious difficulties. First, in a land of Moslems, and where the literacy rate is low, Teilhard is hardly a philosopher with great mass appeal. Secondly, in a society where social engineering is the order of the day, Teilhard's thought reinforces not only scientism but also elitism and hierarchy to the point where his ideal society more closely approximates the beehive than the Garden of Eden. This ideal, which is also Senghor's, is clear throughout Senghor's analysis of *work*, his final image of God and his understanding of Teilhard's notions of socialization and of "totalization."

WORK

The problem of work is a central concern in African literature (particularly in novels like those of Mongo Beti or Peter Abraham). [24] It is interesting, therefore, that Senghor is not concerned with the concept of "work" in his writings. Why has he not attempted an elaboration of a theory of "work" as he has with the concept of "culture" or "Negritude?" The concept of work is central to the problem of alienation with which Senghor is concerned; it is central to the concerns of peoples moving from traditional to industrial economics; it is central, too, to the concerns of his mentor, Teilhard. Why then the apparent lack of interest?

Until recently, at least, Senghor has not been philosophically preoccupied with the problem because ultimately his concern centers upon technological effort rather than manual labor. Also, he views development in a time perspective that cannot place any great immediate value on mass menial effort. While undoubtedly not afraid of getting his hands dirty, Senghor clearly knows how to distinguish between the values of different types of work, as well as between the "cadres of conception" and the "sweat and labor of the masses." [25] Senghor is a modern man: this is the day of invention, organization and the machine. At heart, he is not convinced that the manual labor of the peasant is important or ennobling. In his concept of "work," Senghor is very Marxist to this extent: under conditions of great scarcity, he sees that work can only be the reproduction of necessity. There is neither freedom nor the opportunity for the full development of one's faculties. Work is slavery and suffering. Yet the Marxist schema, precisely because work produces the bitter alienation which results only in the production of stronger chains, gave the strongest impetus to the rapid overthrow of the conditions of exploitation. Senghor is, however, not a Marxist, but a Teilhardian Catholic. The Christian attitude toward work contains a duality and a paradox. Teilhard, regardless of his solution, recognized this as a major problem for believing intellectuals. This duality finds expression in the conflicting injunctions: "Perfection consists in detachment, the world about us is vanity and ashes" versus "Nothing is more certain, dogmatically, than that human action can be sanctified. 'Whatever you do,' says Saint Paul, 'do it in the name of Our Lord, Jesus Christ.' " [26] Teilhard resolves the paradox, giving work meaning by placing it within the framework of a theory of evolution which is appealing to intellectuals because of its materialist grounding and scientific basis. The most mundane work is noble, Teilhard argues, because it is not only the work of God but also practical, for it will lead to a higher humanistic civilization. Similarly, Senghor adopts a long view of history. This perspective gives a definition to his view of rapid change, which is different from that of most Africans. No risk of human life is worth the threat of violence entailed in the mobilization of the population or the pitting of factions against each other. Also, he need not accept as equally ennobling all forms of work. Since everything is touched by an element of the divine, all work has a redeeming quality, no matter how vile, and this attitude is a further counsel to patience. This embodies the brunt of a contradiction between the Catholic and Marxist conceptions of work. For the Marxist, all work in the pre-socialist society is alienated. In the traditional Catholic view, such work is meaningful in divine terms, not because it adds enrichment in any human measure.

Recently Senghor has brought a new approach to the fore with his suggestion that, due to changes in the nature of production, work can be significant in human material terms even before the advent of communism. Industry, he said, is "production considered no longer as a means to satisfy the needs of men, but as itself producing, making Man; production educates, creates men through its very function of creating." Insofar as modern industry is the scientific organization of production, taking advantage of the latest research and modern techniques, it will form humans who are more human.[27] In the past, work deadened man because work was only a prerequisite for meaningful activity that was impossible under the existing social, economic and technical conditions. Today, however, particularly in underdeveloped countries where values are in the process of change, work can be ennobling even while it fulfills material necessities, for the new ethic work incorporates is one that will make men more human.

Appropriately enough, these new values of work are those functional for the new age. They are the values of science, technique and organization. In the final analysis, therefore, work might still be fulfilling only under conditions of universal leisure. Nevertheless, potentially it can become interesting and significant within the framework of scientific organization.

The New Image of God

All things point toward greater organization. Science, technology, development, work and, finally, even God—all are organization. In a moment of great candor, Senghor once revealed his profound religiosity in describing why the existence of God was so personally important:[28]

> At this time of the year which is that of the budgeting session of the National Assembly, at this moment when I spend two-thirds of my time on economic and financial dossiers, I confess my nights are not haunted by the problems of economic expansion or indeed of development alone, but also by the single problem which is really a problem: the one of God. . . . It is not physical death which causes horror in me—I have often viewed it from close—it is the idea of nothing; of no more being. Because the nothing of non-conscience would be the worst of hells. I have, at times, broken out in a cold sweat in the night, and I am always comforted by the reading of Teilhard de Chardin.[29]

Teilhard has thus provided Senghor with a new God, one that a modern man of the twentieth century could believe in:

> His God does not descend, *ex machina,* from the heavens. He emerges from an "internal necessity" . . . as the ultimate stage of a dialectical logic . . . God is the coherent and efficient solution that Teilhard proposes to the problem of alienation. . . . It is no longer the mechanistic and bourgeois God of former times. It is a

new God in a new time when there is developing a new
law, a new morality, a new art. It is a God, let us dare to
say, less creator than personalization. It is the center of
centers who draws towards him all the human centers
in order to expand them in organizing them.[30]

The God of Teilhard is indeed different from that of the traditional Judeo-Christian deity. Teilhard's God is not only for scien-
tific-minded Catholics or the religious intellectual seeking ever-
lasting solace in unity with a suprahuman idea-force; *Teilhard's
God is also for the highly organized community in which the
individual is lost as the bonds of isolation and egoism are burst
and there is a melting away of personalities in a higher totality.*
This is a new kind of total community through belief, and by
believers in a Christian God. But in its religiosity it is reminiscent of the traditional African community as Senghor describes
it. This affinity is undoubtedly one of the reasons for Senghor's
attraction to this image of society, for it emphasizes not the individual but the community.

He rejects traditional African gods, but not with the violence with which the ancient Hebrews and missionaries crushed
the primitive idols. Senghor is famous for his celebration of African art, in which he finds manifestation of a collective as well as
a religious spirit. This collective spirit was precisely what the Hebrews found so abhorrent about idols: the fact that they were
faceless, lacking in personality and inhuman because they did not
represent any individual, but were a *collective* manifestation.
Each son of the Covenant looked upon himself as an individual
with a unique personality. Contractually, the obligations with
God were concluded not simply with the abstract Community,
but with each individual. The Talmud has it that every Jew who
ever lived was at Sinai personally in his "soul" to receive the Ten
Commandments.

Senghor's and Teilhard's God is a God of community. The
individual is submerged into the "masks of unmasked faces,
stripped of the marks of illness and the lines of age," [31] into the

living purgatory, paradise and hell that take away his ego, but from which he re-emerges with the innocent purity that is without sickness or time.

TOTALIZATION AND SOCIALIZATION

Teilhard's basic concepts of "totalization" and "socialization" have further commanded Senghor's attention. "Totalization" Senghor interprets as the existence of the Civilization of the Universal over the planet. It involves the opening of each civilization to every other and from this to the whole world.[32] Explaining the mechanisms by which this occurs, he states:

> This socialization and totalization are rendered possible thanks to the progress of the science and technology of communication: boats, planes, railroads, museums, books, and newspapers, missiles and space-ships. . . .[33] They weave a continuous membrane of thought that encircles the earth.[34]

These factors will bring about the unity of the world. The only question in Senghor's mind is whether this unity will be the projection of any particular civilization or of the Universal Civilization as a "symbiosis," consisting of the complementary contributions of all civilization.

What does this final inevitable great organization involve? "Totalization" has an unpleasant sound to most liberal Western ears. Teilhard does not reassure us when he states: "Monstrous as it is, is not modern totalitarianism really the distortion of something magnificent, and thus quite near to the truth?"[35] Neither does Senghor particularly comfort when he attempts to distinguish between his "totalized" society and all others:

> Although all the present political regimes—democracy, socialism, Communism—have as their goal totalization and socialization with depersonalization, they fail in their attempt. This is because they sacrifice the part to the whole, the person to the collectivity. Since a mate-

rialist postulate underlies this, and since the collectivity is conceived solely as a technical organization, it does not attract; to push the individuals toward it, one must resort to constraint and violence. This is the reason for the failures. But if one conceives of the collectivity as human convergence cemented by liberty, equality, fraternity—terms that Marx scorned—and if one places love of the Super-Person above human life, there will naturally be a powerful attraction to group individuals without constraint. For, once again, "union differentiates," love personalizes.[36]

The key difference between Senghor's projected ideal society and all others does not lie in the degree of "totalization" of organization. This he regards as inevitable. Presumably, the loss of individualism is also inevitable when all societies become highly organized. Senghor, in any event, does not concern himself with the loss of individualism, which he has always considered a manifestation of Western egoism.

According to Senghor, Teilhard does not depict "a great *All* in which individuals were supposed to be merged like a drop in the ocean or like a dissolving grain of salt" (presumably, this is the image of totalitarianism) but "an organized whole" where, like the cells of a body, "the parts perfect themselves and fulfill themselves." [37] This proposed society, however, goes beyond the traditional conservative Burkean type of organic community, because Teilhard is not primarily concerned with functions, divisions and units, but rather with the mergence of self and submergence of ego. Teilhard demands a more total community.

Jacob Bronowski, in perusing *The Future of Man*, found himself brought up short by the following response of Teilhard to the problem of totalitarianism:

> My answer is that I do not think we are yet in a position to judge recent totalitarian experiments finally . . . it is not the principle of totalitarianism that is at

fault, but the clumsy way in which it has been applied.[38]

Commenting on the work of Teilhard, Bronowski noted that:

> Teilhard foresaw a universal community of men who no longer have individual minds, but flow into one all-embracing mind, "an envelope of thinking substance" around the world. It was as if all mankind would become a single clone of cells—or a single insect colony, informed by a common unity of mind instead of common instincts. . . . Nor did he balk at its totalizing implications. . . .
>
> It has been thought that Teilhard was silenced by his superiors, and died in 1955 with his work unpublished, because they would not acknowledge that man has evolved as the other animals have, without a special act of creation. But it seems to me that they must also have shuddered at his picture of the future, in which man will lose his identity in a God who has become a sort of queen-bee of mind. Indeed, they cannot have approved his wish to see man saved by collective rather than personal grace.[39]

To the extent that Senghor shares the perspective of Teilhard, he ultimately directs his ideology toward the disappearance of the "individual" as he has historically existed in Western civilization, as well as of the "materialism" that has sustained and driven man until the present. Hitherto, all men were driven to eke out a living. With the advent of material abundance of modern science and industry, conflict over mundane goods will no longer be necessary; increased leisure will enable men to turn to more ethereal matters. In terms of their social condition, men will become increasingly alike.

With the increasing interdependency and intercommunication brought about by the new technology, values and cultures will become increasingly similar. Ideally, these values, which will be universally shared, will consist of a synthesis of elements from many once diverse peoples and civilizations. Society will, however, be totalitarian in the sense that it will ultimately consist of one total organization of everything human, including one total value system.

In Teilhard's and Senghor's terms, nevertheless, the direction of consciousness and the elimination of ego will keep the individual from being submerged as he was in previous totalitarian regimes. Increasingly alike in beliefs and status, men willingly abandon their self-seeking and turn toward the community. As in the Marxian image, conflict will disappear with the elimination of scarcity. At this point, men will willingly immerse themselves in a broader community, for in so doing they will find the human company necessary for their self-fulfillment. All men acting in this fashion will discover a new unity in aspirations. All mankind finally converges in a new identity. This final convergence is ultimately satisfied by attaining the "final finality," the Omega point, which is God. Ultimately, it is through God that the final miraculous transformation of man takes place—the transformation from egoistic, self-seeking, materialistic individualism to a new community-oriented "personalism." Through the grace of God, man will always be something greater than a grain of sand even though the society in which he lives is totally organized.

Although this final objective remains in the remote future and depends largely upon faith for its realization, for the present the doctrine provides a powerful justification for the development of institutions geared to the total reorganization of society and the ego-centered self.

From this perspective, one cannot truly understand Senghor's thought without appreciating that for him the real beginnings of modern man lie more with the systematic introspection begun with Augustine than with the French Revolution. With the institutionalization of Christianity and its concern with the development of the subconscious, it became possible on a broad scale not only to control physical behavior and command outward allegiance, but also to achieve an inward acquiescence and "freely" given belief in a set of values or suprahuman goal. Teilhard is in this tradition. So are the "process of *encadrement*" and the *prise de conscience* as they operate in Senegal.

Conclusion

Léopold Sédar Senghor has developed a systematically interrelated set of ideas which both justifies close French-African ties and legitimizes an elite rather than mass-based politics. Politically, he has always sought improvements for Senegal and Africa within a framework of a broad community of nations. Economically, he hopes to achieve expansion in the rate of growth of the gross national product and a rise in the standard of living through the systematic application of modern scientific and agronomic techniques.

In seeking both economic and political objectives, Senghor has attempted to accommodate all the powerful interests in Senegal. He has created broad coalitions rather than attempting to use social antagonisms to create a unity which might work to eliminate minority interests. Senghor has been unwilling to strive for rapid economic development at the expense of the sacrifice of the individual. Consistently, he stresses the necessity of an evolutionary policy rather than revolutionary change. He asserts the desirability of a broad non-programatic humanism. A deep religiosity permeates all of his actions.

Two difficulties, however, inhere in Senghor's ideas and programs. First, there is little evidence that Senegal will follow a distinctively African path of development or create a "New African Man" in the future. Rather, the case is that Senghor is a "Man of the West" in the sense that his ideas are rooted in Western civilization and are directed primarily at either a Western or Western-trained audience. Second, despite his concern with humanism, evolution, cooperation and coalitions, Senegal shows a strong tendency toward increased authoritarianism, and the nature of Senghor's ideological contentions furthers this very tendency.

Senghor's immersion in Western civilization began with his student days in Paris. As an outsider, Senghor gained the attention of leading French political and cultural figures by an attack on the alleged superiority of European values.

His attack was noteworthy for the brilliance with which he assimilated supposedly "African" values into categories of French culture. An intellectualized aesthetic, *Africanité* was a doctrine originally directed toward and accepted by the French. Negritude formed the first bridge with which Senghor linked Senegal and France. Later his doctrine of colonialism emphasized not exploitation, but the positive contributions of France to the progress of underdeveloped lands. Further, he argued that conditions of scarcity and technological backwardness in Africa necessitated continued strong ties between *métropole* and dependency. For these reasons, as well as because of ever increasing international interdependency, Senghor also de-emphasized the significance of the nation-state as the central political unit in the modern world. Nationalism, as a political movement in Senegal, did not have the same type of popular support as in the British colonies. An absence of demands for immediate independence, as well as advocacy of membership in a strong French community, further strengthened the ties between Senghor and France. Since Senegal has become independent, Senghor remains closely bound to the West by religion, a non-ideological socialism and a new technicity.

Senghor justifies his non-programatic approach to socialism on the basis of worldwide developments. The historical ability of capitalism to become self-policing and reformatory has outmoded nationalization of the means of production, the doctrine of the class struggle and the moral condemnation of profit, as ideological contentions. Not insisting on the *"passé"* ideological formulations of the nineteenth century, therefore, enables Senghor both to welcome aid from nonsocialistic countries abroad and to tolerate business, traditional and religious elements that

have in the past been the foremost opponents of classical socialism. His categories of analysis and his pragmatic attitude toward
social change place him well within the mainstream of contemporary Western modes of thought. Senghor's technicity involves
the application of the scientific discoveries and organizational
methods developed in the advanced industrial civilization of the
West to the problems of underdevelopment. His deep commitment to Teilhard's perspective of social evolution, in conjunction with his effort to totally reorganize Senegal, also play an
important role in the evolution of Senegal toward increased authoritarianism.

To achieve national unity and development, Senghor has
turned to an *encadrement* of the populations—a total organization and politicalization of the society (even down to sports) so
that the entire community becomes a weapon for some "higher
purpose," such as economic growth. To the extent that control
of the organization of the *encadrement* is crucial in determining
its democratic, socialist or totalitarian character, one can find
little encouragement in the Senegalese situation. Nothing in the
attitudes, values, training or education of the technicians, higher
civil service or army suggests a democratic instinct; by profession,
they are social engineers. The vast gulf between the privileged
and disinherited is filled by, among other things, contempt.[40]

Further, the greatest danger to liberty as it has historically
been known in the West—in the sense of independence of
thought, autonomy and the right of political opposition—comes
not only from the threat of overt political manipulation on the
part of the elite. In the Western tradition, "an individual consciousness and an individual unconscious, *apart from* public
opinion and behavior" have always been highly valued. As Herbert Marcuse suggested, "the idea of 'inner freedom' here has its
reality: it designates the private sphere in which man may become and remain 'himself.' " It is against this inner freedom that
Senghor and Teilhard bring their greatest assault. They encourage the invasion of this private sphere by technological reality.
Senghor acclaims the assimilation of the entire individual to

modern production and allows industrial psychology to emerge from the factory. He seeks—for this is the way to the "Omega point"—the immediate and automatic identification of the individual with his society.

Thus, although Senghor seeks to achieve unity and economic development through humanistic socialism, he, in part, ends with an identity which could construct a social system certainly no less authoritarian than those of the supposedly most radical political regimes. Both in terms of his personal objectives and within the social setting of modern Senegal, his ideology is well suited to his practical politics.

From the beginning of his political and intellectual career, Senghor was committed to an elitist approach. This involved active cooperation first with the established powers in France and then with Senegal's most powerful traditional, religious, commercial and political leaders. As Senegal's administrative, bureaucratic and military structures developed, the technocratic and civil servant elites also entered Senghor's complex political coalitions. Senghor's ideology, which did not recognize the existence of classes or class struggle in Senegal, easily accommodated these new groups with that "community of communities" which was Senghor's way of viewing the organization of the social structure.

Despite Senghor's political ability to compromise, pressures toward authoritarianism have asserted themselves. Senegal shares the realities of underdevelopment confronting all other African states—the acute intensity of the struggle for few material goods; the lack of a variety of articulate, organized, self-sustained interest groups; the demands of awakened expectations; the rise of new classes, such as African business and trade unions, demanding that their aspirations be satisfied, etc. The growth of bureaucratic institutions and the important role accorded to technicians further encourage centralized planning and social engineering.

In the final analysis, however, Senghor's ideology functions not as a block to anti-democratic tendencies, but in their behalf.

It has operated to justify social engineering by technocrats, reliance on the army, de-emphasis of political parties and politics, limited popular political participation, and, finally, an extension of the values of production to the conduct of man's private life. Ultimately, Senghor's doctrines lead to the abandonment of individualism and a loss of egoism. Man can truly find himself only through immersion in a greater union. If in religious terms his higher totality is the "Omega Point," in practical social and political terms it is hardly the type of society envisaged in either democratic liberalism or socialism.

To the extent, however, that Léopold Senghor has not fashioned an ideology suitable to the needs of rapid economic development, there is no cause for rejoicing. His failure again underlines the difficulties of such a task in developing areas, as elsewhere.

NOTES TO CHAPTER VIII

1. Alexis de Tocqueville, *The Old Regime and the French Revolution* (Doubleday & Company, Garden City, 1955), p. 161.
2. Senghor, "The Theory and Practice of Senegalese Socialism," in Cook, *op. cit.*, p. 107.
3. *Ibid.*, pp. 159–160.
4. Senghor, *Planification et Tension Morale, op. cit.*
5. *Ibid.*
6. See, for example, Senghor's statement, "Une Seule Politique Efficace: Celle du Développement," Conseil National, July 12, 1964 (mimeo, N.P.).
7. Senghor, "Préparation du Second Plan Quadriennal ou Pour une Attitude d'Accueil," *op. cit.*
8. *Ibid.*
9. *Ibid.*
10. *Ibid.*
11. "Une Seule Politique Efficace: Celle du Développement," *op. cit.*
12. Senghor, "Message au Peuple Sénégalais," December 31, 1962, *op. cit.*
13. Senghor, "Message au Peuple Sénégalais à l'Occasion de la Célébration du Troisième Anniversaire de l'Indépendance," April 3, 1963, *op. cit.* For an account of what happened to some of the military leaders of the *coup*, see Nara Belly, "Coup Manqué à Dakar," *Jeune Afrique*, No. 161 (December 9–15, 1963).
14. "Message . . . ," April 3, 1963, *op. cit.*
15. *Ibid.*
16. "Discours à l'Assemblée Nationale," *op. cit.*, p. 30.
17. Quoted in *Dakar-Matin*, April 5, 1965. Secretary of Defense Robert McNamara, in an address before the American Society of Newspaper Publishers,

elaborated on precisely this type of military effort for development purposes when he said:

The second—and perhaps less understood category of military assistance in a modernizing nation—is training in civil action.
"Civil Action" is another one of those semantic puzzles. Too few Americans—and too few officials in developing nations—really comprehend what military civic action means.
Essentially, it means using indigenous military forces for non-traditional military projects—projects that are useful to the local population in fields such as education, public works, health, sanitation, agriculture—indeed, anything connected with economic or social progress.
It has had some impressive results. In the past four years, the United States assisted civil action program, worldwide, has constructed or repaired more than 10,000 miles of roads; built over 1,000 schools, hundreds of hospitals and clinics; and has provided medical and dental care to approximately four million people.
What is important is that all this was done by indigenous men in uniform. Quite apart from the development projects themselves, the program powerfully alters the negative image of the military man, as the oppressive preserver of the stagnant status quo. [*The New York Times*, May 19, 1966]

18. Senghor, *L'Unité Africaine*, April 7, 1966.
19. For the most complete single exposition of Teilhard by Senghor, see Senghor's *Pierre Teilhard de Chardin et la Politique Africaine, op. cit.* Particularly interesting is Senghor's discussion of the "Concept of Complexity" as organized heterogeneity (pp. 37 ff). Pierre Teilhard de Chardin's most important works published in English are: *The Divine Milieu* (Harper and Row, New York, 1960), originally published in French as *Le Milieu Divine* (Editions du Seuil, Paris, 1957); and *The Phenomenon of Man* (Harper and Row, New York, 1961), originally published in French as *Le Phénomène Humain* (Editions du Seuil, Paris, 1955).
20. Senghor, *Pierre Teilhard de Chardin et la Politique Africaine, op. cit.*
21. See Chapter V above.
22. Senghor, *Pierre Teilhard de Chardin et la Politique Africaine, op. cit.*, p. 62.
23. *Ibid.*
24. Mongo Beti, *Mission Accomplished* (The Macmillan Company, New York, 1958), originally published under the title *Mission Terminée* (Editions Correa, Paris, 1956); Peter Abrahams, *Mine Boy* (Faber and Faber, London, 1954).
25. *L'Unité Africaine*, May 6, 1965.
26. Quoted by Teilhard in *The Divine Milieu, op. cit.*, pp. 20–21.
27. Senghor, "Les Investisseurs Peuvent Continuer de Nous Faire Confiance," *op. cit.*
28. The rejection of Marx's atheism has been pointed out as a universal characteristic of African socialism. Yet in discussing the importance and significance of religion to Senghor, it is interesting to note that Sekou Touré, whom Hodgkin calls a "muslim pragmatist," handles the problem of Marx's atheism entirely differently. Stating that in Guinea nobody—no African man or woman—will be found who does not believe in God, Touré says that while dialectical materialism "involves a possibility of an interpretation of social or economic facts which could lead, for example, to the negation of the existence of God," this philosophy "doesn't interest us. We have need of the concrete. . . ." Touré wants to learn from Marxism about "principles of organization, democracy, control, etc." All this is concrete and concerns the organic

life of the existing movement. Rather than refute Marx's atheism, Touré chooses to ignore it. Sekou Touré, "Texte des Interviews," p. 108, quoted in Thomas Hodgkin, "A Note on the Language of African Nationalism," *op. cit.*, p. 38.

29. Senghor, *Pierre Teilhard de Chardin et la Politique Africaine, op. cit.*
   Senghor wrote in his poem, *In Memoriam,* of his ancestors:

   O Dead who have always refused to die, who have resisted death
   From the Sine to the Seine, and in my fragile veins you my unyielding
   blood
   Guard my dreams as you have guarded your sons, your slender-limbed
   wanderers.
   Chants d'Ombre, in Reed and Wake, eds., Senghor:
Prose and Poetry, op. cit., p. 103.

   While religiously anathema to a believing Catholic, the idea of eternal togetherness, of a perpetual continuity that envisaged no sharp distinction between the living and the dead, which characterized traditional African religion, was one of tremendous emotional appeal to Senghor.
   Senghor, through Chardin and Catholicism, in a way attempts a resuscitation of or a new synthesis with these African ideals in this finding of a life after death through religion as well as through the re-creation of an individual-less community.
   In the final analysis, however, Senghor accepts the higher synthesis of Teilhard, the merging of all cultures in the "Civilization of the Universal" and of all individuals in the "Omega Point." See below.

30. Senghor, *Pierre Teilhard de Chardin et la Politique Africaine, op. cit.*
31. Senghor, "Prayer to Masks," *Chants d'Ombre,* in Reed and Wake, *op. cit.*, p. 107.
32. Senghor, "Rapport sur la Doctrine et la Politique Générale," *op. cit.*, p. 19.
33. *Ibid.*, p. 9.
34. Senghor, "The Theory and Practice of Senegalese Socialism," in Cook, *op. cit.*, p. 137.
35. Teilhard de Chardin, *The Phenomenon of Man, op. cit.*, p. 257.
36. Senghor, "The Theory and Practice of Senegalese Socialism," in Cook, *op. cit.*, p. 147.
37. See Teilhard de Chardin, *The Divine Milieu, op. cit.*, p. 262.
38. Quoted in J. Bronowski, "Where Do We Go from Here?" *The New York Review of Books,* Vol. IV, No. 2 (February 25, 1965), p. 11.
39. *Ibid.*, p. 12.
40. Totalitarianism is a political form capable of fullest realization only in industrialized societies. The intrusion of the state into all aspects of the individual's life on a full-time systematic basis requires a complex technology and is enormously expensive. No black African country today is capable of any repression much beyond that of classical authoritarianism. Yet there is little doubt that the foundations are now being laid for regimes of potentially the greatest severity. Senegal, with all of its trained technicians, elitist planning, societal reorganization and IBM machines, is in the forefront of this process. The latest and best innovations of modern science and technology will be used—for prestige as well as because of efficiency. Already, for example, IBM computing systems and electronic calculators are used to determine payrolls and employed for other tasks in countries that still do not have significant numbers of trained accountants. In terms of record-keeping that is a concommitant of modern bureaucracy, there are at least three agencies in Senegal that are going to attempt to keep individual files catalogued on every peasant, listing biographical data as well as information on increased productivity.

Bibliography

I. General Works

Abraham, W. E., *The Mind of Africa*. University of Chicago Press, Chicago, 1962.

Abrahams, Peter, *Mine Boy*. Faber & Faber, London, 1954.

Administration et Diplomatie d'Afrique Noire. Europe-Outremer Ediafric, Paris, 1963.

Africa from the Point of View of American Negro Scholars, Alioune Diop, preface, John A. Davis, introduction. Présence Africaine, Paris, N.D.

"African Socialism," special issue of *African Forum*, New York, Vol. I, No. 3 (Winter 1966).

"L'Afrique Se Développe-t-elle," *La Table Ronde*, Paris, No. 231 (April 1967).

Alford, Robert R., *Party and Society: The Anglo-American Democracies*. Rand McNally & Company, Chicago, 1963.

American Society of African Culture, ed., *Pan-Africanism Reconsidered*. University of California Press, Berkeley, 1962.

Ames, David, "Wolof Cooperative Work Groups," pp. 224–237 in W. R. Bascom and M. J. Herskovits, ed., *Continuity and Change in African Cultures*. University of Chicago Press, Chicago, 1959.

Amin, Samir, *Le Développement du Capitalisme en Côte d'Ivoire*. Les Editions de Minuit, Paris, 1967.

Andrian, Charles, "Patterns of African Socialist Thought," *Africa Forum*, Winter 1966.

Angrand, Armand-Pierre, *Manuel Français-Ouolof*. La Maison du Livre, Dakar, 1963.

Annuaire Ministériel et Parlementaire de l'AOF. Paris-Dakar Presse, Dakar, 1958.

Annuaire Parlementaire des Etats d'Afrique Noire: Députés et Conseilleurs Economiques des Républiques d'Expression Française. Annuaire Afrique 1962, Paris, 1962.

Annuaire Politique du Sénégal. Paris-Dakar Press, Dakar, 1957.

Apter, David E., "Some Reflections on the Role of a Political Opposition in New Nations," *Comparative Studies in Society and History*, Vol. IV, No. 2 (January 1962).

———, ed., *Ideology and Discontent*. The Free Press of Glencoe, New York, 1964.

———, *The Politics of Modernization*. University of Chicago Press, Chicago, 1965.

Archaïsme et Modernisme dans l'Islam Contemporain. Cahiers de l'Institut de Science Economique Appliquée, Paris, 1961.

"L'Armée Sénégalaise, au Service de l'Economie Nationale," *Dakar-Matin*, Dakar, May 7, 1965.

Arnault, Jacques, *Du Colonialisme au Socialisme*. Editions Sociales, Paris, 1966.

Asende, Afana, "Les Classes Sociales en Afrique Occidentale," *Partisans*, May-June 1963.

Association Française de Science Politique, *L'Evolution Politique de L'Afrique Noire*. Table Ronde, 2 vols., mimeo, Paris, March 1959.

Austruy, Jacques, *L'Islam Face au Développement Economique*, Economie et Humanisme. Les Editions Ouvrières, Paris, 1961.

Badian, Seydou, *Les Dirigeants Africains Face à Leur Peuple*. François Maspero, Paris, 1965.

Balandier, Georges, *Sociologie Actuelle de l'Afrique Noire*. Presses Universitaires de France, Paris, 1955.

———, *Sociologie des Brazzavilles Noires*, Cahiers de la Fondation Nationale des Sciences Politiques. Librairie Armand Colin, Paris, 1955.

———, *Ambiguous Africa: Cultures in Collision*. Pantheon Books, New York, 1966. Originally published as *Afrique Ambigue*. Librairie Plon, Paris, 1957.

———, "Les Myths Politiques de Colonisation et de Décolonisation en Afrique," *Cahier International de Sociologie*, Paris, Vol. XXXIII, July-December 1962, pp. 85–96.

———, "De la Négritude au Socialisme," *Jeune Afrique*, Tunis, No. 111 (December 3–9, 1962).

———, "Senghor et la Négritude," *Dakar-Matin*, Dakar, January 19, 1965.

Barale, Jean, *Les Etudiants Aixois et la Politique*. Mémoire pour le Diplôme d'Etudes Supérieures des Sciences Politiques, Aix-en-Provence, 1957.

Baran, Paul, *The Political Economy of Growth*. Monthly Review Press, New York, 1957.

Barbé, Raymond, *Les Classes Sociales en Afrique Noire*. Economie et Politique, Paris, 1964.

Bastide, R., "Les Etudiants Africains en France," *Bulletin Interna-*

tional des Sciences Sociales, Paris, Vol. VIII, No. 3 (1956), pp. 496–499.

Battestini, Monique and Simon, eds., *Littérature Africaine 3, L. S. Senghor, Poète Sénégalais*. Fernand Nathan, Paris, 1964.

Behrman, Lucy C., *Ahmadou Bamba*. Paper delivered to African Studies Association, Bloomington, Indiana, 1966, mimeo.

Beier, Ulli, "The Theme of the Ancestors in Senghor's Poetry," *Black Orpheus*, No. 5 (May 1959).

Belly, Nara, "Coup Manqué à Dakar," *Jeune Afrique*, December 9–15, 1963.

Bendix, Reinhard, *Social Science and the Distrust of Reason*. University of California Press, Berkeley, 1951.

Benson, Joseph, and Bernard Rosenberg, *Mass, Class, and Bureaucracy*. Prentice-Hall, Englewood Cliffs, N.J., 1963.

Berg, Elliot, "French West Africa," in Walter Galenson, ed., *Labor and Economic Development*. John Wiley and Sons, New York, 1959.

——, "The Economic Basis of Political Choice in French West Africa," *American Political Science Review*, June 1960.

——, "Socialism and Economic Development in Tropical Africa," *Quarterly Journal of Economics*, Vol. LXVII, No. 4 (November 1964).

——, "The Development of a Labor Force in Sub-Saharan Africa," *Economic Development and Cultural Change*, Vol. XIII, July 1965, pp. 394–412.

Berge, J. L., *Le Sénégal*. Centre de Hautes Etudes Administratives sur l'Afrique et l'Asie Modernes, Paris, November 1962, mimeo.

Beti, Mongo, *Mission Accomplished*. The Macmillan Company, New York, 1958. Originally published as *Mission Terminée*. Editions Correa, Paris, 1956.

Biarnes, Pierre, "Les Charges de la Fonction Publique Pèsent Lourdement sur les Finances du Sénégal," *Le Monde*, Paris, January 5, 1965.

Binder, Leonard, "National Integration and Political Development," *American Political Science Review*, Vol. LVIII, No. 3 (September 1964), pp. 622–632.

Blanchet, André, *L'Itinéraire des Partis Politiques Depuis Bamako*. Librairie Plon, Paris, 1958.

——, "C'est le Vieux Sénégal qui Répondait Oui le 28 Septembre," *Le Monde*, September 15, 1958.

Bohannan, Paul J., ed., *Markets in Africa*. Doubleday & Company, Garden City, N.Y., 1966.

Bonnafé, Pierre, *Nationalismes Africains*. Fondation Nationale des Sciences Politiques, Série D.: Textes et Documents, Paris, 1962, mimeo.

Bourlon, Abel, *Note brève sur l'Organisation Municipale du Sénégal*, CHEAM, Paris, January 1959, mimeo.

——, "Des S.I.P. aux S.M.D.R., l'Effort de l'Administration en Faveur du Développement des Milieux Ruraux en Afrique Noire." CHEAM, January 1959, mimeo.

——, "Actualité des Mourides et du Mourides," *L'Afrique et l'Asie*, first quarter, 1959, pp. 10–30.

Boutillier, J.-L., *et al.*, *La Moyenne Vallée du Sénégal: Etude Socio-Economique*. Presses Universitaires de France, Paris, 1962.

Brigaud, Félix, *Histoire du Sénégal des Origines aux Traités de Protectorat*. Editions Clairafrique, Dakar, 1964.

Brockway, Fenner, *African Socialism: A Background Book*. The Bodley Head, London, 1963.

Bronowski, J., "Where Do We Go from Here?" *The New York Review of Books*, Vol. IV, No. 2 (Febuary 25, 1965).

Carney, David, *The Machinery of Planning: Political, Administrative and Financial Aspects*. Prepared for the University of East Africa, Conference on Public Policy, Kampala, September 1963, mimeo.

Chabas, Jean, "Le Droit des Successions chez les Ouolofs," *Annales Africaines*, Dakar, November 1956, pp. 75–119.

——, *La Propriété Foncière en Afrique Noire*. Librairie Technique, Paris, 1957.

Chaffard, Georges, "L'Armée s'est Adaptée en Afrique Noire à l'Evolution de la Communauté," *Le Monde*, October 23 and 22, 1959.

——, "Aspects du Socialisme Malien," *Le Monde*, December 10, 1964.

Chailly, M., *et al.*, *Notes et Etudes sur l'Islam en Afrique Noire*, CHEAM. J. Peyronnet et Cie, Paris, 1962.

Charbonneau, Jean and René, *Marchés et Marchands d'Afrique Noire*. La Colombe, Paris, 1961.

Charpy, Jacques, *La Fondation de Dakar 1845–1857–1861*. Emile Larose, Paris, 1958.

Checchi & Compagnie, *Projet d'Une Société Sénégalaise d'Investissement*. Prepared for the Governments of Senegal and the United States. Washington, D.C., August 1962.

Chronologie Politique Africaine. Centre d'Etudes des Relations Internationales, Fondation Nationale des Sciences Politiques, Paris, July-August, 1963.

Coffi-Nkamba, Justinien, "Anciens et Nouveaux Blancs d'Afrique," *Jeune Afrique*, November 1964.

Coifman, Victoria Bomba, "Wolof Political and Social Organization Until the Nineteenth Century," unpublished paper presented to the African Studies Association meeting, Philadelphia, 1965.

Coleman, James, and Carl Rosberg, Jr., eds., *Political Parties and National Integration in Tropical Africa*. University of California Press, Berkeley and Los Angeles, 1964.

Colin, Roland, *Les Contes Noirs de l'Ouest Africain*. Présence Africaine, Paris, 1957.

Colloque sur les Conditions de Vie de l'Infant Africain en Milieu Urbain, Dakar, 15–22 December 1964, sponsored by Centre International de l'Enfance, Paris, and Institut de Pédiatrie Sociale, Dakar. Dakar, December 18, 1964, mimeo.

Colonial Students in Britain. Political and Economic Planning, London, 1955.

Compagnie Française de l'Afrique Occidentale, "Notre Politique Commerciale—Les Buts—Les Objectifs." Dakar, November 1959, mimeo.

Comte, Gilbert, "Le Dialogue à l'Escale," *Jeune Afrique*, July 15–21, 1963.

——, "Ni Dieu, Ni Parti Unique," *Jeune Afrique*, July 22–28, 1963.

Conover, Helen F., *Official Publications of French West Africa 1946–1958: A Guide*. Library of Congress, Washington, D.C., 1960.

Cook, Mercer, "The Last Laugh," in *Africa as Seen by American Negroes*, pp. 199–203. Présence Africaine, Paris, N.D.

——: "Léopold Senghor," *Forum-Service: Background Features, Information and Analysis*, London, November 3, 1959.

Correa, Edou, "La Brigande d'Intervention de l'Ecole Nationale de Police Remplit Admirablement son Rôle," *Dakar-Matin*, January 20, 1965.

——, "L'Action Contre le Chômage de l'Office de la Main-d'Oeuvre," *Dakar-Matin*, February 23, 1965.

Courreau, Lt. *Caractères Anciens et Actuels du Maraboutisme Dans le Fouta Toro*. Mémoire d'éntrée au stage 1952, CHEAM, Paris, mimeo, 1952.

Cowan, L. Gray, *Local Government in West Africa*. Columbia University Press, New York, 1958.

Cros, Charles, *La Parole est à M. Blaise Diagne: Premier Homme d'Etat Africain*. Privately printed, Paris, 1961.

Crowder, Michael, *Senegal: A Study in French Assimilation Policy.* Oxford University Press, New York, 1962.

Crozier, Brian, "Six Africans in Search of a Personality," *Encounter,* May 1961.

"Dans Cinq Ans la SICAP Logera 100,000 Dakarois," *L'Unité Africaine,* August 20, 1964.

Dartique, Maurice, *The Planned Development of Education.* United Nations and Planning, African Institute for Economic Development, E/CN.14/CAP.6, November 1964, Dakar, 1964.

Data in Comparative Research, International Social Service Journal, UNESCO, Vol. XVI, No. 1, 1964.

Decraene, Philippe, *Tableau des Partis Politiques de l'Afrique au Sud du Sahara.* Fondation Nationale des Sciences Politiques, Paris, 1963.

——, "Les Etudiants Africains en France," *Le Monde,* July 2, 1964.

——, "Le Sénégal sur la Voie de la Rigueur," *Le Monde,* July 28, 29, 30, 1964.

Delavignette, Robert, *Freedom and Authority in French West Africa.* Oxford University Press, London, 1950.

Delavignette, Robert, and Ch. André Julien, eds., *Les Constructeurs de la France d'Outre-Mer.* Editions Correa, Paris, 1946.

Delcourt, André, *La France et les Etablissements Français au Sénégal entre 1713 et 1763,* Mémoires IFAN, Dakar, 1952.

Deschamps, Hubert, *Le Sénégal et al Gambie.* Que Sais-Je, Presses Universitaires de France, Paris, 1964.

Descloities, R., and J. C. Reverdy, *Le Développement Rural en Milieu Serer: Approche Générale des Structures Sociales et du Regime Foncier.* Centre Africain des Sciences Humaines, Aix-en-Provence, 1964, mimeo.

De Tocqueville, Alexis, *Democracy in America,* Vols. I & II. Vintage Books, New York, 1954.

——, *The Old Regime and the French Revolution.* Doubleday & Company, Garden City, N.Y., 1955.

Deutsch, Karl W., and William J. Foltz, eds., *Nation-Building.* Prentice-Hall, Atherton Press, New York, 1963.

Développement Economique et Evolution Juridique, special issue, *Annales Africaines,* Vol. I, Dakar, 1962.

Développement et Civilisation, special issue, *Sénégal "An 2" par Lui-Même,* Paris, 1962.

Djilas, Milovan, *The New Class: An Analysis of the Communist System.* Frederick A. Praeger, New York, 1957.

Dolci, Danilo, *A New World in the Making*. Monthly Review Press, New York, 1965.

Domenach, Jean-Marie, and Paul Thibaud, "Réponse à Deux Ministres," *Esprit*, Paris, January 1964.

Doublier, R., "La Propriété Foncière en AOF," Imprimerie du Gouvernement Sénégalais, Rufisque, 1957.

Drachkovitch, Milorad M., ed., *Marxism in the Modern World*. Hoover Institute Publication, Stanford University Press, Stanford, Calif., 1965.

Draper, Theodore, *Castro's Revolution: Myths and Realities*. Frederick A. Praeger, New York, 1962.

Drouet, Pierre, "L'Immatriculation Foncière en AOF Depuis le Décret du 20 Mai 1955," *Annales Africaines*, Dakar, 1958, pp. 207–217.

Dresch, J., "Villes d'Afrique Occidentale," *Les Cahiers d'Outre-Mer*, July-September 1950, pp. 201–230.

DuBois, Victor D., "Guinea Educates a New Generation," *Africa Report*, July 1961.

——, *Mali and Senegal and the Dakar-Niger Railroad*. American Universities Field Staff Reports Service, New York, June 1963.

——, *The Trial of Mamadou Dia*. American Universities Field Staff Reports Service, New York, 1963.

Duchenium, G. J., "La République Lebou et le Peuplement Actuel," in *La Presqu'ile du Cap Vert, Etudes Sénégalaises*, November 1, 1949.

Dumont, René, *L'Afrique Noire est Mal Partie*. Editions du Seuil, Paris, 1962.

——, *Choice and Classification of the Basic Aims of Agricultural Development in Africa*, IDEP Paper/ECA-MA/OUS/64, IDEP/ET/XXX1/188, Dakar, 1964, mimeo.

Dunayevskaya, Raya, "Marxist-Humanism," *Présence Africaine*, English ed., 4th quarter, 1963.

Duverger, Maurice, *The French Political System*. University of Chicago Press, Chicago, 1958.

Epstein, A. L., *Politics in an Urban African Community*. University of Manchester Press, Manchester, 1958.

Esperet, S., "Le Syndicalisme en AOF," *Droit Social*, Paris, March 1958.

"Les Etudiants Africains en France," *Connaissance de l'Afrique*, Paris, Nos. 6 and 7, November-December 1963 and January-February, 1964.

Les Etudiants Noirs Parlent. Présence Africaine, Paris, 1953.

Les "Etudiants d'Outre-Mer en France," special issue, *Sondages*, No. 3, 1961.

Fanon, Frantz, *Peau Noire, Masques Blancs.* Editions du Seuil, Paris, 1952.

——, *The Damned.* Présence Africaine, Paris, 1963. Originally published as *Les Damnés de la Terre.* Editions François Maspero, Paris, 1961.

FAO Africa Survey: *Report on the Possibilities of African Rural Developments in Relation to Economic and Social Growth.* Food and Agriculture Organization of the United Nations, Rome, 1962.

Ferkiss, Victor C., *Africa's Search for Identity.* George Braziller, New York, 1966.

Foltz, William J., "Senegal," in James S. Coleman and Carl Rosberg, Jr., eds., *Political Parties and National Integration in Tropical Africa*, pp. 16–64. University of California Press, Berkeley and Los Angeles, 1964.

——, *From French West Africa to the Mali Federation.* Yale University Press, New Haven, 1965.

Fouda, B. J., H. Julliot, and R. Lagrave, *Littérature Camerounaise.* Club du Livre Camerounais, Cannes, 1961.

Fougeyrollas, Pierre, "La Pensée de Marx et l'Avenir de l'Afrique," *Présence Africaine*, No. 63, third quarter 1967, pp. 68–87.

——, *Modernisation des Hommes, l'Exemple du Sénégal.* Flammarion, Paris, 1967.

Fouquet, Joseph, *La Traité des Arachides dans le Pays de Kaolack, et Ses Conséquences Economiques, Sociales et Juridiques*, IFAN, Saint-Louis, 1958.

Friendly, Alfred, Jr., "Resentment Against Senegal's Regime Rises as Economic Woes Increase," *The New York Times*, June 11, 1968.

——, "Senegal's Leader Shuffles Cabinet," *The New York Times*, June 17, 1968.

Furniss, Edgar S., *France: Troubled Ally.* Frederick A. Praeger, New York, 1960.

Fusi, A., "Les Orientations Possibles du Développement du Sénégal," *Industrie et Travaux d'Outre-Mer*, Paris, June 1960.

Gamble, David P., *The Wolof of Senegambia.* International African Institute, Oxford University Press, London, 1957.

Garnier, Christine, *Sénégal Porte de l'Afrique.* Librairie Hachette, Paris, 1962.

Gazier, François, and Lucile Decouflé, *Les Ecoles et Instituts de*

Formation de Fonctionnaires dans les Pays en Voie de Développement. Presses Universitaires de France, Paris, 1963.

Geiger, Theodore, and Winifred Armstrong, *The Development of African Private Enterprise.* National Planning Association, Washington, D.C., 1962.

Gerard, Albert S. "The Neo-African Novel," *Africa Report*, Vol. IX, No. 7 (July 1964).

Gershoy, Leo, *The French Revolution 1789–1799.* Henry Holt & Company, New York, 1932.

Godfrey, Drexel E., *The Fate of the Non-Communist Left.* Doubleday & Company, New York, 1955.

——, *The Government of France.* Thomas Y. Crowell, New York, 1961.

Goldschmidt, W., *The United States and Africa.* The American Assembly, New York, 1958.

Good, Robert C., "Changing Patterns of African International Relations," *American Political Science Review*, Vol. LVII, No. 3 (September 1964), pp. 60–61.

Gorer, Geoffrey, *Africa Dances: A Book About West African Negroes.* W. W. Norton & Company, New York, 1962.

Goussault, Yves, "Participation Paysanne au Développement et aux Structures Nouvelles," *Présence Africaine*, 4th quarter, 1962, pp. 183–189.

Gouvernements et Cabinets, Ministères, Partis Politiques, Annuaire des Etats d'Afrique Noire, 2nd ed. Ediafric, Paris, N.D. (1963).

Gravrand, Henri, "Les Serères (Etude)," *Horizons Africaines*, Nos. 65–68 (1953), pp. 4–8, 15–16, 1–16.

——, "Rites d'Initiation et Vie en Société chez les Serers du Sénégal," *Afrique Documents*, No. 52, 1960, pp. 129–144.

——, *Visage Africaine de l'Englaise.* Orante, Paris, 1961.

Gregor, A. James, *Contemporary Radical Ideologies: Totalitarian Thought in the Twentieth Century.* Random House, New York, 1968.

Gruber, Ruth, ed., *Science and the New Nations.* Basic Books, New York, 1961.

Grundy, Kenneth, "The Class Struggle in Africa," *Journal of Modern African Studies*, Vol. II, No. 7 (November 1964), pp. 379–93.

Guernier, Eugène, *L'Apport de l'Afrique à la Pensée Humaine.* Payot, Paris, 1952.

Guibert, Armand, "Léopold Sédar Senghor," *Encounter*, February 1961.

——, *Léopold Sédar Senghor, L'Homme et l'Oeuvre.* Présence Africaine, Paris, 1962.

Gutteridge, William, *Armed Forces in New States.* Oxford University Press, London, 1962.

"L'Habitat Rural: Premier Pas vers l'Amélioration des Conditions de Vie du Paysannat," *L'Unité Africaine,* August 20, 1964.

"L'Habitat Urbain et le Crédit Immobilier," *L'Unité Africaine,* August 20, 1964.

Hamon, Léo, "La Voie Africaine du Socialisme," *Connaissance de l'Afrique,* Paris, No. 5, July-August 1963.

Hapgood, David, *Africa: From Independence to Tomorrow.* Atheneum, New York, 1965.

Hardy, Georges, *La Mise en Valeur du Sénégal de 1817 à 1854.* Emile Larose, Paris, 1921.

Hargreaves, J. D., "Assimilation in Eighteenth Century Senegal," *Journal of African History,* Vol. VI, No. 2 (1965), pp. 177–84.

Hauser, Arnold, *The Social History of Art, Vol. IV: Nationalism, Impressionism, the Film Age.* Vintage Books, New York, 1958.

Hauser, A., "L'Absentéisme et la Mobilité des Travailleurs des Industries Manufacturières de la Region de Dakar," IFAN, Dakar, 1960, mimeo.

——, "Quelques Données Factuelles et Attitudinales sur un Groupe de Travailleurs en Milieu Urban," in *Urbanization in African Social Change.* Center of African Studies, University of Edinburgh, Edinburgh, 1963.

——, "Facteurs Humains en Productivité des Travailleurs Industriels du Cap Vert." Mimeo, INSEA, Dakar, May 17, 1963.

——, "L'Emergence de Cadres de Base Africaine dans l'Industrie." Communication Faites au Sixième Séminaire de l'Institut International Africain, Ibadan, July 1964.

Hazard, John N., "Negritude, Socialism and the Law," *Columbia Law Review,* Vol. 65, May 1965.

Herskovits, Melville J., and Mitchell Harwitz, eds., *Economic Transition in Africa.* Northwestern University Press, Evanston, 1964.

Hill, Polly, *The Migrant Cocoa Farmers of Southern Ghana: A Study in Rural Capitalism.* Cambridge University Press, Cambridge, 1963.

——, "Markets in Africa," *The Journal of Modern African Studies,* Vol. I, No. 4 (December 1963).

Hodgkin, Thomas, *African Political Parties.* Penguin Books, Baltimore, 1962.

Hodgkin, Thomas, *Nationalism in Colonial Africa*. New York University Press, New York, 1956.

——, "Background to Afrique Occidentale Française: African Reaction and French Rule," *West Africa*, January 16, 1954, p. 313.

——, "Background to AOF," nine articles in *West Africa*, January 2–March 6, 1954.

——, "A Note on the Language of African Nationalism," in *African Affairs: Number One* (St. Antony's Papers No. 10), ed. by Kenneth Kirkwood. Southern Illinois University Press, Carbondale, Ill., 1961.

——, "The Idea of an African University," *Universities Quarterly*, August 1958, pp. 376–84.

Hodgkin, Thomas, and Ruth Schachter, *French-Speaking West Africa in Transition. International Conciliation*, May 1960.

Holt, Robert T., and John E. Turner, *The Political Basis of Economic Development: An Exploration in Comparative Political Analysis*. D. Van Nostrand Company, Princeton, N.J., 1966.

Hoselitz, Bert, ed., *The Progress of Underdeveloped Areas*. Chicago University Press, Chicago, 1952.

Hoselitz, Bert F., and Wilbert E. Moore, eds., *Industrialization and Society*. UNESCO-Mouton, Paris, 1963.

Houis, Maurice, "Préalables à un Humanisme Nègre," *Esprit*, November 1958.

Hughes, H. Stuart, *Consciousness and Society*. Alfred A. Knopf, New York, 1958.

Hymans, Jacques-Louis, "French Influence on Leopold Senghor's Theory of Negritude: 1928–1948," *Race*, April 1966.

Ilboudo, Gilbert, "L'Afrique Noire d'Expression Française à Rendez-vous Littéraire," *Afrique Nouvelle*, Dakar, June 7–13, 1963.

Institut de Science Economique Appliquée, *Séminaire sur les Conditions d'un Dialogue Entre les Différents Echelons du Plan pour la Détermination des Objectifs et des Moyens d'Exécution*. Dakar, 1964, mimeo.

Institut Français d'Opinion Publique, "Les Etudiants d'Outre-mer en France," *Sondages*, Vol. 3, 1961, pp. 50–79.

——, *Les Moyens d'Information (Presse, Radio, Cinéma) en Afrique Occidentale, Enquête Complémentaire Auprès de la Population Africaine de Dakar*. Paris, 1960, mimeo.

——, *West Africa Media Survey*, 4 Vols. London and Paris, 1960, mimeo.

Institut International de Recherche, et de Formation en Vue du

Développement Harmonisée, *Répertoire Analytique des Organisme Français en Matière de Développement.* Paris, N.D., mimeo.

International Social Science Journal, UNESCO, special issue, "Opinion Surveys in Developing Countries," Vol. XV (1963), No. 1.

Irele, Abiola, "Negritude or Black Cultural Nationalism," *Journal of Modern African Studies,* March 3, 1965, pp. 321–48.

——, "Negritude—Literature and Ideology," *Journal of Modern African Studies,* Vol. III, No. 4 (1965), pp. 499–526.

Jadot, J. M., *Les Ecrivains Africains du Congo Belge et du Ruanda-Urundi.* Bruxelles Académie Royale des Sciences Coloniales, Brussels, 1959.

Jahn, Janheinz, *Muntu: An Outline of the New African Culture.* Grove Press, New York, 1961.

——, "Senghor Without Propellor—An English Translation that Does Not Get Off the Ground," *Black Orpheus,* March 1966.

Joachim, Paulin, "African Literature, Part III, French-Speaking Africa," *Africa Report,* March 1963.

Johnson, Wesley, G., "Senegal: Bibliographical Essay," *Africana Newsletter,* Vol. II, January 25, 1964. The Hoover Institute, Stanford University, Stanford, Calif.

——, "The Ascendency of Blaise Diagne and the Beginning of African Politics in Senegal." *Africa,* Vol. XXXVI, No. 3 (July 1966), pp. 235–252.

Julien, C. A., "From the French Empire to the French Union," *International Affairs,* Vol. XXVI, No. 4 (October 1950).

——, *Les Techniciens de la Colonisation XIX-XX Siècles.* Presses Universitaires de France, Paris, 1947.

Julien, C. A., and Robert Delavignette, *Les Constructeurs de la France d'Outre-Mer.* Editions Correa, Paris, 1946.

July, Robert W., *The Origins of Modern African Thought: Its Development in West Africa During the Nineteenth and Twentieth Centuries.* Frederick A. Praeger, New York, 1967.

Kachama-Nkoy, "De Karl Marx à Pierre Teilhard de Chardin dans le Pensée de L. S. Senghor et de Mamadou Dia," *Civilisations,* Vol. XIII (1963), pp. 98–121.

Kahn, Jean-François, "Socialisme et Islam," three articles, *Le Monde,* January 7, 8, 9, 1965.

Kanouté, l'Abbé P., "A Propos du Socialisme Africain," *Afrique Nouvelle,* No. 844 (October 10–16, 1963).

Kesteloot, Lilyan, *Les Ecrivains Noir de Langue Française: Naissance d'une Littérature.* Université Libre de Bruxelles, Institut de Sociologie, Belgium, 1963.

Kilson, Martin, "African Political Change and the Modernization Process," *The Journal of Modern African Studies*, Vol. 1, No. 4 (December 1963).

Kirkwood, Kenneth, ed., *African Affairs: Number One* (St. Antony's Papers No. 10). Southern Illinois University Press, Carbondale, Ill., 1961.

Kitchen, Helen, ed., *The Educated African: A Country by Country Survey of Educational Development in Africa.* Ruth Sloan Associates, Frederick A. Praeger, New York, 1962.

Klein, Martin A., "The Relevance of African History: A Case Study for Senegal," unpublished paper prepared for delivery at the 1965 meeting of the African Studies Association, Philadelphia, October 1965. Mimeo.

——, *Islam and Imperialism in Senegal: Sine-Saloum, 1847–1914.* Stanford University Press, Stanford, Calif., 1968.

La Palombara, Joseph, "Decline of Ideology: A Dissent and an Interpretation," *American Political Science Review*, Vol. LX, No. 1 (March 1966).

Laponce, J. A., *The Government of the Fifth Republic.* University of California Press, Berkeley and Los Angeles, 1961.

Lavroff, Dmitri-Georges, *La République du Sénégal.* Librairie Générale de Droit et de Jurisprudence, R. Pichon et Durand-Auzias, Paris, 1966.

Le Divilec, Marie-Helene, "Les Nouvelles Classes Sociales en Milieu Urbain: Le Cas du Sénégal et Celui du Nigeria du Nord," *Civilisations*, Vol. XVII, No. 3 (1967), pp. 240–251.

Lefebvre, Georges, *The Coming of the French Revolution.* Vintage Books, New York, 1957.

Legum, Colin, *Pan-Africanism: A Short Political Guide.* Frederick A. Praeger, New York, 1962.

Leites, Nathan, *On the Game of Politics in France.* Stanford University Press, Stanford, Calif., 1959.

Lengyel, Emil, *Dakar, Outpost of Two Hemispheres.* Garden City Publishing Company, Garden City, N.Y., 1943.

Leusse, Hubert de, *Léopold Sédar Senghor: L'Africain.* Hatier, Paris, 1967.

Lewis, W. Arthur, *The Theory of Economic Growth.* Richard D. Irwin, Homewood, Ill., 1955.

——, "Science, Men, and Money" in *Science and the New Nations:* ed. by Ruth Gruber. Basic Books, New York, 1961.

——, *Politics in West Africa.* Oxford University Press, New York, 1966.

Lewis, William H., ed., *French-Speaking Africa: The Search for Identity.* Walker & Company, New York, 1965.

Lipset, S. M., "Some Further Comments on 'The End of Ideology,' " *American Political Science Review,* March 1966.

Lo, Cheikh Bara, "La Société Africaine de Confection," *Sénégal d'Aujourd'hui,* September 1964.

——, "La Compagnie Sénégalaise du Sud-Est," *Sénégal d'Aujourd'hui,* October 1964.

Lombard, L., "Pensée Politique et Démocratique dans l'Afrique Noire Traditionnelle," *Présence Africaine,* No. 63, third quarter 1967, pp. 10–31.

Luethy, Herbert, *France Against Herself.* Meridan Books, New York, 1957.

Mackenzie, W. J. M., and Kenneth E. Robinson, eds., *Five Elections in Africa.* Oxford at the Clarendon Press, London, 1960.

Mâitre, Bernard, "Un Problème Urgent: La Formation des Cadres Moyens," *Afrique Nouvelle,* November 28-December 4, 1963.

"Le Malaise du Commerce Privé au Sénégal," *Africa,* No. 32, 1964.

Malraux, André, "Discours à l'Ouverture du Colloque," *L'Unité Africaine,* Dakar, No. 196 (April 7, 1966).

Mannheim, Karl, *Ideology and Utopia.* Harcourt, Brace & Company, New York, 1954.

——, *Man and Society in an Age of Reconstruction.* Harcourt, Brace & Company, New York, 1949.

——, *Essays on the Sociology of Knowledge.* Oxford University Press, New York, 1952.

——, *Essays on the Sociology of Culture.* Oxford University Press, New York, 1956.

Marcuse, Herbert, *Reason and Revolution,* 2nd ed. The Humanities Press, New York, 1954.

——, *One Dimensional Man: Studies in the Ideology of Advanced Industrial Society.* Beacon Press, Boston, 1964.

Marquet, Jacques, *Africanité: Traditionnelle et Modern.* Présence Africaine, Paris, 1967.

Martin, Laurence W., ed., *Neutralism and Nonalignment: The New States in World Affairs.* Frederick A. Praeger, New York, 1962.

Martin, V., *Etudes Socio-Religieuses.* Fraternité, Saint-Dominique, Dakar, 1964, mimeo.

Mathieu, Gilbert, "Le Bilan de l'Effort Français en Faveur du Tiers Monde," *Le Monde Hebdomadaire,* March 10–16, 1966.

Marvick, Dwaine, ed., *Political Decision Makers*. Free Press of Glencoe, New York, 1961.

Masse, L., "Contribution à l'Etude de la Ville de Thiès," *Bulletin de l'Ifan*, Dakar, Série B XVIII, 1956, pp. 255–280.

Maurice, Albert, "Sénégal Terre d'Humanisme," *Bulletin de l'Académie Royale des Sciences d'Outre-Mer*, Brussels, 1964, pp. 11–27.

Mazuri, Ali, "Borrowed Theory and Original Practice in African Politics," unpublished paper, 1965, mimeo.

Meagher, Robert F., *Public International Development Financing in Senegal*, Report No. 7 of the Columbia University School of Law Project in Public International Development Financing. Columbia University, New York, November 1963.

Meier, Gerald M., and Robert E. Baldwin, *Economic Development: Theory, History, Policy*. John Wiley and Sons, New York, 1957.

Melone, Thomas, "The Theme of Negritude and Its Literary Problems," *Présence Africaine*, English Ed., 4th quarter, 1963.

——, *De la Négritude dans la Littérature Négro-Africaine*. Présence Africaine, Paris, 1962.

Mercier, Paul, and Georges Balandier, *Les Pêcheurs Lebou du Sénégal*. Etudes Sénégalaises, No. 3, IFAN, Saint-Louis, 1952.

Mercier, Paul, L. Masse and A. Hauser, *L'Agglomération Dakaroise*. IFAN, Saint-Louis, 1954.

——, "Aspects des Problèmes de Stratification Sociale dans l'Ouest Africain," *Cahiers Internationaux de Sociologie*, Vol. XVI (1954), pp. 59–65.

——, "Evolution of Senegalese Elites," in *African Elites*, special issue of *International Social Science Journal*, Vol. VIII (1956), No. 3, pp. 441–452.

——, "La Vie Politique dans les Centres Urbains du Sénégal," *Cahiers Internationaux de Sociologie*, Vol. 26, July-December 1959, pp. 55–84.

——, "Etude du Mariage et Enquête Urbaine," *Cahiers d'Etudes Africaines*, Vol. I, January 1960, pp. 28–43.

Mercier, Roger, and M. and S. Battestini, eds., *Littérature Africaine I: Cheikh Hamidou Kane*. Fernand Nathan, Paris, 1964.

Mersadier, Y., *Budgets Familiaux Africains*. IFAN, Saint-Louis, 1957.

Meynaud, Jean, and Anisse Salah-Bey, *Le Syndicalisme Africain*. Payot, Paris, 1963.

Michel, C. "L'Organisation Coutumière (Sociale et Politique) de la Collectivité Leboue de Dakar," *Bulletin du Comité d'Etudes Historiques et Scientifiques de l'AOF*, Vol. XXII, No. 3 (1934).

Milcent, Ernest, *L'AOF Entre en Scène*. Témoignage Chrétien, Paris, 1958.

——, "Senegal" in G. Carter, ed., *African One Party States*. Cornell University Press, Ithaca, N.Y. 1962.

——, *Au Carrefour des Options Africaines: Le Sénégal*. Editions du Centurion, Paris, 1965.

Monteil, Vincent, "Une Confrérie Musulmane: Les Mourides du Sénégal," *Archives de Sociologie des Religions*, Paris, No. 14, July-December 1962, pp. 77–102.

——, "Aperçu Historique," *Session d'Information du Personnel d'Assistance Technique*. Ministère de l'Enseignement Technique et de la Formation des Cadres, République du Sénégal, Dakar, November 1963, mimeo.

——, *L'Islam Noir*. Editions du Seuil, Paris, 1964.

Morel, S. C., *Documentation Administratives et Bibliographiques des Problèmes Propres aux Etudiants des Etats, République d'Afrique Noire de Madagascar et des Territoires d'Outre-Mer Faisant Leurs Etudes en France*. Office des Etudiants d'Outre-Mer, Paris, June 1960, mimeo.

Morgenthau, Ruth Schachter, "Single Party Systems in West Africa," *American Political Science Review*, Vol. 55, June 1961, pp. 294–307.

——, "African Socialism: Declaration of Ideological Independence," *Africa Report*, Vol. VIII, May 1963, pp. 3–6.

——, *Political Parties in French-Speaking West Africa*. Oxford University Press, New York, 1964.

Morlan, Robert L., "Foreign Local Government: A Bibliography," *The American Political Science Review*, Vol. LIX, No. 1 (March 1965), pp. 120–137.

Mphalele, Ezekiel, *The African Image*. Frederick A. Praeger, New York, 1962.

——, "The Fabric of African Cultures," *Foreign Affairs*, July 1964.

N'Daw, Amadou Moustapha, "Paysans, Pasteurs," *L'Unité Africaine*, December 17, 1964.

N'Diaye, J. P., *Enquête sur les Etudiants Noirs en France*. Réalités Africaines, Paris, 1962.

N'Diaye, J. P., J. Bassene, D. Germain, *Les Travailleurs Noirs en France: Pourquoi les Migrations*. Réalités Africaines, Paris, May-June 1963.

Neres, Philip, *French Speaking West Africa*. Oxford University Press, London, 1962.

Newbury, Colin, "The Formation of the Government General of

French West Africa," *Journal of African History*, Vol. I, No. 1 (1960), pp. 111–128.

——, "The Government General and Political Change in French West Africa," in *African Affairs: Number One* (St. Antony's Papers No. 10), ed. by Kenneth Kirkwood. Southern Illinois University Press, Carbondale, Ill., 1961.

Nicol, Davidson, "West African Poetry," *African South in Exile*, London, April-June 1961, pp. 115–122.

Nkosi, Lewis, "Some Conversations with African Writers," *Africa Report*, Vol. IX, No. 7 (July 1964).

Nkrumah, Kwame, "African Socialism Revisited," *African Forum*, Winter 1966.

Organski, A. F. K., *The Stages of Political Development*. Alfred A. Knopf, New York, 1965.

Pageard, Robert, *Littérature Négro-Africaine*. Le Livre Africain, Paris, 1966.

Paulme, Denise, "Régimes Fonciers Traditionnels en Afrique Noire," *Présence Africaine*, Vol. XLVIII, No. 4 (1963), pp. 109–132.

Peterson, Wallace C., *The Welfare State in France*. University of Nebraska Press, Lincoln, 1960.

Pickles, Dorothy, *The Fifth French Republic*, rev. ed. Frederick A. Praeger, New York, 1962.

Poirieur, J., Directeur, *L'Islam, l'Economie et la Technique*. Cahiers de l'Institut de Science Economique Appliquée: Humanities, No. 106, Paris, October 1960.

——, *Archaïsme et Modernisme dans l'Islam Contemporain*. Cahiers de l'Institut de Science Economique Appliquée: Humanities, Supplement No. 120, Paris, December 1961.

Poquin, Jean-Jacques, *Les Rélations Economiques Extérieures des Pays d'Afrique Noire de l'Union Française 1925–1955*. Colin, Paris, 1957.

"Prochaine Campagne de Recrutement au Titre de l'Armée Nationale, *Dakar-Matin*, May 21, 1965.

Quesnot, Fernand, *L'Evolution du Tidjanisme Sénégalais Depuis 1922*. Mimeo, Mémoire d'Entrée, CHEAM, Paris, 1958.

——, *Influence du Mouridisme sur le Tidjanisme*, mimeo, exposé CHEAM, Paris, January 1959, pp. 115–125 in M. Chailley *et al.*, *Notes et Etudes sur l'Islam en Afrique Noire*, CHEAM, Paris, 1962.

——, *Panorama de l'Islam au Sénégal*. Mimeo, exposé CHEAM, Paris, December 1958.

Reboux, Michel, "Au Sénégal: Des Emeutes Organisées," *France Eurafrique,* January 1964, pp. 18–20.

Redding, Saunders, "Home to Africa," *The American Scholar,* Spring 1963.

Reed, John, and Clive Wake, *Senghor: Prose and Poetry.* Oxford University Press, London, 1965.

——, translation and introduction to *Selected Poems* by Léopold Sédar Senghor. Atheneum, New York, 1966. Originally published by Oxford University Press, London, 1964.

"Remise au Sénégal d'un Important Stock de Matériels Militaires Cédés par la France," *Dakar-Matin,* March 26, 1965.

"La Répression des Détournements au Préjudice de l'Etat," *Dakar-Matin,* June 23, 1965.

Revue Française de Science Politique, special issue, *La Vie Politique en Afrique Noire,* Paris, Vol. IX, No. 3 (September 1959).

Robinson, Kenneth, "Constitutional Reform in French Tropical Africa," *Political Studies,* Vol. 6, 1950, pp. 45–69.

——, "Political Development in French West Africa," in Calvin Stillman, ed., *Africa in the Modern World.* University of Chicago Press, Chicago, 1955, pp. 140–181.

——, "Senegal: The Elections to the Territorial Assembly, March 1957," in *Five Elections in Africa,* ed. by W. J. M. Mackenzie and Kenneth Robinson. Oxford University Press, London, 1960.

Rosberg, Carl G., Jr., and William H. Friedland, eds., *African Socialism.* Hoover Institute Publications, Stanford University Press, Stanford, Calif., 1964.

Rose, Saul, *Socialism in Southern Asia.* Oxford University Press, New York, 1959.

Rostow, W. W., *The Stages of Economic Growth: A Non-Communist Manifesto.* Cambridge University Press, New York, 1961.

Rous, Jean, *Léopold Sédar Senghor: Un Président de l'Afrique Nouvelle.* Editions John Didier, Paris, 1967.

Safran, Nadav, *Egypt in Search of Political Community: An Analysis of the Intellectual and Political Evolution of Egypt 1804–1952.* Harvard University Press, Cambridge, 1961.

Sainville, Leonard, *Anthologie de la Littérature Négro-Africaine: Romanciers et Conteurs.* Présence Africaine, Paris, 1963.

Sanakle, Marc, and Pierre Pené, *Médecine Sociale au Sénégal. Afrique Documents,* Dakar, March 1960.

Sartre, Jean-Paul. *Black Orpheus,* trans. by S. W. Allen. Présence Africaine, Paris, N.D.

Savonnet, George, "Evolution Démographique de la Ville de Thiès," *Notes Africaines*, Dakar, No. 54, October 1952.

——, "Les Villages de la Banlieue Thièssoire," *Bulletin de l'IFAN*, Dakar, No. 3, 1955, pp. 371–387.

——, *La Ville de Thiès*. IFAN, Saint-Louis, 1955.

Schapper, Bernard, *La Politique et le Commerce Français dans le Golfe de Guinée, de 1838 à 1871*. Mouton & Company, Paris, 1961.

"Second International Congress of Negro Writers and Artists," Rome, March 26–April 1, 1959, special issue, *Présence Africaine*, February-May 1959.

"Sénégal An II de la Deuxième République sur la Voie du Développement," *Afrique Magazine*, May 1964.

"Au Sénégal: Intensification de la Lutte Contre la Corruption," *Le Monde*, December 6, 1964.

Senghor, James E., "Le Congrès des Transporteurs," *L'Unité Africaine*, December 10, 1964.

Seurin, Jean-Louis, "Etudes Sociales et Partis Politiques," *Annales Africaines*, Université de Dakar, Paris, 1958.

Shils, Edward, "Political Development in the New States," *Comparative Studies in Society and History*, Vol. II, 1960.

Sigmund, Paul E., Jr., ed., *The Ideologies of the Developing Nations*. Frederick A. Praeger, New York, 1963.

Signate, Ibrahima, "Les Etudiants Veulent Tout Casser," *Jeune Afrique*, No. 165, January 6–12, 1964.

——, "Les Etudiants en Colère," *Jeune Afrique*, No. 168, January 27–February 2, 1964.

——, "Fin de la Négritude," *Jeune Afrique*, No. 172, February 24–March 1, 1964.

Skurnick, Walter A. E., "Léopold Sédar Senghor and African Socialism," *The Journal of Modern African Studies*, March 3, 1965, pp. 49–69.

Sociétés et Fournisseurs d'Afrique Noire et de Madagascar. La Documentation Africaine, Paris, 1964.

Staley, Eugene, *The Future of Underveloped Countries: Political Implications of Economic Development*, rev. ed. Frederick A. Praeger, New York, 1961.

Stein, Maurice R., *The Eclipse of Community*. Princeton University Press, Princeton, N.J., 1960.

Suret-Canale, Jean, *Afrique Noire Occidentale et Centrale*. Editions Sociales, Paris, 1958.

Tardits, C., "La Notion d'Elite et l'Enquête en Milieu Urbain Africain," *Bulletin International des Sciences Sociales*, Paris, Vol. VIII, No. 3 (1956), pp. 499–502.

Teilhard de Chardin, Pierre, *The Divine Milieu*. Harper & Row, New York, 1966. Originally published as *Le Milieu Divine*. Editions du Seuil, Paris, 1957.

——, *The Phenomenon of Man*. Harper and Row, New York, 1961. Originally published as *Le Phénomène Humain*. Editions du Seuil, Paris, 1955.

Terrise, André, "Senghor, Poète de Son Temps et de Son Peuple," *L'Unité Africaine*, February 20, 1966.

——, "Formation du Caractère et Formation Morale: Rôle de l'Ecole," *L'Unité Africaine*, March 11, 1965.

Tevoedjère, Albert, *L'Afrique Révolté*. Présence Africaine, Paris, 1958.

Thibaud, Paul, "Dia, Senghor et le Socialisme Africain," *Esprit*, Vol. XXXI, No. 9 (September 1963), pp. 332–348.

Thomas, L. V., "L'Organisation Foncière des Diolas Basse Casamance," *Annales Africaines*, Dakar, 1960, pp. 199–223.

——, "Temps, Mythe et Histoire dans l'Afrique de l'Ouest," *Présence Africaine*, Vol. XXXIX, 4th quarter, 1961, pp. 12–58.

——, "Une Idéologie Moderne, la Négritude," *Revue de Psychologie des Peuples*, November 3, 1963, pp. 246–272; November 4, 1963, pp. 367–398.

——, "Le Socialisme de Léopold Sédar Senghor et l'Ame Africaine," *Afrique Documents*, No. 75, 1964.

——, *Les Idéologies Négro-Africaines d'Aujourd'hui*. Dakar, N.D., N.P., mimeo.

——, *Le Socialisme et l'Afrique*, 2 parts. Le Livre Africain, Paris, 1966.

——, "Essai sur le Rôle de l'Idéologie dans les Problèmes du Développement," *Présence Africaine*, No. 63, third quarter 1967, pp. 32–67.

Thomson, David, *Democracy in France*, 3rd ed. Oxford University Press, London, 1958.

Thompson, Virginia, and Richard Adloff, *French West Africa*. Stanford University Press, Stanford, Calif., 1957.

Thoré, Luc, "Mariage et Divorce dans la Banlieue de Dakar," *Cahiers d'Etudes Africaines*, Vol. IV, No. 16, pp. 479–552.

Tlili, Mustapha, "Senghor Se Confie Souvenirs et Projets," *Jeune Afrique*, No. 303, October 30, 1966, pp. 38–46.

Touré, Sekou, *L'Action Politique du Parti, Démocratique de Guinée*. Présence Africaine, Paris, 1959.

———, *La Guinée et l'Emancipation Africaine.* Présence Africaine, Paris, 1959.

———, *Expérience Guinéanne et Unité Africaine.* Présence Africaine, Paris, 1962.

Touze, R. C., *Bigona en Casamance.* Editions SEPA, Dakar, 1963.

Traore, Bakary, *Le Théâtre Négro-Africain et Ses Fonctions Sociales.* Présence Africaine, Paris, 1958.

Traore, Bakary, Mamadou Lo, and Jean-Louis Albert, *Forces Politiques en Afrique Noire.* Presses Universitaires de France, Paris, 1966.

———, "The Trial of Mamadou Dia," *West Africa,* No. 2398, May 18, 1963, p. 547.

Turin, G., "Etapes d'une Enquête sur le Développement: Etude des Structures Economiques du Sénégal," *Economie et Humanisme,* November–December 1960, pp. 72–82.

Ulam, Adam, *The Unfinished Revolution.* Random House, New York, 1960.

U.S. Army Area Handbook for Senegal. Foreign Areas Studies, Division Special Operations Research Office, The American University, Washington, D.C., 1963.

Van Arkadie, Brian, "Allocation of Resources in Africa," U. No. IDEP/ECA-MA/SUT/64, IDEP/ET/SUT/207. Dakar, 1964, mimeo.

Verdier, Raymond, "Féodalités et Etude Critique," *Présence Africaine,* Vol. XXXIX, 4th quarter, 1961, pp. 79–101.

———, "Civilisations Agraires et Droits Fonciers Négro-Africains," *Présence Africaine,* Vol. 30, No. 1 (April-May 1960), pp. 24–33.

Verrière, Louis, "Où en Est, Où Va la Population du Sénégal," mimeo, INSEA, Dakar, 1963.

Von Grunebaum, G. E., *French African Literature: Some Cultural Implications.* Mouton & Company, The Hague, 1964.

Yacouba, Moussa, "Les Problèmes de la Jeunesse Africaine," *Afrique Nouvelle,* Dakar, No. 833, July 26, 1963.

Yahmed, Bechir Ben, "La Révolte des Etudiants," *Jeune Afrique,* No. 165, January 6–12, 1964.

Wade, Abdoulaye, *Economie de l'Ouest Africain.* Présence Africaine, Paris, 1964.

Wallerstein, Immanuel, "The New History: The Search for a National Identity in West Africa," *Présence Africaine,* October 1960.

Wauthier, Claude, *L'Afrique des Africains: Inventaire de la Négritude.* Editions du Seuil, Paris, 1964.

Ziegler, Jean, *Sociologie de la Nouvelle Afrique.* Gallimard, Paris, 1964.

Zolberg, Aristede R., *Creating Political Order: The Party States of West Africa.* Rand McNally & Company, Chicago, 1966.

Zuccarelli, F., *La Formation de l'Unité Nationale du Sénégal.* Mémoire CHEAM, mimeo, Paris, September 1963.

II. THE WRITINGS OF LÉOPOLD SÉDAR SENGHOR

A. *Poetry*

Chants d'Ombre. Editions du Seuil, Paris, 1945.

Hosties Noires. Editions du Seuil, Paris, 1948.

Chants pour Noett. Seghers, Paris, 1950.

Chants d'ombre—Hosties Noires. Editions du Seuil, Paris, 1956.

Ethiopiques. Editions du Seuil, Paris, 1956.

Nocturnes (includes *Chants pour Noett*). Editions du Seuil, Paris, 1961.

Poèmes. Editions du Seuil, Paris, 1964 (includes *Chants d'ombre, Hosties Noires, Ethiopiques, Nocturnes,* as well as poetry not previously published.

Selected Poems, translated and introduced by John Reed and Clive Wake. Atheneum, New York, 1966. Originally published by Oxford University Press, London, 1964.

B. *Political, Social, Literary and Other Writings*

"Le Problème Culturel en AOF," *Paris-Dakar,* Dakar, Nos. 489–492, September 7–11, 1937.

"Ce Que l'Homme Noir Apporte," in *L'Homme de Couleur.* Librairie Plon, Paris, 1939.

"Défense de l'Afrique Noire," *Esprit,* Paris, July 1945.

"Vues sur l'Afrique Noire, ou Assimiler, Non Etre Assimilés," in *La Communauté Française Impériale.* Editions Alsatia, Paris, 1945.

"L'Afrique Noire, la Civilisation Négro-Africaine," *Les Plus Beaux Ecrits de l'Union Française et du Maghreb.* La Colombe, Paris, 1947.

"Les Négro-Africains et l'Union Française," *Revue Politique et Parlementaire,* June 1947.

Anthologie de la Nouvelle Poésie Nègre et Malgache de Langue Française, with a preface by J.-P. Sartre, "Orphée Noir," Presses Universitaires de France, Paris, 1948.

"Flavien Ranavio, Poète Malgache," *Présence Africaine*, January 1948.

"Marxisme et Humanisme," *Revue Socialiste*, March 1948.

"Le Message de Goethe aux Nègres-Nouveaux," in *Hommage à Goethe*, UNESCO, Publication 410, 1949.

"L'Afrique S'Interroge: Subir ou Choisir," *Présence Africaine*, special issue, *Le Monde Noir*, March 1950.

Le Problème de la Culture. Journées d'Etudes des Indépendants d'Outre-Mer, July 1950, mimeo, N.P.

"De la Liberté de l'Ame ou Eloge du Métissage," *Liberté de l'Esprit*, October 1950.

"Jeunesse de Victor Hugo," *Liberté de l'Esprit*, February 1952.

"Les Elites de l'Union Française au Service de Leurs Peuples," preface to *L'Inventaire Linguistique de l'Afrique Occidentale et du Togo*. IFAN, Dakar 1953.

"Contre le Courant Centrifuge de l'Etat Assoie, une Seule Solution: La République Fédérale Française," *Marchés Coloniaux*, April 4, 1953.

"Contribution Négro-Africaine à l'Edification d'une Civilisation Mondiale," *Liberté de l'Esprit*, June–July 1953.

"Une République Fédérale Française," *Le Monde*, July 4, 1953.

"La Méthode et la Doctrine du Bloc Démocratique Sénégalais," *Marchés Coloniaux*, March 27 and April 3, 1954.

"L'Avenir de la France dans l'Outre-Mer," *Politique Etrangère*, August–October 1954.

"Les Conditions de l'Unité d'Action," *Condition Humaine*, September 10, 1954.

"La République Française et les Problèmes de l'Outre-Mer," *Politique Etrangère*, November 4, 1954.

"Langage et Poésie Négro-Africaine," in *Poésie et Langage*. Editions de la Maison du Poète, Brussels, 1954.

"La Poésie du Monde Nouveau," introduction to *Anthologie des Poètes du XVIe Siècle*. Bibliothèque Mondiale, Paris, 1955.

"Pour une Solution Fédéraliste" in *Ou Va l'Union Française?* special issue, *La Nef*, June 1955.

Preface to Flavien Ranavio, *Mes Chansons de Toujours*. Privately printed, Paris, 1955.

"Réponse au Débat sur la Poésie Nationale," *Présence Africaine*, December 1955–January 1956.

"L'Esprit de la Civilisation ou les Lois de la Culture Négro-Africaine," *Présence Africaine*, June–November 1956.

"Esthétique Négro-Africaine," *Diogène*, October 1956.

"Pour une Communauté Franco-Africaine," *Les Cahiers de la République*, May–June 1957.

"La Décolonisation, Condition de la Communauté Franco-Africaine," *Le Monde*, September 4, 1957.

"Le Réalisme d'Amadou Koumba," preface to Roland Colin, *Contes Noirs de l'Ouest Africain*. Présence Africaine, Paris, 1957.

"Le Problème des Langues Vernaculaires ou le Bilinguisme Comme Solution," *Afrique Nouvelle*, January 3, 1958.

"Il y a une Négritude," *Preuves*, April 1958.

"Vers l'Indépendance dans l'Amitié," *Cahiers de la République*, November–December 1958.

"La Lucidité et la Franchise, Conditions de la Communauté Franco-Africaine," preface to Ernest Milcent, *L'AOF Entre en Scène*. Témoignage Chrétien, Paris, 1958.

"D'Amadou Koumba à Birago Diop," preface to B. Diop, *Les Nouveaux Contes d'Amadou Koumba*. Présence Africaine, Paris, 1958.

Recueil des Interventions Faites a l'Assemblée Nationale Française par le Président Léopold Sédar Senghor de 1946 à 1958 en sa Qualité de Député du Sénégal (a collection of 47 speeches). Mimeo, Dakar, N.D.

African Socialism: A Report to the Constituent Congress of the Party of African Federation. The American Society of African Culture, New York City, 1959.

"Les Nationalismes d'Outre-Mer et les Peuples de Couleur," in *Encyclopédie Française*, Vol. XX, 1959.

"Eléments Constructifs d'une Civilisation d'Inspiration Négro-Africaine," *Deuxième Congrès des Artistes et Ecrivains Noirs*, Vol. I, Présence Africaine, March–April 1959.

"Discours Devant l'Assemblée Fédérale du Mali," Dakar, April 6, 1959.

"Inauguration de l'Hôtel de Ville de Thiès," mimeo, N.P., April 28, 1959.

"Comité Directeur du PFA, Résolution, Déclaration du Président Senghor," Dakar, September 23 and 24, 1959.

"Réception du Général de Gaulle à l'Assemblée Fédérale du Mali," mimeo, Dakar, Dec. 13, 1959.

"L'Université de Dakar," *L'Unité Africaine*, January 16, 1960.

"Installation de la Cour Suprème," mimeo, N.P. March 14, 1960.

"Les Accords Franco-Maliens," *L'Unité Africaine*, April 30, 1960.

"Proclamation de l'Indépendance du Mali," mimeo, N.P. June 20, 1960.

"Rapport de Politique Générale au Deuxième Congrès U.P.S. à Saint-Louis," mimeo, N.P., July 2, 1960.

"Conférence de Presse du 23 août 1960," Ministre de l'Information, de la Presse, et de la Radiodiffusion de la République du Senegal, Dakar, 1960.

"Message de Monsieur Léopold Sédar Senghor, Président de la République au Peuple Sénégalais," Ministre de l'Information, de la Presse, et de la Radiodiffusion de la Republique du Sénégal, Dakar, 1960.

"Pour une Coopération entre L'Islam et le Christianisme," mimeo, N.P., 1960.

Nation et Voie Africaine du Socialisme. Présence Africaine, Paris, 1961.

"West Africa in Evolution," *Foreign Affairs*, Vol. XXXIX, January 1961, pp. 240–246.

"Inauguration de la Route Dakar–Saint-Louis," mimeo, N.P., January 7, 1961.

"Discours au Banquet Affecté par le Gouverneur Général, le Docteur Nnamdi Azikiwe," mimeo, N.P., January 8, 1961.

"Allocution à Kaolack," mimeo, N.D., January 21, 1961.

"Discours à Kaffrine," mimeo, January 22, 1961.

"Discours Devant le Parlement du Ghana," mimeo, N.P. February 15, 1961.

"Discours à l'Occasion de la Visite à l'Université d'Achimota," mimeo, N.P. February 16, 1961.

"Troisième Message du Président à l'Occasion des Fêtes de l'Indépendance du Sénégal," mimeo, N.P., April 4, 1961.

"Sorbonne et Négritude," mimeo, N.P., April 21, 1961.

"Visite à Thiès," mimeo, N.P., May 21, 1961.

"Discours à Khombole," mimeo, N.P., May 22, 1961.

"Distribution des Prix au Lycée Van Vollenhoven," mimeo, N.P., June 15, 1961.

"Allocution Devant le Parlement Malgache," mimeo, N.P., June 28, 1961.

"Réception à l'Académie Malgache," mimeo, N.P., June 29, 1961.

"Première Conférence de l'U.A.M. à Tananarive," mimeo, N.P., June 29, 1961.

"Discours Devant l'Assemblée Nationale Tunisienne," mimeo, N.P., October 19, 1961.

"Quatrième Message du Peuple Sénégalais sur la Journée des Nations Unies," mimeo, N.P., October 24, 1961.

"Conférence prononcée à Chatam-House," mimeo, N.P., October 25, 1961.

"Discours Prononcé à l'Université d'Oxford," mimeo, N.P., October 26, 1961.

Allocution du Président de la République du Sénégal à la XVIe Session de l'Assemblée Générale des Nations Unies Tenue le 31 Octobre 1961. Présence Africaine, Paris, 1961.

"Réponse au Toast du Président de la République Fédérale d'Allemagne," mimeo, N.P., November 8, 1961.

"Cinquième Message au Peuple Sénégalais," mimeo, N.P., December 31, 1961.

Pierre Teilhard de Chardin et la Politique Africaine. Editions du Seuil, Paris, 1962.

"Socialisme Africain et Développement de la Voie Sénégalaise," *Sénégal "An II" par Lui-Même, Développement et Civilisation,* Paris, 1962.

Messages de Monsieur Léopold Senghor, Président de la République, au Peuple Sénégelais. Direction des Services de l'Information, République du Sénégal, Dakar, 1962.

"De la Négritude," *Psychologie du Négro-Africaine, Diogène,* No. 37, 1962.

Rapport sur la Doctrine et la Politique Générale ou Socialisme, Unité Africaine, Construction Nationale, III Congrès de l'U.P.S., mimeo, Thiès, February 4–6, 1962.

"Deuxième Conférence de l'UAM à Bangui," mimeo, N.P., March 25, 1962.

"Some Thoughts on Africa: A Continent in Development," *International Affairs,* Vol. XXXVIII, April 1962, pp. 189–195.

"Sixième Message au Peuple Sénégalais," mimeo, N.P., April 3, 1962.

"Discours d'Ouverture de la Semaine Linguistique," mimeo, April 12, 1962.

"Négritude et Civilisation de l'Universel," *Présence Africaine,* 2nd quarter, 1963.

"Message au Congrès des Villes Jumelées à Dakar," mimeo, N.P., April 19, 1962.

"Saint-John Perse ou la Poésie du Royaume d'Enfance," *La Table Ronde,* May 1962.

"Toast en l'Honneur de Monsieur Tubman," mimeo, N.P., May 1, 1962.

"Réponse à l'Allocution Prononcée par le Président Sekou Touré," mimeo, N.P., May 27, 1962.

"Voyage Officiel au Dahomey: Réponse au Toast du Président Maga," mimeo, N.P., July 1, 1962.
"Allocution à la Chambre de Commerce et d'Industrie du Dahomey," *Chambre de Commerce Bulletin*, Dakar, July 1962.
"Discours à Florence," mimeo, N.P., October 4, 1962.
"Rapport sur la Formation de Cadres, Conseil National de l'U.P.S., mimeo, October 21, 1962.
"Le Français, Langue de Culture," *Esprit*, November 1962.
"Présentation du Premier Gouvernement Senghor," mimeo, N.P., December 19, 1962.
"Les Données du Problème," in *Développement et Socialisme; Colloque sur les Politiques de Développement et les Diverses Voies Africaines vers le Socialisme, Dakar, 3–8 Decembre 1962.* Présence Africaine, Paris, 1963.
Preface to A. Fofana and A. Terrisse, *L'Education Civique au Sénégal.* Fernand Nathan, Paris, 1963.
"Troisièmes Journées Médicales de Dakar," mimeo, N.P., January 5, 1963.
"Inauguration du Lycée Charles de Gaulle," mimeo, N.P., January 6, 1963.
"Discours à Ziguincher," mimeo, N.P., January 14, 1963.
"Message à la Nation," mimeo, N.P., February 18, 1963.
"Message au Peuple Sénégalais sur le Festival Mondial des Arts Nègres," mimeo, N.P., February 20, 1963.
"Discours à Diourbel," mimeo, N.P., February 28, 1963.
"Discours à Conakrey," mimeo, N.P., March 8, 1963.
"Ouverture de la Deuxième Conférence des Chefs de Mission Diplomatique Sénégalaise," mimeo, N.P., March 18, 1963.
"Discours d'Ouverture du Colloque sur la Littérature Africaine d'Expression Française de l'Université de Dakar," mimeo, N.P., March 26, 1963.
"Negritude and the Concept of Universal Civilization," *Présence Africaine*, Eng. ed., 2nd quarter, 1963.
Message au Peuple Sénégalais à l'Occasion de la Célébration du Troisième Anniversaire de l'Indépendance, April 4, 1963. Ministre de l'Information, Dakar, April 1963.
Discours à l'Assemblée Nationale, Avril 19, 1963. Republic of Senegal, mimeo, Dakar, April 1963.
"Les Accords Franco-Maliens," *L'Unité Africaine*, April 30, 1963.
"Toast en l'Honneur de S. E. Monsieur Hubert Maga," mimeo, N.P., May 2, 1963.

"Visite Officielle du Président A. Sekou Touré," mimeo, N.P., May 13, 1963.

"Discours d'Addis-Ababa," mimeo, N.P., May 23, 1963.

"Discours à l'Assemblée Nationale," mimeo, N.P., June 6, 1963.

"Inauguration de la Mosquée de Touba," mimeo, N.P., June 7, 1963.

"Discours à l'Ouverture de la Discussion Budgétaire," June 25, 1963.

Conseil National de l'U.P.S., mimeo, N.P., July 7, 1963.

"Magal de Touba," mimeo, N.P., July 11, 1963.

Les Mésures de Rigueur et d'Austérité: Allocution à la Nation Sénégalaise 13 Septembre 1963. Ministre de l'Information, République du Sénégal, Imprimérie A. Diop, Dakar, 1963.

"Message sur le Premier Festival Mondial des Arts Nègres, *Afrique Nouvelle*, No. 840, September 13, 1963.

"Instructions d'Application sur la Réorganisation du C.E.R." Directive No. 90 PR, Présidence de la République, Dakar, September 21, 1963.

Planification et Tension Morale: Rapport sur la Politique Générale, IVe Congrès National de l'U.P.S. les 10–11 et 12 Octobre 1963 à Dakar, mimeo, 1963.

"Ouverture de l'Institut Africain de Développement Economique et Planification," mimeo, N.P., November 4, 1963.

"Toast en l'Honneur de Sir Ahmadou Bello," mimeo, N.P., November 6, 1963.

"Les Elections Présidentielles et Législatives ou Liberté et Défense de la Patrie," mimeo, N.P., November 8, 1963.

"Hommage à Gaston Berger," mimeo, N.P., November 12, 1963.

"La Tâche la Plus Difficile," *Jeune Afrique*, November 18–24, 1963.

"Meeting de Clôture de la Campagne Electorale," mimeo, N.P., November 20, 1963.

"Allocution à l'Issue des Elections," mimeo, N.P., December 2, 1963.

"Message à la Nation Sénégalaise," mimeo, N.P., December 9, 1963.

"Campagne de Commercialisation de l'Arachide," mimeo, N.P., December 13, 1963.

"Inauguration de l'Ecole Nationale d'Economie Appliquée," mimeo, N.P., December 16, 1963.

"Déclaration à l'Assemblée nationale," mimeo, N.P., December 17, 1963.

"Serment Devant la Cour Suprème," *Afrique Nouvelle*, December 13–19, 1963.

"Allocution sur les Logements Administratifs," mimeo, N.P., December 20, 1963.

"Réponse aux Vœux du Corps Diplomatique," mimeo, N.P., December 31, 1963.

"Message à la Nation," mimeo, N.P., December 31, 1963.

Liberté I: Négritude et Humanisme. Editions du Seuil, Paris, 1964.

"Preface" to *Reliefs* by Malick Fall. Présence Africaine, Paris, 1964.

"Preface" to *Aubades* by Ibrahima Sourang. Poètes de Notre Temps, Monte Carlo, 1964.

On African Socialism. Trans. and intro. by Mercer Cook. Frederick A. Praeger, New York, 1964.

"Ouverture de la Troisième Conférence des Techniciens Ferroviaires Africains et Malgaches," mimeo, N.P., January 1, 1964.

"Entretien des Logements Administratifs," mimeo, N.P., January 10, 1964.

"La Santé Publique," mimeo, N.P., January 17, 1964.

"Elaboration du Deuxiéme Plan Quadriennal," mimeo, N.P., January 24, 1964.

"Inauguration de la S.A.R. de M'Bab," mimeo, N.P., January 27, 1964.

"I'Emprunt National," mimeo, N.P., January 31, 1964.

"Hommage à André Peytavin," mimeo, N.P., February 5, 1964.

"Licenciement des Non-Fonctionnaires de l'Etat pour Limite d'Age," mimeo, N.P., February 7, 1964.

"Les Elections Municipales Partielles ou l'Ordre Public Sera Maintenu," mimeo, N.P., February 14, 1964.

"Service de Réclassement des Anciens Militaires Libérés," mimeo, N.P., February 21, 1964.

"Installation du Conseil Economique et Social," mimeo, N.P., February 26, 1964.

"Inauguration des Installations de Dakar de l'Usine Berliet," mimeo, N.P., February 27, 1964.

Théorie et Pratique du Socialisme Sénégalais: Séminaire des Cadres Politiques. Services de Presse du Ministre de l'Information, Dakar, March 1964.

"Allocution de Bienvenue, à l'Occasion de'l'Ouverture de la Conférence des Chefs d'Etat de l'U.A.M.," mimeo, N.P., March 7, 1964.

"Un Message de Léopold Senghor au 'Populaire.'" *Le Populaire de Paris.* Paris, March 10, 1964.

"Le Problème de l'Urbanisme," mimeo, N.P., March 13, 1964.

"Préparation de la Prochaine Campagne Agricole," mimeo, N.P., March 20, 1964.

"Allocution de Bienvenue à Sa Majesté Hassan II," mimeo, N.P., March 24, 1964.

"Inauguration de la Mosquée de Dakar," mimeo, N.P., March 27, 1964.

"Message aux Jeunes de l'U.P.S.," mimeo, N.P., March 27, 1964.

"Message à la Nation," mimeo, N.P., April 3, 1964.

"Examens, Concours et Justice Sociale," mimeo, N.P., April 17, 1964.

"Animation du Building," mimeo, N.P., April 24, 1964.

"Allocution sur le Projet de Loi sur le Domaine National," mimeo, N.P., May 1, 1964.

"Les Impayées du Crédit Populaire," mimeo, N.P., May 22, 1964.

"Distribution des Prix," mimeo, N.P., June 26, 1964.

"Pèlerinage Annuel de Touba," mimeo, N.P., June 30, 1964.

"Distribution de Prix," mimeo, N.P., July 4, 1964.

"Une Seule Politique Africaine: Celle du Développement," Conseil National, mimeo, N.P., July 12, 1964.

"Le Problème de l'Urbanisme," *L'Unité Africaine*, August 20, 1964.

"Message à l'Internationale Socialiste à l'Occasion de la Commémoration de Son Centenaire," *L'Unité Africaine*, Dakar, September 17, 1964.

Voyage Officiel aux Etats-Unis du Brésil, 19–25 Septembre 1964. Commissariat à l'Information, Dakar, October 1964.

"Négritude et Civilisation Gréco-Latine ou Démocratie et Socialisme," *L'Unité Africaine*, November 26, 1964.

"Message," *L'Unité Africaine*, Dakar, December 31, 1964.

"Dialogue et Développement, Assemblée Eurafricaine," mimeo, N.P., December 8, 1964.

"Message du Président de la République du Sénégal," *Paysan Noir*, No. 2, January 1965.

"Préparation du Second Plan Quadriennal ou Pour une Attitude d'Accueil, Conseil National," mimeo, N.P., January 3, 1965.

"Rapport du Secrétaire Général," *L'Unité Africaine*, Dakar, January 7, 1965.

"La Remise des Insignes de Grand Officier de l'Ordre Nationale du Professeur Monod," *Dakar-Matin*, January 26, 1965.

"Le Président Senghor dans le Sine-Saloum," *Dakar-Matin*, February 19, 1965.

"La Troisième Journée du Président dans le Sine," *Dakar-Matin*, February 20, 1965.

"Fin de la Visite du Chef de l'Etat dans la Région du Sine-Saloum," *Bulletin Quotidien de Synthèses de Nouvelles*, Dakar, February 26, 1965.

"Dan le Sine-Saloum: Onze Jours en Février," *L'Unité Africaine,* Dakar, March 4, 1965.

"Inauguration de l'Ecole Nationale des Cadres Ruraux de Bambey," *L'Unité Africaine,* Dakar, May 6, 1965.

"Discours à Taiba," *L'Unité Africaine,* Dakar, May 20, 1965.

"La France et Nous: Le Sénégal Etat Pilote de l'Afrique Occidentale Francophone," supplement, *Le Monde,* June 8, 1965.

"Les Investisseurs Peuvent Continuer de Nous Faire Confiance à l'Inauguration du Nouvel Ensemble Peyrissac," *L'Unité Africaine,* Dakar, June 24, 1965.

"Les Objectifs Essentiels du II Plan Quadriennal du Sénégal, Conseil National de l'U.P.S. April 25, 1965," *Sénégal d'Aujourd'hui,* No. 21, July 1965.

"L'Animation dans le Développement Economique," *Sénégal d'Aujourd'hui,* No. 21, July 1965.

"The African Road to Socialism," *African Forum,* New York, 1966.

"Negritude and the Germans," *Africa Report,* February 1967, pp. 46–48, trans. by Ellen Conroy Kennedy from *Sind die Deutschen Wirklich So?* Horst Erdmann Press, Herrenalb, West Germany, 1966.

Les Fondements de l'Africanité ou Négritude et Arabité. Présence Africaine, Paris, 1967.

Politique, Nation, et Développement Moderne: Rapport de Politique Générale, VIe Congrès de l'Union Progressiste Sénégalaise, 5, 6, 7 Janvier, 1968. Rufisque, Imprimerie Nationale.

III. Other Senegalese Writers

Baudin, A. N'Diaye, "A l'Ecoute du Monde Rural," *L'Unité Africaine,* April 22, 1964.

Boissier-Palum, Léon, "Au Conseil Economique et Social," *L'Unité Africaine,* March 25, 1965.

Bouly, Drame, *La Réforme Domaniale, Bigona,* mimeo, mémoire E.N.A.S., Dakar, 1962.

Boye, Moustapha, *Urbanisme et Développement au Sénégal,* mimeo, E.N.A.S., Dakar, 1962.

Cabou, Daniel "La Stabilisation des Prix au Sénégal," Conseil National, U.P.S., Dakar, mimeo, January 3, 1965.

"Le Centre d'Expansion Rurale Polyvalent, Lieu du Dialogue Entre l'Etat et les Collectivités Rurales," *L'Unité Africaine,* December 24, 1964.

Cissé, Ben Mady, *Socialisation et Re-Structuration Rurales: La Communauté Rurale Cellule de Base du Développement Rural,* mimeo, Dakar, April 25, 1962.

Correa, Daniel, *L'Etat et les Confessions Religieuses au Sénégal,* mimeo, mémoire, E.N.A.S., Dakar, 1962.

Daffe, Amadou L. Amine, "Economie Planifiée et Non Marasme," *L'Unité Africaine,* November 12, 1964.

Danfakha, Lamine, "Histoire du Sénégal Oriental," *L'Unité Africaine,* June 24, 1965.

D'Arboussier, Gabriel, *L'Afrique Vers l'Unité.* Editions Saint-Paul, Paris, 1961.

———, "La Législation du Sénégal, Législation de Développement," Colloque des Facultés de Dakar, mimeo, Dakar, 1962.

Dia, Mamadou, *Contribution à l'Etude du Mouvement Coopératif en Afrique Noire,* 3rd ed. Présence Africaine, Paris, 1952.

———, *Réflexions sur l'Economic de l'Afrique Noire,* Editions Africaines, Paris, 1953.

———, *L'Economie Africaine, Etudes et Problèmes Nouveaux.* Presses Universitaires de France, Paris, 1957.

———, "L'UPS au Lendemain du Referendum; Devant le Comité Exécutif de l'UPS Réunie à Rufisque, October 4, 1958," *Info-Sénégal,* Service de l'Information du Sénégal, Dakar, new series, No. 248, October 6, 1958.

———, "Le Développement de Tout l'Homme et de Tous les Hommes," *Déclaration d'Investiture,* Dakar, April 4, 1959.

———, "La Construction Nationale, Doctrine Objectifs, Moyens, Discours au Premier Séminaire National d'Etudes pour les Responsables Politiques, Parlementaires et Gouvernmentales," mimeo, Dakar, October 26, 1959.

———, "Déclaration Devant l'Assemblée Législative du Sénégal," mimeo, Dakar, June 9, 1966.

———, *Principes et Méthodes du Développement du Sénégal: Le Plan,* Présidence du Conseil, Dakar, August 1, 1966.

———, *Déclaration d'Investiture Devant l'Assemblée Nationale,* mimeo, Dakar, June 9, 1960.

———, *Discours à l'Assemblée Générale des Nations Unies,* mimeo, Dakar, December 8, 1960.

———, *Nations Africaines et Solidarité Mondiale.* Presses Universitaires de France, Paris, 1960. Translated into English as *The African Nations and World Solidarity.* Frederick A. Praeger, New York, 1961.

———, *Déclaration Devant l'Assemblée Nationale,* Présidence du Conseil des Ministères de la République du Sénégal, Dakar, April 4, 1961.

——, A l'Occasion de l'Inauguration de l'Iséa, Dakar, November 28, 1961.

——, Declaration à l'Ouverture de la Conférence Syndicale Panafricaine, Dakar, January 9, 1962.

——, Rapport Economique, 3rd Congrès Thiès de l'U.P.S., January 4, 1962.

——, "Le Parti et le Développement," L'Unité Africaine, April 4, 1962.

——, Doctrine et Problèmes de l'Evolution du Mouvement Coopératif au Sénégal, Instructions Circulaires, No. 032/PC, mimeo, Présidence du Conseil, République du Sénégal.

——, "Discours de Clôture," in Colloque sur les Politiques de Développement et les Diverses Voies Africaines du Socialisme. Présence Africaine, Paris, 1963.

——, "Organisation Foncière et Dominale," Assemblée Législative au Sénégal, mimeo, N.D., N.P.

Diagne, Lamine Mamadou, Organisation du Travail Législatif à l'Assemblée Nationale du Sénégal, mimeo, Mémoire ENAS, Dakar, 1962.

Diakhate, Lamine, "Le Nègre de Demain ou la Civilisation de Synthèse," mimeo, Rufisque, 1963.

——, "Essai sur la Poésie de Senghor," L'Unité Africaine, February 6, 1960.

——, "Le Mythe dans la Poésie Populaire du Sénégal et Sa Présence dans l'Oeuvre de Léopold Sédar Senghor et de Birago Diop," Présence Africaine, 4th quarter, 1961.

——, Primordiale du Sixième Jour. Présence Africaine, Paris, 1963.

——, La Nation en Question, Sénégal 1963. Ministère de l'Information, Dakar, 1963.

——, "The Acculturation Process in Negro Africa and Its Relations with Negritude," Présence Africaine, Eng. ed., 4th quarter, 1965.

Diallo, Bakary, Force Bonté. Editions Rieder et Co., Paris, 1926.

Diao, Momar, Plan Quadriennal de Développement 1961–1964 dans le Cercle de Kaffrine, mimeo, Mémoire ENAS, Dakar, 1962.

Dione, Kjibril, "Rapport de Politique Générale," 4e Congrès National de l'U.P.S., mimeo, Dakar, N.D.

Diop, Abdoulaye, "Enquête sur la Migration Toucouleur à Dakar," Bulletin de l'IFAN, Dakar, Vol. XXII, No. 3–4 (1966), pp. 393–418.

Diop, Birago, *Les Contes d'Amadou Koumba.* Edition Tasquelle, Paris, 1947.

Diop, Caroline, "Sénégal, L'Animation Féminine," *Organisation Africaine & Malgache de Coopération Eurafrique,* No. 5, March 1964, pp. 50–56.

Diop, Cheikh Anta, *Nations Nègres et Culture.* Présence Africaine, Paris, 1955.

——, *L'Unité Culturelle de l'Afrique Noire.* Présence Africaine, Paris, 1959.

——, *Les Fondements Culturels, Techniques et Industriels d'un Futur Etat Fédéral d'Afrique Noire.* Présence Africaine, Paris, 1966.

——, "African Sociology and Methods of Research," *Présence Africaine,* Eng. ed., 4th quarter, 1963.

——, "Histoire Primitive de l'Humanité: Evolution du Monde Noir," *Présence Africaine,* 3rd quarter, 1964.

Diop, David, *Coup de Pilon.* Présence Africaine, Paris, 1956.

Diop, Majmout, *Contribution à l'Etude des Problèmes Politiques en Afrique Noire.* Présence Africaine, Paris, 1958.

——, "L'Unique Issue: Indépendance Total, La seule Voie: Un Large Mouvement d'Union Anti-Impérialiste," *Présence Africaine,* 4th quarter, pp. 145–184.

——, "Pan Africanisme et Socialisme, Rapport Presenté à la Conférence des Peuples de l'Afrique (Accra 5–12 Dec. 1958)," reprinted in *La Lutte,* Dakar, March 1959.

Diouf, Coumba N'Doffene, *La Participation des Organisations à l'Application de la Politique Economique et Social,* Mémoire, ENAS, mimeo, Dakar, 1963.

Diouf, Khar Ndofine and Habib Thiam, "Lettre Ouverte à M. Jean-Marie Domenach, Directeur de la Revue 'Esprit.'" *Esprit,* January 1964, pp. 157–174.

Diouf, Mohamed, *La Réforme Foncière Diourbel,* mimeo, Mémoire ENAS, Dakar, 1962.

——, *La Réforme Foncière et l'Aménagement Rationnel des Terroirs dans Notre Circonscription,* mimeo, Dakar, 1962.

Diouf, Patrice, "Paroles d'un Chef," *Sénégal Actualités,* Service de Presse, Dakar, March 21, 1963.

Dioum, Aly, "L'Union Nationale des Etudiants de Sénégal Se Veut Apolitique et Réaliste," *L'Unité Africaine,* December 1964.

Dramé, Bourley, *La Réforme Domaniale et l'Aménagement du Territoire Bigona 1962,* mimeo, Mémoire ENAS, Dakar, 1962.

Eléments pour un Manifeste du Socialisme Africain, Etude Realisée

Bulletin de l'IFAN, Vol. XXVIII, Series B, No. 3–4 (July-October 1966), pp. 731–70.

⸺ce, Ousmane, *Karim, Roman Sénégalais*. Editions F. Sorlot, Paris, 1935.

⸺, *Mirages de Paris*. Nouvelles Editions Latines, Nevers, 1955.

⸺urang, Ibrahima, *Aubades*. Poètes de Notre Temps, Monte Carlo, 1964.

⸺iam, Doudou, *La Portée de la Citoyenneté Française dans les Territoires d'Outre-Mer*. Sociétés d'Editions Africaines, Paris, 1953.

⸺, *La Politique Etrangère des Etats Africains*. Presses Universitaires de France, Paris, 1963.

⸺iam, Habib, "La Civilisation du Plans dans l'Europe et l'Afrique de Demain," Vichy, June 23, 1963.

⸺, *Rapport sur l'Exécution du Plan Quadriennal et sur l'Evolution de l'Economie Sénégalaise*. Conseil Nationale de l'U.P.S., mimeo, N.P., July 7, 1963.

⸺, *Deuxième Session de Planification Régionale*, Rapport sur la Session Tenue à Rufisque. Ministère du Plan, mimeo, Rufisque, May 1964.

⸺, *Rapport sur le Plan Quadriennal de Développement et la Situation Générale de l'Economie*. Conseil National de l'U.P.S., mimeo, N.P., July 12, 1964.

⸺, *Communication Relative à la Création d'Une Société pour la Mise en Valeur de 30,000 Ha dans le Delta du Fleuve-Sénégal*. Mimeo, Dakar, September 29, 1964.

⸺, *Conference of African Planners*, Dakar, November 16–27, 1964. Economic Commission for Africa 1NF/10, mimeo, Dakar, November 1964.

⸺, *Note sur l'Etat d'Exécution des Investissements Privées au 31 Décembre 1964*. Mimeo, N.D., N.P.

⸺, "Coopération et Développement," *Paysan Noir*, No. 2, January 1965.

⸺, *Le Deuxième Plan de Développement Economique et Social*. Conseil National de l'U.P.S., mimeo, April 25, 1965.

⸺, "Le Deuxième Plan de Développement: Conseil National de l'U.P.S.," *L'Unité Africaine*, May 2, 1965.

⸺, Medoune, *Cheickh Ahmadou Bamba Fondateur du Mouri⸺isme 1850–1927*. Imprimerie Nationale Patrice Lumumba⸺onakrey, 1964.

⸺ Générale des Etudiants Sénégalais, *Deuxième Congrès: Text⸺s Motions et Résolution*. Dakar, mimeo, July 27–29, 1963.

par le Groupe d'Etudes pour le Socialisme Africaine, mimeo, Dakar, March 29, 1961.

Fal, Babacar, *Le Place du Crad en Diourbel*, mimeo, Mémoire ENAS, Dakar, 1962.

⸺, "L'Etat d'Avancement du Plan Quadriennal dans Notre Circonscription Kebemer*, mimeo, N.D., N.P.

Fall, Cheikh Ibrahima, *L'Economie de l'Arachide dans les Etats de l'Ouest Africain*, mimeo, Mémoire, CHEAM, 1961.

Fall, Malick, *Reliefs*. Présence Africaine, Paris, 1964.

Ficaja, M., *La Sécurité Sociale au Sénégal*, mimeo, N.D., N.P.

Fofana, Abdoulaye, *Projet de Rapport*, Congrès de U.P.S. mimeo, October 1963.

⸺, "La Réforme Municipale," *Dakar-Matin*, May 4, 1965.

Fofana, Abdoulaye, and A. Terrisse, *l'Education Civique au Sénégal*. Fernand Nathan, Paris, 1963.

Gaye, Amadou Lamine, *Le Financement du Développement*, mimeo, ENAS, Dakar, 1962.

Gaye, Karim, *Rapport sur le Situation de l'Agriculture Sénégalaise au Seuil de la Campagne Agricole 1963, 1964*, Conseil National de l'U.P.S., mimeo, N.P., July 7, 1963.

⸺, *Bilan de la Campagne Agricole 1964–1965 et Préparation de la Campagne 1965–1966*, Conseil National de l'U.P.S., mimeo, N.P., April 25, 1965.

⸺, "La Situation de l'Agriculture Sénégalaise," *L'Unité Africaine*, July 1, 1965.

Gaye, Mohammadou, *Les Principes Fondamentaux du Droit de la Fonction Publique de Sénégal*, mimeo, mémoire, ENAS, Dakar, 1962.

Gueye, Lamine, *Etapes et Perspectives de l'Union Française*. Editions de l'Union Française, Paris, 1955.

⸺, *Itinéraire Africain*. Présence Africaine, Paris, 1966.

Kaba, Manka, "L'Animation Féminine au Sénégal," *Dakar-Matin*, January 13, 1965.

Kane, Cheikh Hamidou, "Le Sénégal Veut Promouvoir Son Développement Economique et Social," *L'Economie*, No. 809 (February, 8, 1962), pp. 9–10.

⸺, "Le Plan National et l'Option Sénégalaise pour une Politique de Développement Socialiste," mimeo, Dakar, December 1962.

⸺, *Ambiguous Adventure*. Walker and Company, New York, 1963. Originally published as *L'Aventure Ambigue*. Julliard, Paris, 1962.

Kebé, Moctar, "Exode Rural et Sous Prolétariat Urbain," *Sénégal d'Aujourd'hui*, Dakar, April 1965.

Lo, Lamine, *L'Etat d'Aménagement du Plan Quadriennal 1961–1964 dans le Cercle de Gossas au 30 Juin 1962*, mimeo, Mémoire ENAS, Dakar, 1962.

Ly, Abdoulaye, *Les Masses Africaines et l'Actuelle Condition Humaine*. Présence Africaine, Paris, 1956.

——, *Mercenaires Noirs*. Présence Africaine, Paris, 1957.

——, *La Compagnie du Sénégal*. Présence Africaine, Paris, 1958.

——, *L'Etat et la Production Paysanne*. Présence Africaine, Paris, 1958.

——, *Sur le Nationalisme dans l'Ouest-Africain*, Publication du PRA-Sénégal No. 1, Imprimerie A. Diop, Dakar, August 1959.

——, *Un Navire de Commerce sur la Côte Sénégalienne en 1685*, IFAN, Dakar, 1964.

Ly, Bocar, *Politique Rurale Sénégalaise: Cercle de Ziguinchor*. Mimeo, Mémoire, ENAS, Dakar, 1963.

Ly, Souleymane, *Exposé sur la Régionalisation*. Direction de la Planification, République de Sénégal, mimeo, Dakar, March 24, 1964.

Mathiam, Joseph, "Quelques Réflexions sur le Développement du Sénégal," *L'Unité Africaine*, March 17, 1964.

——, "Loi de Finances et d'Habilitation," *L'Unité Africaine*, June 10, 1965.

M'Bengue, Alioune Badara, "La Réforme Agraire," *L'Unité Africaine*, June 10, 1965.

M'Bengue, Mamadou Seyni, *La Sirène Noire*, Editions Bingo, Dakar, N.D.

——, *L'Animation dans le Développement Economique du Sénégal*, mimeo, Dakar, N.D.

N'Diaye, Albert, *L'Originalité du Mouvement Coopératif au Sénégal*, mimeo, N.P., 1962.

N'Diaye, Amadou N'Deme, *Le Gouverneur de Région*, mimeo, Mémoire, ENAS, Dakar, 1962.

N'Diaye, Amadou Racine, "Le Ministre de l'Education Populaire," *L'Unité Africaine*, December 31, 1964.

N'Diaye, Bouma, *Réflexions sur le Mouvement Coopératif Sénégalais*, mimeo, N.P., 1962.

——, "La Coopération Rurale," *Sénégal Documents*, Dakar, No. 1, October 1963.

N'Diaye, Massata Abdou, *Afrique Unie et Rénovation Mondiale*. France, 1963.

——, *Le Mouvement Syndical Africain Devant Ses Résponsabilités*.

Collection Continent Africain, 1964, Imprimer Lumumba, Conakry.

N'Diaye, Nalla, "La Formation des Cadres Admir dans les Pays d'Expression Françaises en ment," Mémoire, ENAS, 1962, Dakar.

Niang, M. M., *Etude sur la Fusion des Service Coopération*. Direction de la Coopération November 1964.

Oumar, Dia, *Mémoire sur le Régime des Stag France*, typescript, ENAS, Dakar, 1962.

Ousmane, Sembene, *Le Docker Noir*. Les No bresse, Paris, 1956.

——, *O! Pays Mon Beau Peuple*. Le Livre 1957.

——, *Bouts de Bois de Dieu*. Le Livre Cont Trans. by Francis Price as *Gods' Bits o* Company, Garden City, N.Y., 1962.

——, *Voltaïque*. Présence Africaine, Paris, 196

——, *L'Harmattan*. Présence Africaine, Paris,

Sadji, Abdoulaye, *Education Africaine et Ci* Diop, Dakar, 1964.

Sankale, Edourd, *Les Rapports du Gouvern Nationale au Sénégal*, mimeo, Mémoire

Sar, A., *et al.*, "Esprit et Situation de l'E Noire," *Présence Africaine*, December

Seck, Assane, "La Formation d'Une Classe dentale Française," pp. 159–163 in Differing Civilizations, ed., *Developm Tropical and Sub-Tropical Countries*. ilizations, Brussels, 1956.

——, "Education in French West Africa York, April 30, 1960.

——, *Dakar*. Faculté des Lettres, Dakar, 1

Seck, Charles B., "La Presqu'île du Ca 17, 1965.

Seck, Moustapha, Ministre de l'Energie, du Fleuve-Sénégal," *L'Unité Africa* 1964.

Silla, Ousmane, "Le Système des Cast *Franco-Eurafrique*, January 1964, pr

——, "Persistence des Castes dans la So

——, *La Voix de l'Etudiant Sénégalais*, Dakar, No. 1, November-December 1964.

Wane, Amadou Moctar, "L'Organisation du Service de la Santé Publique au Sénégal," *Panorama*, Agence de Presse Sénégalaise, Dakar, No. 7, April 16, 1965.

IV. SENEGALESE GOVERNMENT DOCUMENTS

Archives Nationales, Centre de Documentation
   Porges, Laurence, *Eléments de Bibliographie Sénégalaise 1959–1963*. Senegalese Archives, mimeo, Dakar, 1964.
   Bibliographie de M. Léopold Sédar Senghor au Oct. 1959, mimeo, N.D., N.P.
   Discours, Messages, Allocutions de Monsieur Léopold Senghor," mimeo, N.P., 1964.
   Bulletin Bibliographique des Archives du Sénégal, January 1963–October-December 1967.
Assemblée Nationale
   Déterminant la Nationalité Sénégalaise (Loi No. 61–09), February 21, 1961.
   Plan Quadriennal de Développement 1961–1964 (Loi Sénégalaise No. 61–32), N.P., N.D.
   Budget du Sénégal, Exercise 1961 (Loi Sénégalaise No. 60–055), Rufisque, Imprimerie Officielle, N.D.
   Budget Général, Gestion 1962–1963 (Loi de Finances No. 62–49, June 20, 1962, Rufisque, Imprimerie Nationale, 1962.
Chambre de Commerce d'Agriculture et d'Industrie
   "Rapport d'Etude sur le Projet et Décret Instituant un Code du Travail en AOF et au Togo," *Bulletin Mensuel*, Dakar, April 1949.
   L'Economie du Sénégal. Dakar, April 1961.
   Aperçu sur le Sénégal et Son Economie. Mimeo, Dakar, December 1964.
Codes des Investissements (Loi No. 62–33, March 22, 1962), Imprimerie Nationale, Rufisque, 1962.
Comité d'Etudes Economiques
   Rapport sur les Investissements au Sénégal, mimeo, Dakar, June 1959.
   Etudes sur le Milieu Rural, 3 vol., mimeo, Dakar, 1959.
   Commerce et Exchange, Comptes et Circuits Financier, mimeo, Dakar, 1959.

Sur la Réforme du Régime Foncier Rural au Sénégal, mimeo, Dakar, April 25, 1960.

Comité d'Etudes pour les Problèmes Sociaux, *Etudes des Besoins de l'Enfance au Sénégal,* mimeo, N.P., N.D.

Ecole Nationale d'Economie Appliquée
Rapport sur le Déroulement de la Première Partie du Stage de Formation d'une Nouvelle Promotion d'Agents de la Coopération, mimeo, N.D., N.P.
Programmes des Cours du Tronc Commun, mimeo, N.D., N.P.
Mersadier, Yves, *Connaissance de l'Exploitation Agricole, Résumés du Cours,* mimeo, N.P., N.D.

Institut de Science Economique Appliquée
Marchat, Ph., *L'Organisation du Crédit au Sénégal,* mimeo, Dakar, June 22, 1962.
Justification Théorique d'une Etude de la Consommation Alimentaire Exprimée en Nutriments, Denrées, et Valeur Monétaire de Trois Villages de la Région de Thiès, mimeo, Dakar, March 1963.
La Diffusion du Progrès Technique en Milieu Rural Traditional, mimeo, Dakar, March 1963.
Méthodologie d'une Enquête de Consommation Alimentaire dans 3 Villages de la Région de Thiès, mimeo, Dakar, July 4, 1963.
Les Industries du Cap Vert, mimeo, Dakar, January 1964.

Ministère du Commerce
Fall, Medoune, *Notes sur les Organismes Stockeurs,* mimeo, Dakar, January 26, 1962.
Communication en Conseil Inter-Ministériel du 14 Janvier 1965 sur la SONADIS, mimeo, Dakar.

Ministère de l'Economie Rurale, Direction de la Coopération
Note sur la Reprise de la Fonction Consommation des Coopératives Agricoles, mimeo, N.P., N.D.
Programme Intermédiare pour le Développement de la Casamance, mimeo, N.P., January 15, 1961.
L'Essor du Mouvement Coopératif au Sénégal, mimeo, Dakar, 1962.
Colombain, Maurice, *Rapport sur le Mouvement Coopératif dans le République du Sénégal et Ses Perspectives de Développement,* Dakar-Paris, 1962.
Desroche, H., *Etudes des Questions Relatives à l'Enseignement Coopératif au Sénégal,* mimeo, Dakar, March 1962.
Bilan des Opérations-Texts-Fonction Consommation, N.P., 1963.

Les Coopératives Comme Investissements de Développement, College Coopératif, mimeo, Dakar, 1963.

Etat de la Situation Actuelle de l'Opération Consommation en Casamance, Rapport de Mission, College Coopératif, Dakar, 1963.

Situation de l'Encadrement Rural, mimeo, N.P., October 1963.

Etude Expérimentale du Centre d'Expansion Rurale de Thiadiaye, Rapport de Zone Soumis au C.L.D. de M'Bour, Méthode de l'Elaboration des Programmes Locaux de Développement, mimeo, Thiadiaye, November 1963.

Note à l'Attention de Monsieur le Directeur de la Coopération sur la Situation des Coopératives de Consommation dans les Régions de Thiès, de Diourbel et du Sine-Saloum, typescript, N.P., 1963.

Note Pédagogique Concernant les Stages de Président et Peseurs des Coopératives, N.P., N.D.

Belloncle, Guy, *Le Mouvement Coopératif au Sénégal, Bilan et Perspectives,* mimeo, Dakar, May 1964.

Weuleresse, Hubert, *Bilan Quantitatif de l'Opération Complexe, Crédit Agricole–Commercialisation par les Coopératives Arachidières du Sénégal,* mimeo, March 1965.

Buffet, H., *Inspection Général d'Etat, Rapport No. 15* (On Senegalese Agriculture), mimeo, Dakar, May 3, 1965.

Note sur un Projet de Structuration des Coopératives Rurales, mimeo, S.A.T.E.C., Dakar, December 1964.

Note sur les Structures Coopératives, typescript, Dakar, 1965.

Ministère de l'Education Nationale, *Statistiques des Etudiants Inscrits à l'Université de Dakar, Année Universitaire 1964–1965,* mimeo, N.P., N.D.

Ministère de l'Enseignement Technique

Enquête sur les Besoins en Main-d'Oeuvre du Secteur Privé au Sénégal, mimeo, Dakar, 1962.

Session d'Information du Personnel d'Assistance Technique, mimeo, Dakar, November 23–24, 1963.

Ministère de l'Information, *Livre Blanc sur le Coup d'Etat Manqué du 19 au 20 Août 1960,* Dakar, 1960.

Commissariat à l'Information, *Sénégal Faits et Chiffres, Nouvelle Edition 1965,* Dakar, 1965.

Ministère de l'Intérieur, M. Dieude, *La Police,* Direction de la Sûreté, mimeo, Dakar, February 26, 1962.

Ministère du Plan et du Développement, *Deuxième Plan Quadriennal 1965–1969,* mimeo, Dakar, 1965.

Ministère du Plan et du Développement, Aménagement du Territoire

Odient, Bernard, *Aspects de la Politique du Logement à Dakar*, mimeo, Dakar, 1962.

Pour une Politique Cohérente en Matière d'Equipements Administratifs (Document de Travail), mimeo, Dakar, 1962.

Dottelonde, A., *L'Ecole Primaire en Milieu Rural*, Dakar, 1963.

Rocard, M., *Propositions pour un Code de l'Aménagement Urbain*, mimeo, Dakar, 1963.

Marie-Sainte, Yves, *Quelques Données Relatives au Principales Cultures au Sénégal*, mimeo, Dakar, 1963.

———, *La Culture Attelée au Sénégal*, mimeo, Dakar, 1963.

Bugnicourt, J., *Aspects de la Démographie de l'Agglomération Dakaroise*, mimeo, Dakar, January 1964.

Camara, Camille, *Pikine, Etude d'une Nouveau Quartier d'une Quartier de Saint-Louis*, mimeo, Dakar, August 1964.

Metge, Pierre, *Structure du Peuplement du Delta, Conséquences sur l'Exploitation et l'Habitat dans la Cuvette de Boundoun-Nord*, mimeo, Dakar, November 20, 1964.

———, *Aperçu sur l'Orientation des Courants Migratoires au Cours des Phases Futures du Développement*, mimeo, Dakar, December 1964.

Cros, Claude, *Peuplement du Delta: Résultats Complémentaires de la Première Enquête*, mimeo, Dakar, December 1964.

Ministère du Plan et du Développement, Commission de la Regionalisation

Situation Economique Régionale, Région de Diourbel, Comité Régional de Développement, 1963.

Premier Schéma de Synthèse Interrégional des Perspectives 1980, mimeo, Dakar, August 18, 1964.

Proposition d'une Méthode d'Elaboration de Projets Locaux de Développement, mimeo, Dakar, August 18, 1964.

Commission de la Régionalisation: Groupe de Travail, Liaisons Sectorielles, Rapport sur les Perspectives Regionales, mimeo, Dakar, 1964.

Rapport de Synthèse, mimeo, Dakar, 1964.

Mise en Route des Travaux des Commissions Régionales de Préparation du Deuxième Plan Quadriennal: Rapport sur la Session Tenue à Rufisque les 23, 24, 25 Janvier 1964, mimeo, Dakar, January 31, 1964.

Elaboration du 2ème Plan 1965–69, Rapport–Phase "RO," Région du Sénégal Oriental, 1964.

Elaboration du 2ème Plan 1965–1969, 2ème Rapport–Phase "RI," July 15, 1964, Région du Fleuve, 1964.

Elaboration du Deuxième Plan 1965–1969, 1er Rapport–Phase "RO," Région du Fleuve, 1964.

Elaboration du Deuxième Plan Quadriennal de Developpement, Tableau de Bord (Dossier RO) Rapport Provisoire, Région du Cap Vert, Dakar, 1964.

Rapport sur la Session tenue à Rufisque les 13, 14 et 15 Mai 1964, Deuxième Session de Planification Régionale, Dakar, 1964.

Données de Base pour la Préparation du 2ème Plan Quadriennal de Développement, Tableau de bord, Régions de Thiès, Thiès, 1964.

Ministère du Plan et du Développement, Compagnie d'Etudes, Industrielles et d'Aménagement du Territoire (CINAM) and Société d'Etudes et de Réalisations Economiques et Sociales dans l'Agriculture (SERESA)

Rapport Général sur les Perspectives de Développement du Sénégal, 2nd ed., 2 Vols., Dakar, July 1960.

Notes sur l'Industrialisation du Sénégal. Mimeo, Dakar, March 1961.

Henry, J. P., *Enquête sur la Commercialisation par les Organismes Stockeurs et sur la Commerce de Détail,* N.P., 1963.

Les flux des Transports dans la République du Sénégal, 2 vols., Paris, N.D.

Etudes Préparatoires à l'Elaboration et à l'Exécution de Programmes Régionaux et Locaux de Développement. Premier volume: *Rapport de Synthèse,* Dakar and Paris, mimeo, 1964. Quatrième Volume: *L'Administration Locale du Développement,* Etude Réalisée par le Centre Africain des Sciences Humaines Appliquées (CASHA), Aix-en-Provence, à la demande de la CINAM, mimeo, February, 1964.

Note Provisoire Concernant la Mise au Point de Méthodes d'Elaboration de Programmes Locaux et l'Elaboration du Deuxième Plan, Dakar, mimeo, November 1963.

Rapport de la Mission d'Aide à l'Elaboration des Perspectives Régionales, 2 vols., N.P., November 1964.

Secteur de Sebilcotane Enquêtes Cooperateurs, mimeo, N.P., March 8, 1964.

Rapports d'Analyse Présenté par les Equipes Polyvalents des CER de Bambyor, April 1965, mimeo, N.P.

Ministère du Plan et du Développement, Direction de l'Animation

L'Animation Rurale au Sénégal, Etude Générale, Orientations et Résultats, I.R.A.M., N.D., 1960.

Animation et Participation des Masses au Plan Quadriennal du Sénégal, Note sur les Problèmes d'Orientation et d'Organisation, mimeo, N.P., Dec. 1961.

Problèmes d'Adaptation des Structures au Développement Socialiste, mimeo, N.P., 1962.

Pensons à Demain. Imprimerie A. Diop, Dakar, 1962.

Les Observations Relatives au Projet de Création des Centres de Formation Professionalle Rurale, mimeo, Dakar, 1962.

Note de Travail Concernant le Stage de Premier Degree, mimeo, Dakar, 1962.

Note au Sujet de l'Action à Mener l'Animation Rurale Concernant les Problèmes de Santé, mimeo, Dakar, 1962.

Méthode d'Approche pour le Structuration du Monde Rural, Dakar, 1962.

Stage des Cadres Supérieurs du Développement—les Méthodes Concrètes de l'Animation, mimeo, Dakar, 1962.

Projet de Plan Cadre Régional pour le Développement des Structures Rurales, mimeo, Dakar, 1962.

Participation des Masses à la Réalisations du Plan. M. Sow Ibrahima, mimeo, Dakar, 1962.

La Structuration des Populations Animées, mimeo, Dakar, 1962.

L'Animation au Sénégal ou le Socialisme en Marche, mimeo, Dakar, 1962.

Note de Synthèse sur l'Organisation de l'Animation au Sénégal, mimeo, Dakar, January 20, 1962.

Séminaire des Instituteurs et des Cadres Intermédiares Animés, Région de Thiès, Cercle de Tivaouane, mimeo, Thiès, 1962.

L'Investissement Humain dans le Développement Socialiste, mimeo, N.P., 1962.

Note au Sujet des Journées de Développement, Dakar, N.D.

Rapport sur l'Action de Structuration dans le Cercle de Kolda, mimeo, N.P., N.D.

Observations sur le Rapport Dumont, typescript, N.P., N.D.

Animation Rurale, Programme 1963, mimeo, IRAM, N.P., N.D.

Orientations Générales pour 1963: Note sur l'Investissement Humain, mimeo, Dakar, 1963.

L'Animation du Building Administratif, mimeo, Dakar, 1963.

Note de Synthèse sur la Session Nationale des Cadres de l'Animation, mimeo, Dakar, March 1963.

Rapport sur les Problèmes d'Animation, Situation Actuelle et Perspectives, Dakar, mimeo, July 3, 1963.

Stage des Cadres Intermédiaires, Région du Sine-Saloum, Dept. de Gossas, mimeo, Dakar, 1963.

Stage des Cadres Intermédiaires, Région de Diourbel, Dept. de Bambey, mimeo, Dakar, 1963.

Stage des Cadres Intermédiaires, Région de Casamance, Dept. de Oussoye, mimeo, Dakar, 1963.

Stage des Cadres, Schéma d'Exposé, mimeo, N.P., 1964.

Compte-Rendu de la Réunion des Responsables Régionaux, mimeo, Dakar, August 8, 9, 1964.

Etat d'Avancement du Premier Plan et Projets pour la Fin du Premier Plan, January 1964–July 1965, mimeo, N.P., N.D.

Ministère du Plan et du Développement, Service de la Statistique

Commune Mixte de Ziguinchor: Recensement de 1951, Imprimerie A. Diop, Dakar, 1953.

Commune Mixte de Thiès: Recensement de 1953, Dakar, N.D.

"La Structure de l'Industrie Sénégalaise d'après la Comptabilité Economique 1959–1960," supplément au *Bulletin Mensuel No. 9,* Dakar, 1961.

Verrier, M., *Sondage Démographique 1960–1961,* mimeo, Dakar, N.D.

Service de la Statistique et de la Mécanographie, *Recensement Démographique de Dakar, 1955,* N.P., March 1962.

"La Structure de l'Industrie Sénégalaise d'après la Comptabilité Economique 1959–60," Dakar, 1962.

Diop, Serigne Lamine, Oumar Thiaw, Louis Verrière, *Situation Economique de Sénégal,* 1962, mimeo, Dakar, 1962.

Comptes Economiques Années 1959–1962, mimeo, Dakar, December 1963.

Rapport Provisoire sur les Comptes de la Nation des Années 1959 à 1962, mimeo, Dakar, December 1, 1963.

Résultats de l'Enquête Démographique 1960–61, Données Régionales, mimeo, Dakar, 1964.

Situation et Perspectives dans le Commerce en Fevrier 1964 d'après les Commerçants, mimeo, Dakar, 1964.

Mas, J. B., *Le Rôle de l'Arachide dans la Croissance Economique de Sénégal,* mimeo, Dakar, July 1964.

Situation Economique du Sénégal 1963, mimeo, Dakar, August, 1964.

"Situation et Perspectives dans l'Industrie en Juillet 1964 d'après les Chefs d'Enterprise," *Supplément à Bulletin Mensuel,* No. 3–4, 1964, Dakar, August 1964.

Présidence du Conseil

Rapport sur les Perspectives du Développement—Rapport Hygiène-santé, 2 vols., Dakar, December 1962.

Plan Quadriennal 1961–1964: *Bilan d'Exécution Matérielle et Financière des Investissements Publics au 31, Decembre 1962,* June 1963.

Grosmaire, Jean, *Eléments et Documentation pour une Réforme Agraire Rurale Foncière du Sénégal,* Commission de Réforme du Régime Foncière du Sénégal, mimeo, Dakar, 1960.

Dumont, René, *Notes Provisoires sur les Principales Conditions du Développement Agricole du Sénégal,* mimeo, Dakar, July–August 1961.

Note sur le Planification de l'Evolution Structurelle et le Développement Socialiste, mimeo, Dakar, August 21, 1962.

Présidence du Conseil, Secrétariat d'Etat Chargé du Plan et du Développement

Rapport sur la Première Année de l'Exécution du Plan Quadriennal 1961–64, mimeo, June 20, 1962.

Moity, M., *Note au Sujet de la Régionalisation,* mimeo, Dakar, April 1963.

Laville, Pierre, *Rapport sur l'Activité et les Perspectives de Développement du College Coopératif,* mimeo, Dakar, 1963.

Présidence de la République

Conseil Supérieur de l'Urbanisme, mimeo, Dakar, January 20, 1964.

Compte-Rendu de la Réunion du Comité Interministérial sur le Domaine National et l'Urbanisme, Dakar, mimeo, February 1964.

Conseil Interministériel, Peuplement du Delta, mimeo, Dakar, October 8, 1964.

Senegal, Laws, Statutes, etc., *Code du Travail* (Loi No. 61–34, June 15, 1961), Rufisque, Imprimerie Officielle, 1961.

V. French Government Documents

General

Rapport sur le Régime des Tenures de la Vallée du Sénégal au Fouta antérieurement à l'Occupation Française par le Commandement H. Gaden., mimeo, Mission d'Aménagement du Sénégal, N.P., N.D. (1910).

Questionnaire Relatif au Régime Foncier Chez les Indigènes de l'AOF, Imprimerie du Gouvernement Générale, Gorée, 1915.

Réglementation Dominale et Foncière: Textes Organiques, Textes Généraux, Réglementation Speciale à la Circumscription de Dakar, Imprimerie du Gouvernement Général, Gorée, 1939.

Mission Roland Portères, Aménagement de l'Economie Agricole au Sénégal, 3 vols., Gouvernement Général de l'AOF, Grande Imprimerie Africaine, Dakar, March–April 1952.

Les Salaires en AOF: Salaires Minima Hiérarchisés, mimeo, Haut-Commissariat de l'AOF, Dakar, March 1958.

Etude Statistique sur les Etablissements et les Salaires Réels Pratiques au Sénégal en 1956 et 1957, mimeo, Dakar, March 1958.

Mission Socio-Economique du Fleuve (MISOES), Les Budgets Familiaux, N.P., 1958.

Mission Socio-Economique du Fleuve (MISOES), L'Etat de Santé de la Population, Dakar, 1959.

Mission Socio-Economique du Fleuve (MISOES), La Structure Foncière au Fouta-Toro, N.P., 1959.

Mission Socio-Economique du Fleuve (MISOES), L'Exploitation Agricole Toucouleur, 2 vols., N.P., 1959.

Sénégal (République du) Economie et Plan du Développement, Secrétariat d'Etat aux Relations avec les Etats de la Communauté, Paris, October 1960.

La Documentation Française

Quelques Données Statistiques sur les Etats Africains et Malgache de la Communauté, Paris, December 1959.

La Politique de Coopération avec les Pays en Voie de Développement, Rapport de la Commission d'Etat Institutée par le Décret du 12 Mars 1963, Paris, 1963.

L'Evolution Economique du Sénégal, Paris, January 1964.

Ministère de la Coopération

Facteurs Psychologiques dans la Lutte Contre la Sous-Alimentation en Afrique Noire d'Expression Française, mimeo, N.P., N.D.

Rapport d'Exécution du Stage de Formation et de Perfectionnement pour les Agents de la Coopération de la République du Sénégal, mimeo, N.P., 1961.

Portères, R. et al., Problèmes d'Economie Agricole et Rurale en Casamance, Rapport Préliminaire, Paris, March 1961.

La Rosa, J. L., and M. Belmont, Enquête Agricole, 1960–61 Résultats Provisoires, Paris, 1962.

Blanc, Robert, Manuel de Recherche, Démographique en Pays

Sous-Développé, Paris, 1962.

Manuel pour la Formation d'Agents Recenseurs dans la Cadre d'une Etude Agricole par Sondage dans un Pays en Voie de Développement, 2nd ed., Paris, March 1962.

Leroux, Henri, *Revenu et Consommation des Ménages*, mimeo, France, March 1962.

Desroche, H., *Etude des Questions Relatives à l'Enseignement Coopératif au Sénégal*, mimeo, Paris, March 1962.

Rollot, M. *Rapport de Mission en République du Sénégal*, mimeo, Paris, 1962.

Julienne, Pierre, *La Contribution de la Taxe Régionale à Réalisation du Plan de la République du Sénégal en 1961*, mimeo, Paris, June 1962.

Lacroix, J., *Possibilité d'Action Coopérative dans la Domaine de la Distribution du Sénégal*, mimeo, Paris, December 1962.

Leroux, H., *Politique Fiscale et Développement*, mimeo, February 1963.

Perspectives de Population dans les Pays Africains et Malgache d'Expression Française: Etude de Synthèse des Enquêtes Démographiques Récentes, Paris, December 1963.

Réunion sur les Problèmes de Planification et de Développement, Deuxième Session, Paris, April 20–27, 1964.

Économie et Plan de Développement, République du Sénégal, Paris, 3rd ed., May 1964.

Dix Responses sur l'Afrique: Opinions sur la Coopératives Entre l'Afrique et la France, Paris, N.D.

Ministère d'Etat Chargé de la Réforme Administrative

La Politique de Coopération avec les Pays en Voie de Développement, Annexes, Paris, 1963.

VI. Periodicals

L'Action, publication of Mouvement Populaire Sénégalais (Section-Sénégalaise du RDA, Dakar (weekly).

Africa Report, Washington, D.C. (monthly).

Afrique Noire, principal publication of Rassemblement Démocratique Africain, Dakar (weekly).

Afrique Nouvelle, Dakar (weekly).

Annales Africaines, Dakar (yearly).

Bulletin de la Chambre de Commerce d'Agriculture et d'Industrie de Dakar, Dakar (weekly).

Bulletin de la Chambre de Commerce de Kaolack, Kaolack (weekly).

Bulletin Quotidien de Synthèse de Nouvelles, Présidence de la République, Dakar (daily).

Clarté, Parti Socialiste Sénégalais, Dakar (irregular).

Combat, official publication of Fédération des Etudiants (Union Progressiste Sénégalaise), Dakar (irregular).

Condition Humaine, publication of Bloc Démocratique Sénégalais, Dakar (weekly).

Dakar-Matin, Dakar (daily).

L'Etudiant d'Afrique Noire, publication of Fédération des Etudiants d'Afrique Noire en France, Paris (irregular).

L'Etudiant Sénégalais, Paris, mimeo (irregular).

Indépendance Africaine, publication of Parti du Regroupement Africain-Sénégal, Dakar (monthly).

Info Sénégal, daily bulletin of Agence de Presse Sénégalaise, Dakar (weekly).

Lutte, publication of *Parti Africain de l'Indépendance*, Dakar (irregular).

Le Monde, Paris (daily).

Perspectives, journal of Fédération des Croupements Economiques Africains, Dakar (monthly).

Présence Africaine, Paris (quarterly).

Reveil d'Aujourd'hui, publication of Union Démocratique Sénégalaise —Section Sénégalaise du Rassemblement Démocratique Africain, Dakar (monthly).

Senegal Actualités, publication of Service de Presse du Ministère d'Information, Dakar (monthly).

Unité, publication of Bloc Populaire Sénégalais, Dakar (weekly).

L'Unité Africaine, Dakar (weekly).

La Voix de l'Etudiant Sénégalais, publication of Union Générale des Etudiants Sénégalais, Dakar (irregular).

Voix de l'Islam, publication of Association du Culture et d'Education Islamique, Dakar (irregular).

West Africa, London (weekly).

Index

Abraham, W. E., 63–64
Abrahams, Peter, 224
"Accommodation," Senghor's, African critics of, 63–68
African democracy, toward, 195–200
Africanization, 87
African Socialism, 5, 34, 119, 120, 128, 129, 150n., 159
Afrique Equatoriale Française, 43
Afrique Occidental Française, 43
Agricultural development, 190n.
Algerian war, 23, 64, 65, 81, 92, 93–94
Alienation, 133
America and the Americans, see United States of America
Angola, 109
Animation Rurale, 215, 219
   changing nature of, 168–72
Anthologie de la Nouvelle Poésie Négre Malgache (Senghor), 61
Anti-nationalism, 133–34
Apartheid, policy of, 69
Apathy, 5
Apter, David, 37n.
Army, Senegalese, 30
   reliance on, as logical culmination of technicity, 220–22
Art, African, 228
Assembly of the French Union, 21
Assimilation, racial, 54, 67, 68, 82, 89, 103, 115
Association, policy of, 54
Atheism, 132–33, 134, 238–39n.
Augustine, St., 232
Authoritarianism, 30, 197
Autonomy, 84, 104, 106

Balandier, Georges, 152n.
Balante tribe, 14
Bamba, Amadou, 22
Bambara, 14
Bandung Conference, 84
Baol, 13
Bassari tribe, 14
Batouala (Maran), 47
Bendix, Reinhard, 130
Bernanos, Georges, 89
Beti, Mongo, 224
Bilingualism, 62
Black Intellectuals, 3, 50–55
"Black is beauty" doctrine, 4
Black Orpheus (Sartre), 50
Black, symbol and hope, 46
Bloc Démocratique Sénégalais (B.D.S.), 22, 23
Bloc des Masses Sénégalaises, 24, 209n.
Bloc Populaire Sénégalais (B.P.S.), 23
Bonnafé, Pierre, 81
Bourguiba, 101n.
Bourlon, Abel, 17
Brazil, 110
Brockway, Fenner, 121
Bronowski, Jacob, 230–31
Brotherhoods, see Religious brotherhoods
Bureaucracy, 30, 213

Cameroun, 99n.
Canada, 110
Capitalism, 31, 53, 84, 119, 123, 140, 141, 157, 158
   image, policy and theory of, changing, 142–46
Cartier, Raymond, 99n.
Casamance district, 14

Caste and the caste system, 15
   in traditional society, 139–40
Catholicism, 14, 88, 119, 239n.
Cayor, 13
Centers for Rural Expansion (C.E.R.), 173
Centralization of power, 202–05
Centres d'Expansion Rurale, 173, 215, 219
Centres Regionaux pour le Développement (C.R.A.D.), 174, 178
Césaire, Aimé, 45, 52
Chad, 99n.
Chieftainship, 15–16
China, 110, 116
Christianity, 120, 133, 232
Civilization of the Universal, *see* Universal Civilization
Civil service and civil servants, 201–202, 213–14
   appeal to, economic development and, 177–80
Class, *see* Social class
Class conflict, 136
   post-independence period, development and, 146–47
Class relationships, 15, 19–20, 25–27
Class struggle, 134–47
Classless society, 135, 136, 146, 181
Coalition, creating, 8
Cold War, 109, 117n.
Collective soul, search for, 52
Collective will, 106
Collectivism, 84
Colonialism, 69, 70, 234
   appeal of, for dependent countries, 80–98
   criticism of, post-independence, 94–98
   faults of, 163
Commerce and commercialization, 16
Common experience, theory of, 56
Communalism, 72

Communism, 92–93, 116, 119
Communist Manifesto, 84
Communist Party, 122
Community of Communities, 114
Complexity, 34
Concentration of power, 202–05
Condorcet, Marquis de, 9
Congo-Brazzaville, 99n.
Coniqui tribe, 14
Constituent Assembly, French, 104
Constitution of 1946, French, 20–21, 83–84
Constitution of 1956, French, 104
Constitution of 1958, French, 21, 22, 85
Constitutional Assembly, French, 88
Contribution of Africa to Human Thought, (Guernier), 47
Cook, Mercer, 33, 77n.
Cooperative movement, 72, 173
Cooperatives, the, 18, 19, 30, 172–176, 217, 218, 219
Cotonou Conference (1958), 22, 23
Council of Planning, 167
Council of the Republic, 21
Coup d'état of 1962, attempted, 200, 203, 220
Cri des Nègres (journal), 47
Crime in Senegal, 26
Criticism, constructive and destructive, 197–200
Culture, African, 45, 55–56, 71, 86, 108, 112, 225
   inventory of, need for, 162–65
   traditional, 145–46

Dahomey, 22, 99n., 110, 117n.
Dai, Bao, 93
Dakar, Senegal, 10, 15, 22, 23, 25, 55, 97, 143, 170, 176, 179, 188n., 192n.
   University of, 27, 182
Damas, Léon, 45n., 52

Damnés de la Terre, Les (Fanon), 64
Delafosse, 44
Delavignette, Robert, 76n.
Democracy, 88, 194–95
  economic development and, 194–209
    African democracy, toward, 195–200
    political party in, role of, 205–209
    politics, futility and despair of, 200–02
    power, centralization and concentration of, 202–05
Dependent countries, appeal of colonialism for, 80–98
Depoliticization of the masses, 216
Determinism, 130, 151n.
Developing nations, ideology for, functions of, 3–35
  processes in, 6–8
Development, agricultural, 190n.
  economic, *see* Economic development
  industrial, 123, 125
    class and, 140–42
  social, 59, 92
  socialism and, 155–86
    Animation Rurale, changing nature of, 168–72
    appeal to the privileged, 177–186
    concrete, the, search for, 160–162
    cooperatives, the, 172–76
    inventory of culture and resources, need for, 162–65
    planning, need for, 165–68
    politics and institutions of socialism, 168–72
Dia, Mamadou, 18, 21, 22, 24, 70, 160, 198, 200, 213, 214, 220
Diagne, Blaise, 10–11, 12, 14

Dictatorship, 197
Dieme, Amadou Lamine, 39n.
Diola tribe, 14, 118n.
Diop, Cheikh Anta, 24, 209n.
Diori, Hamani, 99n.
Discrimination, *see* Racial discrimination
Divine mileu: Technology, totalization and totalitarianism, 222–32
  God, new image of, 227–29
  socialization, 229–32
  work, 224–27
Dominant party system, 197, 199, 205–97
Dunayevskaya, Raya, 181
Durkheim, Emil, 122

Economic development, 59, 92, 116, 156, 175
  appeal to the privileged and, 177–186
    civil service, the, 177–80
    elites, the, 184–86
    peasants, the, 180–82
    students, the, 182–84
    trade-union leaders, the, 184–186
    youth, the, 182–84
  democracy and, 194–209
    African democracy, toward, 195–200
    political party in, role of, 205–209
    politics, futility and despair of, 200–02
    power, centralization and concentration of, 202–05
  Negritude and, 70–74
  problem of, 5, 34
Economic growth, 156, 157, 159, 194
Economists, the, 212
Education, 18–19, 26, 28, 43, 55, 73, 91, 182

Elites, the, and elitism, 19–20, 25–27, 86–87, 177, 182, 184, 194, 224, 236
appeal to, economic development and, 184–86
genesis of, 43–44
Negritude as link between French and African, 44–49
Embezzlement, 174
Encadrement (framework) of the population, 217, 218, 219
problem of, 8
Engels, Friedrich, 134, 140, 165, 223
England, see Great Britain
English-speaking Africans, 59–60, 102, 104, 105, 213
Enlightenment, the, *philosophes* of, 9
Equality of all men, 194
European Economic Community (Common Market), 157, 176
Executive branch of the government, Sengalese, 203, 214
Exploitation, 217

Fall, Medouane, 189–90n.
Fanon, Frantz, 57, 64–65, 81, 116
Fatherland, nation, state and, 112–117
Fèbvre, Lucien, 118n.
Federalism, 110–12
Federal state, 110
Federation of French West Africa (A.O.F.), 19, 21, 202
Feudalism, 135
Feurbach, 127
Fon country, 113
Fond d'Investissement pour le Développement Economique et Social (F.I.D.E.S.), 92
Forced labor, policy of, 20
Fourth French Republic, 195
France, 13, 127
black intellectuals in, during the

France (*continued*)
thirties, 43–44
colonial policy of, 8–24, 59
military intervention in Africa, 99n.
Negritude as link between French and African elites, 44–49
Senegal and, appeal of colonialism, 80–98
French Community, 106, 107, 115
French Revolution, 9, 232
French-speaking Africans, 59–61, 107, 115, 217
French Union, citizenship and democracy within, 87–94
French West Africa, 11, 21, 90, 185
Frobenius, Leo, 44
Fromm, Eric, 127
Front Nationale Sénégalaise, 210n.
Future of Man, The (Teilhard de Chardin), 230

Gabon, 99n.
Gaulle, Charles de, 22, 100n., 103, 106, 194
Gavroche, 103
Ghana, 23, 117n.
Ghana-Guinea Union, 117n.
God, new image of, 227–29
Gods, African, 228
Gold Coast, 11, 90
Gorée, Senegal, 10, 13
Grand Council (A.O.F.), 21
Great Britain, 11, 13, 121
colonial policy of, 59, 90
Griffin, John, 51
Guernier, Eugène, 47–48
Gueye, Lamine, 11–12, 13, 20, 22, 23
Guinea, 7, 22, 105, 117n., 134–35, 205, 238n.

Hamalliste religious brotherhood, 39n.
Hamon, Leo, 150n., 175
Hazard, John N., 150n.

Hegel, Georg Wilhelm Friedrich, 127, 130
Henry the Navigator, Prince, 13
Heraclitus, 130
Historical background, 8–27
Ho Chi Minh, 93
Hodgkin, Thomas, 99n., 238n.
Holland, 11, 13
Hughes, H. Stuart, 126, 151n.
Humanism, 125, 127, 155
   Marxism, science and, 130–34
   technicity and the new, 212–37
   history of technicity, 216–20
   technology, totalization and totalitarianism, 222–32
Humanitarianism, 119
Humanization, 114

Identities, search for, 49, 75
Ideology, 4
   evolution of, 27–32
   functions of, for developing nations, 3–35
   need of, 5–8
   uses of, 5–8
Imperialism, 28, 83, 98n., 115, 141
Income, distribution of, 156
   per capita, 156
Independence, 102, 103–04, 105–108, 115, 119, 197
   period of, evolution of Negritude during, 58–68
India, 23, 110, 124, 134
Indifference, problem of, 6
Indigénat, policy of, 20
Individual, the, 196
Indochina, 23, 92, 93
Indonesia, 11
Industrial development, 123, 125
   class and, 140–42
Innate differences, theory of, 57
Innovation, 120–21
Institutions of socialism in Senegal, 168–72
Interdependence, theme of, 109–12

International, Communist Party, 122
Internationalism, 116
Inventory of culture and resources, need for, 162–65
Investissement Humain projects, 7
Irele, Abiola, 75n.
Islam and the Moslems, 14, 16, 88, 224
Italy, 127
Ivory Coast, 92–93, 110

Jahn, Janheinz, 76n.
Juene Afrique, 101n.
Julien, Charles-André, 76–77n.

Kenya, 138
Kesteloot, Lilyan, 47, 76n., 120

Labor, *see* Trade unions
Labor Party, British, 121
Laissez-faire, policy of, 144, 158
Laleau, Léon, 61
Land tenure, problem of, 181
Language in Senegal, 26, 61–63
La Palombara, Joseph, 36n.
Law on the National Domain (1964), 181
Layene religious brotherhood, 39n.
Lebou tribe, 14–15
Legislative branch of government, Sengalese, 203
Lengyel, Emil, 26
Lenin, Nikolai, 116, 122, 141
Liberty, 196, 235
Literature, 62, 65
Living standard, 180
Local assemblies, 21, 80
Loi-Cadre of June 23, 1956, 21, 184
London League of Communists conference (1847), 84
Ly, Abdoulaye, 23, 211n.

MacKay, Claude, 47
Maga, Hubert, 99n.

Mali, 7, 205
Mali Federation, 22, 187n., 202
Mandingue, 14
Mandjaque, 14
Marabout-talibé relationship, 16–17
Marabouts, 14, 16–19, 31, 86, 180, 182
Maran, René, 39n., 47
Marchés Tropicaux (journal), 167
Marcuse, Herbert, 235
Marginal men, 43
Marx, Karl, and Marxism, 84, 86, 114, 116, 119, 122–23, 125, 126–27, 128, 129, 131, 132–134, 141, 143, 165, 166, 185, 217, 223, 224
  confrontation of Marx, need for, 126–29
  science, humanism and, 130–34
Materialism, 72, 119, 130, 231
Mauretania, 99n.
Mazuri, Ali, 138
M'Ba, Léon, 99n.
M'Bow, Amadou Moctar, 23, 211n.
McNamara, Robert, 237–38n.
Medina, the, 26
Melone, Thomas, 76n., 77n.
Mentalities, changes in, 7
Mercier, Paul, 153n.
Métis, 9, 10
Milcent, Ernest, 151n.
Militant racism, 53–54
Ministery of the Interior, Sengalese, 221
Monde, Le, 97
Monod, Théodore, 53
Monteil, Vincent, 39n.
Moral awakening, 5
Moral tension, 5–6
Morocco, 23
Moslems, *see* Islam
Mouride religious brotherhood, 16, 17, 22, 39n., 189n.
Mozambique, 109

Mphalele, Ezekiel, 66–68
Multi-party system, 197

Napoleon I, Emperor, 9
Narayan, Jayaprakash, 124, 125
Nation, fatherland, state and, 112–117
National Assembly, French, 14, 21, 33, 44, 80, 87–94, 142
  Senegalese, 181, 203
National construction period, evolution of Negritude during, 68–74
National realities, 116
National School of Applied Economy, 215
National Society of Distribution in Senegal (S.O.N.A.D.I.S.), 175
National Union of the Workers of Senegal (U.N.T.S.), 180
National unity, 112
Nationalism, 68, 102–03, 109, 113, 116–17, 134, 158, 199, 234
Nationalization, 158
Negritude as an ideology, 5, 86, 108, 120, 121, 129, 225, 234
  appeal to the French elites, 44–49
  birth of, 50–53
  black intellectuals in Paris during the thirties, 43–44
  development and, 70–74
  doctrine of, 4, 28, 29, 31, 34
  elite, the, genesis of, 43–44
  evolution of, 41, 49–74
    independence period, 58–68
    national construction period, 68–74
    pre-establishment period, 49–58
  link between French and African elites, 44–49
  militant racism of, 53–54
  overview of, 41–42
  philosophy of, 40–41

Negritude as an ideology
    (*continued*)
  social functions of (1931–1966),
    changing, 40–75
Neocolonialism, 97–98
Nepotism, 207
New man, the, creating, 163–64
Niasse, Ibrahim, 39n.
Niger, 99n., 110, 117n.
Niger, Paul, 58
Nigeria, 117n.
Nkrumah, Kwame, 90, 152n.
Nouakchott, 99n.

Office de Commercialisation Agricole (O.C.A.), 174, 175,
  176, 178
Office de Commercialisation du Sénégal (O.C.A.S.), 176
Office Nationale de Coopération et d'Assistance pour le Développement (O.N.A.D.), 176
Olympio, Sylvanus, 99n.
Oxford University, 50

Palabre, the, 195
Pan Africanism, 5
Parti Africain de l'Indépendance (P.A.I.), 24, 209n.
Parti de la Fédération Africaine, 105
Parti du Regroupement Africain (P.R.A.), 22, 24, 210n.,
  211n.
Parti du Regroupement Africain-Sénégal (P.R.A.-Sénégal),
  23
Parti Sénégalais d'Action Socialiste (P.S.A.S.), 23n.
Paul, St., 225
Pax Française, 14
Peasants, the, 216–17
  appeal to, economic development
    and, 180–82
Perroux, François, 105–06
Peulh tribe, 14
Peyrefitte, Alain, 99n.

Philosophical Works (Marx), 143
Physiocrats, the, 212
Planning, 216
  need for, 165–68
Poetry, black, 45n., 61
Political parties, 81, 184–85, 197–
  200
  role of, in the state and in economic development, 205–09
Politics, 213
  futility and despair of, 200–02
  mass, 25
  of socialism in Senegal, 168–72
  technique replaces, 216–20
Population of Senegal, 14–15, 17,
  39n.
Port Etienne, 99n.
Portugal, 13, 109
Portuguese Guinea, 221
Post-independence period of national development, class conflict and, 146–47
  evolution of Negritude during,
    68–74
Power, centralization and concentration of, 202–05
Pre-establishment period, evolution of Negritude during, 49–58
Présence Africaine, 45, 58
Price-Mars, Dr., 47
Prise de conscience (self-consciousness), 5, 218, 219
Proprietorship, 158
Proudhon, Pierre Joseph, 111
Pure race, 68

Quadriya religious brotherhood, 16,
  39n.

Racial discrimination, 20, 28, 45
Racial oppression, 85
Racial superiority, 54, 56, 68
  theory of, 56
Racial supremacy, 56, 57
Racism, 52, 56–58, 104
  militant, 53–54

Rassemblement Démocratique Africain (R.D.A.), 92
Regional Committee for Development, 176
Regional divisions, 113
Reification, 128
Religious brotherhoods, 14, 16–19, 38–39n., 134
Resources, inventory of, need for, 162–65
Restructuring, problem of, 8
Revolutionary doctrines, 40
Revolutions of 1848, 9
Revue du Monde Noir, 47
Rose, Saul, 124
Rufisque, Senegal, 10
Russia and the Russians, *see* Soviet Union

Saint-Louis, Senegal, 10, 23
Sanctification, dogma of, 17
Sankole tribe, 14
Sartre, Jean-Paul, 3, 42, 46, 50, 57, 60, 74, 75n., 120
Science, Marxism, humanism and, 130–34
Seck, Assane, 23, 211n.
Senegal, army of, 30
  reliance on, as logical culmination of technicity, 220–22
  caste system in, 15
  chieftainship in, 15–16
  class relationships in, 15, 19–20, 25–27
  colonial reform in, 20–22
  communes of, 10
  conquest of, 14
  coup d'état of 1962, attempted, 200, 203, 220
  crime in, 26
  France and, appeal of colonialism, 80–98
  French colonial policy in, 8–24
  historical background, 8–28
  ideology in, problems of, 5

Senegal, army of (*continued*)
  independence of, from France, 24
  institutions of socialism in, 168–172
  language in, 26, 61–63
  Mali Federation membership of, 22
  mass politics in, 25
  nationalism in, 68, 102–03, 109, 113, 116–17, 134, 158, 199, 234
  politics in, 25, 168–72, 200–02, 216–20
  population of, 14–15, 17, 39n.
  religious brotherhoods of, 14, 16–19, 38–39n.
  social context, changing, 8–27
  socialism in, *see* Sengalese socialism; Socialism
  society in, 13
  suffrage in, 12, 13
  taxes and tax-collectors in, 26
  urban migration in, 72–73
Senegal River, 13
Sengalese socialism, class struggle in African society, 134–47
  capitalism, changing image, policy and theory of, 142–46
  class and caste in traditional society, 139–40
  class and industrial development, 140–42
  confrontation of Marx, need for, 126–29
  definition of, 119–50
  development and, 155–86
  Animation Rurale, changing nature of, 168–72
  appeal to the privileged, 177–186
  concrete, the, search for, 160–162
  cooperatives, the, 172–76
  inventory of culture and resources, need for, 162–65
  planning, need for, 165–68

Sengalese socialism (*continued*)
  politics and institutions of so-
    cialism, 168–72
  Marxism, science, and human-
    ism, 130–34
  post-independence period and,
    146–47
  theory of, 120–21, 122–26
Senghor, Léopold Sédar, "accom-
    modation" of, African critics
    of, 63–68
  appeal of, 32–34
  appraisal of, 233–37
  career of, rise of, 12–13
  colonialism for dependent coun-
    tries, appeal of, 80–98
  criticism, constructive and de-
    structive, 197–200
  of colonialism, post-independ-
    ence, 94–98
  democracy and economic devel-
    opment, 194–209
  development, socialism and, 155–
    186
  French National Assembly mem-
    ber, 87–94
  ideology for developing nations,
    functions of, 3–35
  ideology in evolution, 27–32
  independence advocated by, 103–
    104, 105–08, 115
  interdependence, theme of, 109–
    112
  nation, fatherland and state, 112–
    117
  nationalism, views on, 102–03,
    109, 113, 116–17
  Negritude as an ideology, *see*
    Negritude as an ideology
  Official Grammarian of the Con-
    stitution, 33
  political unity with France em-
    phasized by, 81–82
  politics, futility and despair of,
    200–02

Senghor, Léopold Sédar
    (*continued*)
  politics of, 3–4
  ideas and, marriage of, 4
  power, centralization and concen-
    tration of, 202–05
  socialism, definition of, 119–50
  style of, 32–34
  technicity and, 212–33
  Teilhard de Chardin and, 222,
    223–24, 225–26, 227–28,
    229–31, 232–33, 235, 239n.
Serer country, 113
Serer tribe, 10–11, 14, 118n., 139
Sigmund, Paul E., Jr., 36n.
Sine, Kingdom of, 13, 139
Skurnick, Walter A. E., 75n.
Slave trade and slavery, 9, 13, 15,
    52, 83, 94–95, 131
Social class, industrial development
    and, 140–42
  in traditional society, 139–40
  one country, two nations, 25–27
Social context, changing, 8–27
Social democracy, 120
Social development, 59, 92
Social engineering, 212
Social justice, 159, 181–82
*Social Science and Distrust of Rea-
    son* (Bendix), 130
Socialism, 3, 18, 30, 84, 87, 116,
    216, 218
  African, *see* African Socialism
  historical factors of, 121–26
  Sengalese, *see* Sengalese socialism
Socialism in Southern Asia (Rose),
    124
Socialist Party, French, 11
Socialization, totalization and, 229–
    232
Songhai country, 65, 113
Soudan, 22
Sovereignty, 106
Soviet Union, 98, 109, 110, 116,
    127, 142, 148, 165
Stability, problem of, 5

State, federal, 110
   nation, fatherland and, 112–17
   political party in, role of, 205–09
Stein, Maurice R., 153n.
Strasbourg University, 204
Students, 201
   appeal to, economic development
      and, 182–84
Sudan, 106, 110
Superior Council of the Public
      Service, 180
Sy, Khalifa Abdoul Aziz, 39n.
Synthesis, racial, 68–69

Talibés, 17–18, 19
Tall, Seydou Nourou, 39n.
Talmud, the, 228
Taxes and tax-collectors, 26
Technicity, *see* Technology and
   technicians
Technique, definition of, 212–13
   politics replaced by, 216–20
Technocracy, 212–13
Technology and technicians, 29, 71,
      72, 89, 123, 129, 142, 172,
      183
   army as the logical culmination
      of technicity, reliance on,
      220–222
   history of technicity, 216–20
   new humanism and, 212–37
   totalization, totalitarianism and,
      222–32
      God, new image of, 227–29
      socialization and, 229–32
      work, 224–27
Teilhard de Chardin, Pierre, 68,
      78n., 84, 90, 109, 110, 111,
      158, 222, 223–24, 225–26,
      227–28, 229–31, 232–33,
      235, 239n.
Territorial General Council, 10
Thiam, Habib, 189n.
Tidjane religious brotherhood, 16,
      38n., 39n.

Tirolien, Guy, 58
Tocqueville, Alexis de, 212
Togo, 99n.
Totalitarianism, technology, totali-
      zation and, 222–32
Totalization, socialization and,
      229–32
   technology, totalitarianism and,
      222–32
Toucouleur tribe, 14, 118n.
Touré, Sekou, 134–35, 136, 152–
      153n., 238–39n.
Trade unions, 20, 87, 184–86, 201
Traditional society, 145–46, 147
   class and caste in, 139–40
Transport Company of Senegal, 222
Tribes, 14, 112, 113
Tunisia, 23, 92, 93

Ulam, Adam, 122–23, 223
Unfinished   Revolution,   The
      (Ulam), 122
Unitary state, 110, 111
United Gold Coast Convention
      party, 90
United Nations, 109
United States of America, 98, 109,
      110, 142
Unity, problem of, 5
Universal Civilization, 63, 68–70,
      88, 90, 110, 115, 116, 125,
      129
Upper Volta, 22, 110
Urban migration, 72–73

Vichy Government, 20
Violence, use of, 65, 136

West African society, 153–54n.
Wolof tribe, 14, 15, 16, 22, 118n.
Work, concept of, 224–27

Youlou, Fulbert, 99n.
Youth, the, appeal to, economic de-
      velopment and, 182–84

Irving Leonard Markovitz

Irving Leonard Markovitz, a native of McKeesport, Pennsylvania, received his bachelor's degree in politics from Brandeis University in 1956. A Fellow of the African Studies Program, Boston University, where he received a Master's degree, he went on to earn a Ph.D. from the University of California at Berkeley. In 1964–1965, on a fellowship from the Foreign Area Program of the Ford Foundation, Mr. Markovitz and his family lived in Paris for six months, and Senegal for a year, doing research for this study. A grant from the Committee on Comparative Urban Studies of the City University of New York made possible a return visit to West Africa during 1968. In 1969 he was granted an award by the National Endowment of the Humanities. Mr. Markovitz is the editor of *African Politics and Society: Basic Issues and Problems,* to be published in early 1970, and his articles have appeared in *Africa Report, Africa Today,* and elsewhere. He has taught at the University of California at Berkeley, New York University at University Heights, and Queens College of the City University of New York, where he is currently a member of the Department of Political Science.